Advance Praise

"A riveting tale based on a real-life woman who traversed the Wild West in the 1800s, dealing cards to gold-seekers and demanding respect on her own terms. From high society New Orleans to the dusty saloons of California, Walsh's latest heroine is a seductive risk-taker who doesn't suffer fools. A rollicking ride of a story." — **Fiona Davis**, *New York Times* bestselling author of *The Lions of Fifth Avenue*

"Engaging and empathetic, Eleanor Dumont's adventures provide a compelling picture of how women created lives for themselves in the hardscrabble boomtowns of the American West." — **Elise Hooper**, author of *The Other Alcott* and *Learning to See*

"Based on a true story, a historical novel that focuses on an unconventional young woman who introduces the game of twenty-one to mid-19th century San Francisco during the California Gold Rush ... The beginning of a unique Western adventure, with an indomitable female protagonist who repeatedly finds herself rising out of the ashes ... An enjoyable search-for-identity tale with a strong female protagonist." — *Kirkus Reviews*

"Walsh has written a fast-paced, original tale of the Gold Rush, complete with gun and gambling, bar brawls and boomtown. Highlighting the life of Madame Dumont, mother of Blackjack and the queen of fresh starts, *A Betting Woman* is a Wild West adventure featuring an ambitious, gutsy, independent woman as its driving force." — **Amy Poeppel**, author of *Small Admissions*, *Limelight*, and *Musical Chairs*

"*A Betting Woman* is an engrossing story, very well done and hard to put down. Hopefully, it will reach beyond historical fiction audiences and into enthusiasts of women's literature who look for powerful voices, experiences, descriptions, and growth in their novels. It's very highly recommended reading." — *Midwest Book Review*

"When Eleanor Dumont's family perishes in a fire in downtown New Orleans, she cuts her ties to the city and leaves on the next steamboat to anywhere. Soon she embarks on a wild adventure that ultimately leads to her renowned nickname—Madame Moustache—and a legend is born. A clever and cunning heroine, Madame Moustache outwits the best card shark in the west, makes her own fortune, and does it all with enough panache to impress nearly every saloon-goer she's ever met. Walsh's snappy voice, innate sense of pacing, and skillful narration make for a rollicking good read. *A Betting Woman* is a winner!" — **Heather Webb**, *USA Today* bestselling author of *The Next Ship Home*

"*A Betting Woman* is a fascinating read that expertly weaves sparse fact and imaginative fiction into a story that introduces readers to a little-known but remarkable woman. Bold, pioneering, romantic, and intriguing, this novel will delight historical fiction fans and all who love a good tale about the strength and resilience of women." — **Camille Di Maio**, bestselling author of *The Memory of Us, Before the Rain Falls, The Way of Beauty, The Beautiful Strangers,* and *The First Emma*

$\mathcal{A}$
BETTING WOMAN

♠

OTHER BOOKS BY JENNI L. WALSH

Becoming Bonnie
Side by Side

A
BETTING
WOMAN

♠

A Novel of Madame Moustache

JENNI L. WALSH

Wyatt-MacKenzie Publishing
DEADWOOD, OREGON

A Betting Woman
A Novel of Madame Moustache

Jenni L. Walsh

ISBN: 978-1-948018-95-1

Library of Congress Control Number: 2021933965

Wyatt-MacKenzie Publishing
DEADWOOD, OREGON

Wyatt-MacKenzie Publishing, Inc.
Deadwood, Oregon
www.WyattMacKenzie.com

For a little-known woman of history.

Born as Simone Jules, reinvented as Eleanor Dumont,
and largely remembered as Madame Moustache...

PART 1

Simone Jules

Chapter 1

1849

San Francisco, California

I HAD ARRIVED; ready to start anew, with nothing but two trunks, a mouth of deceptions, and my broken memories. Opportunity whistled through San Francisco, where its gold was discovered accidentally, unexpectedly. One could've said the same about my coming here.

Unexpected.

I stepped from the ship to the congested pier, not as Simone Jules, daughter of Phillipe and Adélaïde, sister to Patricia, but as Simone Jules, unknown.

At once, my sea limbs failed me. A young porter was all too eager to lend an arm, his cheeks reddening at our contact.

"*Merci.*"

The boy, perhaps fifteen to my nineteen, blushed further, presumably at the exotic nature of my French, a novel response to the language commonly used in my *Nouvelle-Orléans*. Already, the thought of the birthplace I'd fled nearly caused me to retreat onto the charter ship I'd only just exited. Instead, I took a steadying breath, my ribcage pressing against my corset's boning and the few remaining bills I'd hidden there, and gently patted my turban, concealing my unclean hair, to ensure its place.

"Is your husband fetching your trunks? If not, I'd be happy to do so," the porter offered. The question was innocent enough, yet guilt flooded me like a failing levee. Every day of my six-month journey, waves of doubt and guilt had rocked me more than the Pacific. But here I was, alone, without my fiancé, on the threshold of reinvention. Wasn't that why most people came here, no matter where they were from?

On the boat, I had listened intently; secretly playing a game with myself to name the different languages I overheard, relying on my studies as a child. And now, on the dock, I saw men with dark skin, light skin, and shades in between. The land that stretched before us was once known as Yerba Buena, an outback settlement of the Spanish. It had been renamed San Francisco three years ago, after a U.S. flag was raised here. Then, only last year, precious metal was found in its foothills and rivers. Thus, all of America, and even many around the world, rushed to the shores of this boomtown.

The dreams of my fellow passengers seemed as plentiful as the gold. As the only woman aboard the ship, I had kept a safe distance and eavesdropped on their words.

One man said he had no mind for mining, but he'd run a laundry. Those digging would need their clothing cleaned, would they not?

Another, arguing the same for whiskey, planned to open a saloon.

Countless others were dead-set that bonanzas awaited them. All those men who had tried their luck and left penniless were doing it incorrectly, apparently.

They said the population swelled from only hundreds to tens of thousands.

They said with enthusiasm how the gambling halls and saloons didn't close for the Sabbath.

They said with less enthusiasm, but a competitive spirit, how there were dozens of men to every available woman.

With only myself to blame, I now fell into that category, a realization that made my neck prickle with unease.

I answered the young porter, "No, it is only me."

"Miss." He scratched his hairline, averted his eyes. "Are you certain this is a suitable place for you? As a refined woman, such as yourself, a husband offers safety."

"I understand your meaning. Yet"—I winked, feigning a confidence I didn't fully embody after months of insinuations and advances from the men—"it is only me, as I've said."

His cheeks flushed again. "Please, let me call you a carriage and see to your belongings."

I took his thin arm, his jacket oversized, and the porter navigated me away from the bustling bay. The rising summer sun warmed my back, a gentle push toward the shoreline, littered with wood shacks, makeshift tents, and was that a boat, on dry land?

I asked the boy, who spoke hesitantly and too softly to overcome the bibble-babble of men, horses and dogs.

"Louder, please." I leaned closer to him, and I felt his body tense before his chest rose with a breath. "She was brought on land and converted to a warehouse." How inventive; I noticed a doorway cut into the oaken hull. A sign read REST FOR THE WEARY AND STORAGE FOR TRUNKS. "See there," my wide-eyed porter continued, "now they're erecting a hotel on top."

"Fascinating," I said, the word punctuated by the men's hammering. I'd never seen anything like it. *La Nouvelle-Orléans* was more established; the fourth largest city in America, even owning railways that weren't pulled by horses. I considered, "But why is the ship on land?"

He shrugged, though it was clear with his smile he was pleased to be well-informed and informing me. "Her crew abandoned her for the mines, so she was only clogging up the bay. Plenty more out there. Hundreds. They become buildings, get broken down for lumber, their sails used for tents."

He shrugged a second time.

It was impossible not to notice the volume of vessels, their masts—sometimes bare—jutting into the sky. I hadn't realized many were crewless. Though I didn't blame the desire of these men to scoop gold from rivers when the alternative was to complete a return journey to New York. Or in my case, to *La Nouvelle-Orléans*.

It had been several weeks into my voyage around the whole of South America when a fellow passenger had complained of a quicker route, one that left from New York's port, sailing south, before travelling seventy-five miles up Panama's Chagres River, then twenty-five miles on mules through the jungle, with its insects, poisonous snakes, and potential for yellow fever and malaria. But once the perils of Panama were crossed, there was the Pacific, with only forty-five hundred miles to San Francisco.

For those fortunate souls, their voyage was shortened from six months to four weeks; lessening the time spent with rats and weevils, with rancid butter and already breathed air. It reduced the threat of scurvy and cholera, with many passengers not surviving our trip. On my longer voyage, I still found unnerving how an unlit candle, while we crossed the equator, melted in my hand. And also, how the winds as we rounded the tip of Cape Horn had done their darndest to pull us toward the Antarctic.

I'd have preferred that alternative, quicker course. However, I didn't know the route via Panama only originated from New York's port. Had I known—and had I not impulsively fled my birthplace—I would've made the necessary preparations and taken the necessary week to travel the seaways north and sailed from there. The men had said the route was double the price at four hundred dollars. During my escape, when I emptied Papa's safe, I had procured less than that.

Soon, though, I'd have more than enough, as I assumed

my family's estate had been sold in my absence. No longer mine. Another family filling its rooms with laughter and love, as we'd once done. I'd be forced to stomach that information in the coming weeks, after I posted a letter to my family's lawyer and received his response.

"Here we are," the porter said, stopping at a carriage. "I'll only be a minute to get the trunks from your cabin."

"Very well." What was a minute more, after it'd taken me those long six months to arrive, and when my future had been set in irrevocable motion, only four months before that, when I had come of marriageable age?

Chapter 2

Ten months earlier
La Nouvelle-Orléans

HURRYING, while trying not to appear hurried wasn't the easiest of tasks. Not when each step felt infused with champagne bubbles. Not when my left hand, in particular my ring finger, felt heavier. Not when I couldn't wait to gabble with my sister about it all.

The backward glance I gave my minutes-old fiancé couldn't be resisted. David stood, handsome as ever, outside our carriage, watching me, happiness written upon his own face.

Truth be told, I hadn't expected David's proposal this afternoon. My twin and I had been introduced to society only last night, at the start of the Carnival season. David wasted no time in claiming me. His grasp had been so sure and so steady as he helped me from the carriage after our ride. When he dropped to a single knee, I thought he wasn't equally as surefooted. But no, it wasn't clumsiness that left David in a position to tilt his head back and ask me his life-changing question.

"Simone," he had said. "Last year, I became the victim of a cliché, love at first sight. But that's truly how it was for me. Now"—he grinned—"don't dampen my sentiments by saying it took you longer to fall. I know I stumbled through our first meeting."

"I was smitten from the start," I had assured him, and now I fell deeper into a memory of our first words, the very first time David had come into Papa's shop.

"We're closing soon," I had called out from behind the counter, without looking up from the books. I'd already reconciled the register and moved the money to the safe. Finishing the books was my final step before going home.

The response I received wasn't quite words, but a noise. I looked up, but he quickly turned, showing me only his back. He sidestepped around the store, from one jewelry display to another. He fidgeted, wiping his palms down his trousers.

It'd been a long day. The sun would set soon. But I took pity on him and his nerves, plain as a pikestaff. "Are you shopping for anyone specific?"

He turned. Pleasing to the eye. It took me by surprise, with his light features, almond-shaped eyes, and a neatly trimmed beard. His dress indicated he came from a respectable family. His cravat was straight and snug. Perhaps too snug with how he forced a swallow. "Not yet."

I found his response obscure, which I supposed was his point, as he followed it with a sly smile.

"Well, please let me know if I can be of any help." I nodded to the door. "That is, before we close."

"Actually..." He took a giant step closer, the movement exaggerated. "I should be truthful about why I'm here."

I closed my ledger and folded my hands on top of it, forcing a look of calm. Papa had left for the day. My sister held no interest in the work and came in only to socialize. I was alone in the shop. Nerves prickled. "I do prefer honesty."

"As do I. You see," he said, "I've seen you at the docks a number of times."

His cheeks reddened, obvious even on his already flushed skin. The day was warm. I guessed he was of Irish descent. Many came to Louisiana decades ago because of persecution. Those who could emigrate—who had the resources to manage the journey—became financiers, doctors, attorneys, or worked in printing, journalism. Others, who lacked the resources, came to the American colonies as indentured servants, taking on roles of farm laborers or domestic servants or the rare apprenticeship with a craftsman.

He went on, "The fellas down at the docks said how you worked at your father's shop. One said your name was Simone?"

After a pause: "Yes."

Encouraged, he said, "Well, this was the fifth store I tried."

I laughed, for a multitude of reasons, one of which was that this young man meant me no harm. He meant to woo me. Which, he couldn't, not until my coming-out party. But I daresay I liked his purposefulness. His gumption. Many of those Irish immigrants I'd mentioned had swiftly integrated into *La Nouvelle-Orléans's* society by marrying Creoles. Perchance it was their assertiveness as well. Still, I teased him, "I'm not certain you're supposed to admit that you went to such great lengths."

He met my smile. We seemed of a similar age, seventeen or so. "I know I should've waited for a proper introduction, but I truly do need a watch. For work," he added.

"Let me guess, a businessman?"

He nodded. "Port trade."

"Another guess, your first job?"

"First one of consequence. Is it that obvious?"

I laughed. Papa would approve of his line of work. I did, too, but I hadn't wanted to show this boy too much approval. "I'd be happy to help you find a watch. Tomorrow." Reticule and shop keys in hand, I rounded the counter and led him toward the door. "As I said, we are about to close."

"Tomorrow, then, when your father is also here. I'd like to see you again."

I stopped myself from returning the sentiment. Instead, I offered, "Very well. But on one condition."

He fidgeted once more. "Of course."

"First, you must tell me your name."

He closed his eyes at his mistake, missing my smile. "David Tobin."

And soon, I thought as I emerged from my memories and neared my family's front door, I was to become Madame Tobin. I entered my home and went straight for the parlor to tell my sister of David's proposal. Patricia's head turned, from where she sat at the card table.

She knew in an instant—and so did I—that we shared identical news.

"David," she whispered.

"And your Charles," I responded, awe in my voice.

I ran to her and we clasped our jeweled hands. We fell into a fit of giggles, as if we were five years old again sharing a secret no one else knew. I hadn't realized our oldest girlfriend Sophie was also in the room until she spoke. "You mean to tell me you both received proposals this very day? How delighted your mother will be."

Maman was delighted, indeed. In fact, she threw herself into preparations straight away, beginning by telling every soul in the French Quarter who possessed ears about the engagements of her shining jewels. Maman never told us who was born first. "That matters little," she had said. "What matters is you're a pair. You complete one another, see?" She named us as such: Patricia's name meaning *clear-sighted* and mine *one who hears*.

That night, we dressed for sleep, but we both knew sleep was far off. Patricia moved from her bed to mine, lying so close we may've been adjoined. She spoke into the darkness, "This must be a dream."

"Do you think the boys were in cahoots, proposing like that?"

"Papa says they were not. They came to him separately. But they surely didn't waste any time, both proposing the first night possible after our party."

I smiled at the ceiling. "Can you imagine all that's to come?"

Patricia squeezed my hand. "We'll live side by side."

"Perhaps add an interior door between our two homes."

Her head nodded next to mine. "That'd surely make things simpler. Our children can come and go, as if it's one big home."

I asked, "Two children?"

"Each. *Oui.*"

"They'll have brown eyes."

"Brown hair."

"Our olive skin," I said.

"Shouldn't we factor in the appearances of our husbands, too?"

"*Non.*"

She laughed and I felt her roll to her side to face me. "And it's all to begin on our wedding day. We'll have it together, won't we?"

"As if there was ever a question of that."

As winter progressed, so did our wedding plans, set for the spring. I was continually overjoyed at the *idée fixe* of a joint wedding with Patricia. However, a better word than *sulky* couldn't have been found to explain David's reaction to the mirrored proposal, and more so to the double wedding.

"But don't you wish the day to be special for us?" David asked me. He'd called on me, and now wandered my parlor, his distraction evident.

I watched from a settee as he flipped through one of Papa's books and countered, "I can't reason how sharing the day with Patricia will make ours any less special."

David's idle flipping of pages continued and the tip of his tongue poked from his mouth while he thought. With a thud, he returned the book, then sat beside me. David took my hands, fingering my engagement ring. "I understand you are close with your sister."

"My twin."

Nearly every memory of mine was intertwined with Patricia's. Even now, the simple act of sitting on this settee had the ability to rouse the recollection of Patricia and me—identical from bow to toe—perched here, our matching petticoats surrounding us like clouds, while we giggled and watched Maman play cards with friends.

"Yes. Only, Simone, I see our wedding as the start of *our* life together. Can we not have it for ourselves?"

The honest answer, no. Maman's planning had progressed too far, the wedding within the month, and she saw nothing greater than her two jewels shining together. I didn't disagree. Our dresses, nearly identical save for embellishments we'd chosen separately, already hung in our bedroom. But I also didn't wish to bring the hammer down on my fiancé's wishes too abruptly. I fibbed, "I could try to talk to Maman. I didn't realize the ceremony meant such a great deal to you."

"How could it not?" He checked his watch. David was set to meet a stagecoach for an out-of-town business endeavor. I had plans, as well, but to meet my family at the opera. I'd yet to change. "If the wedding is shared, does that not set precedent?"

"For what?"

He was slow to answer, "For everything."

"David, dear, I'd like to understand your worry, but it's eluding me. *Dis-moi.*"

His right eyebrow rose slightly higher than his left, as it so often did when I spoke French.

I clarified, "Please tell me. It's obvious this is important to you."

"Couldn't we marry first? I proposed first."

"By mere minutes, if at all."

He licked his lips. "Our future is important, is all. The wedding, the shop—"

"The shop?"

Papa's grandfather clock chimed, announcing the quarter hour. We both turned to look at it, as if the device was also saying, *you'll both be late.*

"David," I said, "what does Papa's shop have to do with proposing first?"

"Because..." He dropped his head, then met my eyes. "I thought it was to become ours."

I nodded. Papa had told us as much over brandy one evening. Then, it dawned on me. "It's not about our wedding being special, is it? It's about whoever marries first. You're huffy over whether or not you still gain to inherit the store. You've always showed such a great interest in it."

Naturally, he'd come by the store to see me. But he had also joined Papa in his workshop. They had put their heads together. They tinkered over gears. They appraised merchandise. Quite simply, they talked shop. Patricia's Charles never did the same, his interest in medicine. Patricia's interests also lay elsewhere. So why David felt this concern caused nothing but my irritation. I stood from the settee and David reached for me. A quick step thwarted his efforts. "You wish to marry first," I said into the window's panes, seeing only his reflection. "You believe that if Patricia and Charles marry first—or even at the same time—then Charles may get a portion of the family store."

"Simone, I—" He let the remainder drop like a leaf. "Please don't ever think I pursued you only for your Papa's store."

"I never did." Our courtship had consisted of laughter, stolen kisses, and entertaining banter. But now I wondered if he had proposed so quickly only for his own gains. In an attempt to secure his stake in Papa's shop. And even to achieve the next level in our intimacy. Once we'd been promised to each other, neither of us had wanted to wait until the wedding. With a sigh, I faced him. "We'll continue this conversation later. We both have someplace to be."

Like a puppy that'd been kicked, David accepted my dismissal. He'd be doubly sorry if he missed his coach; his business ventures clearly were important to him. And I turned my attention to what was important to me: my family and our evening at the opera. I dressed as quickly as possible, already minutes late, and ventured toward the *Théâtre d'Orléans* off Bourbon Street.

I was rounding Jackson Square, still two blocks from the theater, when I heard the sounds of commotion. There was shouting. Unrest. Over the buildings, a glow lit up the darkening sky. It was all happening in the direction I was going. I bustled my heavy skirts and quickened my pace, my heartbeat matching my stride. The air thickened as my breathing labored. Others hurried alongside me. We eyed each other with curiosity, but no one spoke, as if not wanting to voice the horrible event awaiting us. Or, more likely, give voice to which building, in particular, was in flames.

As I overtook a hotel, the last obstacle obscuring my view of the theater, my worst fears were realized. Smoke poured from the eight upper windows of the *Théâtre d'Orléans*. Its arched entrances spewed flames.

For a moment, I couldn't bring myself to go any closer. A horse-drawn fire truck arrived. Men scurried. They extended a hose. They pumped. I stood on wobbly legs and watched as the water streamed toward the arched entryways. Their efforts seemed to only enhance the flames, where it flicked. The fire danced. The fire, I realized now with a horrified gasp, wasn't letting anyone in or out of the doors.

Someone brushed my shoulder as they ran past. I stumbled, continued stumbling, until I was running. "Monsieur," I called after him. "Did the people get out?"

He didn't answer. I called to whoever would listen, "Where are the people who were inside?" Frantically I searched the faces for one identical to mine, for my parents', for Charles's. I saw neighbors. I saw other business owners. I recognized a girl from the charm school I'd attended. I put my weight on them all and asked if they'd seen my family. No one had. My former classmate clutched me back and blathered on, but I couldn't comprehend her words beyond how her maman also had attended this evening.

Clutching each other, we searched. But the faces and clothing outside the theater weren't dirtied by soot or ash. Those faces only displayed sheens of sweat. Hands covered their mouths. Tears leaked from their eyes. One woman was on her knees, praying. I had a mind to join her, to pray and plea that my family had arrived late as I had. My family couldn't be inside, where no one was bursting free.

With an ear-splitting pop, the theater's insides gave way. The finality of the sound released a sob and turned my bones to butter. I went limp in my classmate's arms and collapsed on the cobble.

Chapter 3

MY HEAD SCREAMED AT ME, from when I had crumpled outside the theater and from all it had endured in the few days since. Sophie sat patiently across from me in my parlor. My friend's face held a sorrowful expression, but with a forced smile. It was as if she wanted to comfort me and uplift me simultaneously. I appreciated her efforts.

On my side of the card table, I shuffled a deck, performing the second-natured motion. Card playing preceded the majority of my extensive schooling, learned from years of watching Maman play *vingt-et-un* with friends. She'd take bets, deal the cards, sip on champagne. It was all in good fun, though she regularly had provoked her friends' card totals to go beyond twenty-one to cause them to lose. I regularly had done the same.

Today, I only shuffled. I couldn't bring myself to deal, not with Patricia's chair empty. Staring at the upholstered chair, it was as if it was the first time I had ever seen it. Had I ever played without my sister? I must've. A time when either she or I was ill? But I couldn't remember such a moment.

"Simone," Sophie said, her voice gentle. "How are you feeling today?"

"Tired," I said simply. I tended to have trouble sleeping at night, resembling Maman in that regard, but now sleep was even harder to find. Sleep was plagued by the sound of a deafening pop.

Sophie nodded, using the time to perhaps find the correct words. "I can imagine. Yesterday was...."

A wake, a burial at St. Louis Cemetery, a houseful of people continuing to pay their respects for my deceased family and for me—the newly created orphan who'd skirted death for something so frivolous as tardiness. Now here I was, upon Sophie's insistence, attempting something habitual.

"I'm sorry," she said. "I thought a game would lift your spirits."

Her motives weren't unjustified. But I'd lost my *joie de vivre* and I wanted nothing more than to be elsewhere, anywhere but in this room of reminders.

Beside me lay Papa's last will and testament. The papers were read to me this morning. I'd known Papa intended to pass his business to me, but today I saw his wishes, in black and white. The shop was to be transferred to David Tobin, Simone Tobin.

As it was, his directive was premature. I was still Simone Jules. Only, Simone Jules was a daughter and a sister. Simone Jules wasn't set to become Madame Tobin for another twenty-three days, in the same moments that Patricia took Charles's name. Children were to follow. A shared future was to come, that no longer would. Who was I now, I wondered, if not the Simone Jules I've always been and not yet Simone Tobin, the wife, the mother, the shopkeeper?

I knocked the deck of cards against the table, the thud consuming the ticking of Papa's grandfather clock. I once found comfort in the steady din of it. Now it roared in my aching head, sounding too loud.

Sophie opened her mouth, but the electric doorbell chimed. My head snapped in the sound's direction. Yesterday, I had asked for the wires to be snapped, cut, whatever needed to be done to make the noise stop. The mourners and sympathizers meant well enough, but the noise. Oh how that noise had taken on a life all its own.

They're dead.

They're dead.

It appeared the doorbell had been put back together. The butler now stood at the parlor's doorway. "Mr. Tobin is here."

David's hurried entrance into the room saved me from deciding if I desired to see him or not. With him out of town, I hadn't since we bickered. "Simone." He rushed to me, lifting me by the elbows and into his arms. He smelled of springtime perspiration and day-old clothing. "I came as soon as I heard. Your family... all those people..." His head shook into mine. I shuddered a breath, willing myself not to cry. Not to feel the guilt of my own accidental survival, unscathed, beyond a burn in my throat and the gaping fissure in my heart. But my heart still beat. For what, I didn't feel certain.

"Simone," David repeated. He pulled back, ran a thumb down my cheek. "I'm sorry I've been unable to be with you these past days."

It was fine; I held no resentment that he was conducting business a town away while my life came undone and foreign to me. I messaged him the information, and based on his arrival time, he'd come straight away. Even still, I wasn't able to look at him, and not because we had quarreled. It was because I couldn't see David without seeing Patricia's Charles.

It made little sense. David was light where Charles was dark. David's eyes were blue, Charles were a gray. David was a shorter height, closer to my own, while Charles was tall, towering over my sister.

But even while it felt senseless, the rationale was built—layer by layer—by the fact that David was still here, while Patricia and Charles were not. How would I ever be able to stand at an altar meant for four?

I turned away, fingering my engagement ring, and went to the window. I peered out at a horse and carriage, a couple arm in arm, another row of three-story homes, but my gaze remained unfocused. My breath clouded the window. "I need air," I declared, my voice's volume too high.

David crossed the room in giant steps. "Simone?"

I looked from him to Sophie. "I'd like to go alone," I said with a slight raise of my palm. "There's no need to worry; I'll be back before twilight."

Outside, humidity hung in the air. I began walking, any which direction; it mattered little. It was the docks at the Mississippi where my feet led me, a place I so often had gone with Papa, him overseeing the unloading of jewelry, silverware, and other goods he purchased for the store. With a mind for numbers, I had helped him take inventory and keep the books. I'd been his assistant as he assembled the gears in his clocks.

I quickened my pace, an aimless escape, not stopping until my stomach hit a stack of crates. My hands flung on top. I dropped my head to my arms, my forehead coming to rest on the gold-dusted watch my Papa had given me for my eighteenth birthday. I held my breath, and wondered how long Patricia had held hers until the smoke filled her lungs. Until it took my twin's life.

"Mademoiselle," I heard.

The voice startled me and my remaining breath puffed free.

"Are you well?" a dockworker asked. I nodded, to which he was undoubtedly relieved to trade comforting a woman to continuing his work. With a gloved hand, he motioned to the wooden crate I had draped myself over.

"Of course," I said, stepping away, rubbing a hand over my watch and wrist. Without my family, I felt lost, misplaced, unsure of my own identity. But I knew one thing for certain: I was incapable of carrying on, as planned, without them. I wondered, "Where's the ship headed?" The dock was full of crates, of piled sacks, of trunks, of awaiting passengers.

"Gold Country."

"Out west?" I asked. I personally hadn't given the hullabaloo of the most recent gold rush much consideration beyond the inventory it could've brought Papa, but every newspaper sang of the opportunity there, of the many people reinventing their lives, their futures, their beings in the mountains' foothills.

He smiled. "The Wild West."

The word *wild* jumped out at me. That word cut through my grief and spoke to me. My family and I had gone to the opera for as long as I remembered. It was refined. It was respectable. It was enjoyable, but there was nothing *wild* about it. Yet, that venture turned out to be gravely dangerous.

That evening stripped me of my future as Madame Tobin. And I couldn't remain in *La Nouvelle-Orléans* without my family as Simone Jules. But perhaps she could rise from the ashes elsewhere, in a new way.

I asked, "When does the ship leave?"

"Two hours."

I checked my watch—enough time to return to the house, to transcribe a letter to our lawyer, and to pack my trunks. But not enough time for the glimmer of an escape to a booming gold town and a new existence to fade.

Chapter 4

1849
San Francisco

I GAZED UPON THE SHORELINE of Gold Country, both eager and uneasy, and ran a hand down my black cloak. The garment felt too heavy for the warm August air. Underneath, my dress was black, honoring my family while also hiding the grime of a seafarer. I wore no jewelry, no engagement ring, only the watch from Papa.

Getting on the ship had been rash, impulsive, but to this day, it felt necessary. I spent my six-month *grand deuil* with little more than my thoughts. I spent it determining who Simone Jules was supposed to now be. Surely I was meant to be more than a woman willing to leave behind what her father—and his father before him—had built. A woman willing to abandon the man she had promised to marry. I'd been certain guilt was going to pull me to the ocean's depths, especially in regard to David. I left him only his ring. No note, no word, no explanation of why I'd forsaken him. There were unkind names for what I did to him; I knew it, but as it was, on the twenty-third day of my voyage, I had tried to imagine how our wedding would've gone. Yet, my vision never fully formed. Not with Patricia missing.

But here, in this new world, my family was never meant to be.

The coachman and my young porter gave a final tug on the ropes holding my trunks atop the flat-roofed carriage. I tipped my porter before he was off at a jog, back toward the ship. "Where to?" the coachman called to me over the racket of the wharf.

A bull broke free from his carrier and made a mad dash down the dirt-packed street. Three men jumped on him, roped him, the beast snorting. The commotion died down. My heart beat rapidly for all involved. "The Plaza," I managed.

My all-too-talkative and lewd acquaintances on the voyage spoke of it. The area's full name was Portsmouth Square, where the discovery of gold was first announced, but anyone who knew better called it by the simpler name. The Plaza.

The coachman seemed unimpressed with my familiarity and instead pressed, "Any lodgings there will do?"

I tilted my head, softened my voice. "Any recommendations? Surely you, monsieur, would know the best accommodations."

I'd learned at Papa's shop, while bartering with countless customers, that men often needed a velvet voice and a smattering of flattery for encouragement. The trick was subtlety, a sleight of hand.

I extended mine, silently asking for assistance to climb inside the coach.

He took it. "The two biggest establishments are The Palmer House and Bella Union Hotel."

"The latter will do." *Bella* sounded encouraging. The carriage ambled up a sloping hill, then there sat the Plaza. Jackson Square in the French Quarter had a looming cathedral, walkways, vegetation. This was a patch of dirt with ample foot traffic, steers, frolicking children, and merchants with stalls advertising sweetmeats, newspapers, toys, and other goods. Surrounding the disorder—in the expected square shape—were buildings, most built in wood with a fancier brick or stone front. A false front, I later learned, to give the building a lovelier look without the cost. The coachman maneuvered a right turn onto flat land, the remainder of the square still sloping uphill, and proceeded down Kearny Street. I made mental notes of the buildings we passed.

Florence Dining Saloon, Delmonico's Dining Saloon, then Hughs, Noel & Crenshaw. I leaned out the open window for a better view of the last. Onions piled high in a barrel by the door. It appeared to be a grocer. Then came the United States Restaurant, Dennison Exchange. A-ha, the aforementioned Parker House. Out front, lumber sat in stacks and a man worked a circular saw, the metal disc screaming as it completed each rotation. I craned my neck. Another story to the building was in the process of being built. With the Plaza being only a block in each direction, I was certain the banging would reach me anywhere I lay my head. I was also certain I didn't need to feel the hammering in my bones as I struggled to sleep. The coach carried on.

El Dorado, a gambling hall, its doors wide open, was next and last to complete the strip of buildings on this street. I looked left, up Washington Street, past the Miners' Bank and spotted the Bella Union Hotel. The building sat two levels tall. A man climbed a ladder to the roof. A dark wood sign awaited him, half painted in the building's name. My gaze caught on the rolling land beyond the signage. Small dwellings and buildings dotted a steep hill, a mountain by my account, with pathways beaten into the terrain.

"We're here," the coachman announced, his holler trailing back. A moment later, he stood at my window. "I'll inquire about vacancy."

Vacancy, yes. I steeled myself, determined to keep moving forward, and helped myself out of the carriage. The building had shutters, something I saw as a promising sign. Few others in the Plaza had those. However, every house on my previous street did, with balconies for each level. I pushed aside the thought, the memory, the pang in my stomach. I convinced myself it was only hunger.

The coachman returned, and I greeted him with an exaggerated smile.

"I'll take your belongings in. Second floor, second room."

"Easily enough to remember," I attempted to say easily. The man grunted.

I followed him inside, my eyes needing a moment to adjust to the darkness. The building may've been labeled a hotel, but this room was clearly a barroom. An empty one, at the moment. I'd never stepped foot in a gambling hall or saloon before. Ladies didn't work in such establishments. Furthermore, ladies only played cards amongst friends in well-lit and civilized parlors, that didn't smell overwhelmingly of cigarettes and alcohol. This room unnerved me; but in an odd way, its uses for gambling provided a sense of familiarity. *La Nouvelle-Orléans* opened the first legal gambling house over twenty years ago. Not long after, the first bluffing game, now called poker, was played. It was as if this building was a secret nod to my former city.

The coachman said gruffly, "Sullivan rents by the week or by the month. Not the day. He expects his money up front."

I licked my lips, tasting the room's foul smell in my mouth. "And where is this Sullivan?" As it was, I was without the necessary means to pay. In my haste to leave home, I'd taken all that was inside our family's safe. It had been enough to bribe the cook's son to discreetly bring my trunks to the ship, and enough to bribe myself onboard, as there were no more tickets to be had, but all that bribery left me nearly desolate. The few remaining wrapped bills were hidden beneath my clothing, no one the wiser, and I'd been peeling off dollars as I went to pay for odds and ends. My cache was nearly gone.

"Sullivan isn't in. He'll find you later."

It sounded like a threat. I quickened my pace behind the coachman. He heaved my first trunk up the stairs, remarkably fast. At the top, he progressed to my room and shouldered his way in. He used his boot to push my trunk across the oaken floor, then turned on his heel to fetch my second piece of luggage.

"Very well," I said to myself.

I stood there, taking in my new quarters. My fellow passengers had spoken of boarding house rooms, shared by many men on many bunks. Amongst my numerous apprehensions while sailing here, I feared those accommodations for myself. But that was not this. It was a private room. There was a single window, its dusty panes letting in little light, obscured further by the outlines of a ladder, belonging to the man painting from the roof. There was a wash-stand, surprisingly a claw-foot tub, a writing table with candles, and a looking mirror.

I held my breath, and squared my shoulders to the glass. I hadn't seen myself—or my twin—in over six months. I let out a small gasp. My sister's large dark eyes and thin lips stared back at me. But my cheeks were sunken, my usually olive skin was pallid, my dark hair hidden beneath a wrap. I looked changed.

"Do you want me to carry in water?"

My hand flew to my chest.

My second trunk rested next to the first. The coachman motioned to the bathtub, not reacting to my alarm.

"Yes, please."

I assumed the water would be frigid, bucketed from a well. I was right. Still, after I paid the coachman and he left to aid another newcomer, I sunk a toe, then my body into the water. It felt novel, after months of only a washbowl. There was no way to secure the door, a worrisome feeling as the proprietor was set to find me, but hesitantly I submerged myself. My entire body went cold, numb. I decided in the twenty seconds I held my breath, that it was a glorious feeling. It was invigorating.

After washing the voyage from my hair and body, I chose a dress of many colors, and set to writing my lawyer. The letter I had left on my bed in *La Nouvelle-Orléans* provided specific directions. I wished for him to give references for the servants and to sell the estate and all that was in it. As far as Papa's shop, it had been left to me, but also to David. *David Tobin*, it had said in the will. I instructed that full ownership should go to him.

In my new letter, new instructions were written about where to send the money acquired from the sale of my old home and the considerable funds from our bank account. The aptly named Miners' Bank did fine.

While there was no other option, I was hesitant to provide my location. What if David saw, despite my lawyer's supposed confidentiality? Would he pursue me? Even after my treatment of him? If he were to board a ship—I counted on my fingers, from the current month of August, the length of time it'd take for my letter to arrive and then for David to follow—it'd be April or May before he disembarked. Unless, he traveled to New York and sailed from there. Then, only ten weeks? As early as November?

He wouldn't. Not after I left him without a single word. I could've tried to find words for David now, after hypothetical apologies chirped in my head throughout my voyage louder than the seabirds. But I hoped he'd have moved on. Hearing from me could only be a disruption in what he had rebuilt. Maybe it'd even prompt him to pack a trunk, my contact encouraging him.

My stomach grumbled, and that was that, a reason to put down my pen.

For the first time, I left my room to mail the letter and venture into the wild on my own.

♣

Task complete, I set my eyes upon my new town. A bell rung. Bells, in fact. I startled at the noise and the effect the noise had. Men began to swarm, much like a hoard of animals, toward the United States Restaurant, and the other eateries.

I followed.

Inside, they rushed to buffets, which very well could've been troughs. As they ate, many didn't use forks or spoons, having mastered the skill of using a knife to both scoop and shovel food, no matter a liquid or solid, into their mouths.

Admittedly, this was an unusual experience for me, beyond the men's primal eating habits. I'd been to coffee shops but I had mostly dined at home. Travelers were the ones to frequent eateries, if they were without a host family. Though, my family had made a big show of eating at Antoine's when it first opened—when was it—eight years ago. And, Antoine's certainly served more than travelers' fare.

I remembered it well, even though Patricia and I had been only twelve. We had begged Maman to join her and Papa. Maman's lips had twisted, no doubt debating bringing children.

"Bring your jewels, Adélaïde," Papa had said with a smile. "They'll shine."

I felt as if we had. Patricia and I had worn our best dresses and were on our best behavior with each small bite of our *Escargots à la Bordelaise*, catching the favor of our server and the adults dining around us.

Now, within the United States Restaurant, it didn't surprise me that the majority of the room's eyes fell on me. I was new, undiscovered—and I guessed, to them, exotic: a *femme française*, despite being of their same country.

As I put together my own plate and crossed to a free table, the jaws of the men slackened, whereas the lips of the few women thinned and their noses visibly rose in the air. Self-consciously, I touched my hair, which I'd blindly styled and pinned atop my head. The women here wore severely tight hairstyles, parted down the middle. And their clothing resembled what my family's servants would've worn. Plain. Simple. A stark contrast to my colored silk gown. I stood out like a sore thumb, and the women let me know it with their more-than-occasional and less-than-discreet glances. I left half of my oyster and eggs untouched, and returned to my room, unable to meet the gaze of anyone from here to there.

I sat on my hair-filled mattress, my apparently overly-coiffed head in my hands, and could only think: *I don't belong* while I also thought *how dare those women.* Beyond day-trips, I'd never left my hometown. I'd never received such unjust scrutiny. My breath came out slow, shaky, and then I raised my head at the sounds of carefree and high-pitched laughter. The glee came from women, but surely not the surly type I'd experienced in the eatery, who I imagined incapable of such gaiety. The footsteps of the joyful women trailed down the hallway, then the stairs. Soon, deep-toned voices joined them. Glasses clinked. Music began. The downstairs saloon and gambling den came alive.

In truth, it sounded like one of the *soirées* my parents had frequently thrown, Patricia and I giggling from our bedroom at the sounds we hadn't yet experienced below.

"I want to see," she had whispered. But even as she said it, I'd already slipped from my bed, reaching for her hand, and our bare feet padded against the floors.

The memory put me on my feet. My slippers were soundless and I slowly crept from my room, toward the stairs. With a hand on the banister, I gained my bearings. Hadn't Patricia and I snuck to the top of the stairs to peer down, to catch a glimpse of whatever scandalous things our parents and their friends did downstairs, before we were old enough to join them?

Here, the staircase was open to the smoke-filled saloon

and ran down the wall opposite the bar. What lay beneath me looked nothing like I'd seen upon my arrival. Rather, what little I had seen. Now, the oil lamp chandeliers were lit, hanging from the ceiling, gilded in a beautiful gold pattern. Light was seemingly everywhere, twinkling around the room like an explosion of stars in a cloudy night.

There were men at the bar, at tables playing cards, merely drinking around tables, dancing with women. It was all so casual. Too casual. Where I was from, being asked to dance by a stranger would've incited scandal for days. I breathed deeply, coughing as my lungs filled with the rising smoke, and descended another step. An unexpected laugh bubbled up my throat at what I noticed next. Portraits, nestled between the numerous mirrors and candled sconces. Those portraits were of *femme française*, in various stages of undress. I no longer wondered why my young porter had blushed upon learning I was French. He must've spent an evening with his mouth hanging open in this very room.

My amusement was fleeting, cut short when a body was thrown, banging against the stair's railing. I gasped, my hand flying to my mouth. Amidst the shouting, profanity, and commotion, a woman bent to whisper a smattering of words into the fallen man's ear before helping him to his feet. She led him toward the other dancing women.

Saloon girls, they were called. The men I had avoided on the ship had been eager to make the acquaintances of such women. "For seventy-five cents, they'll dance with you for fifteen minutes," I'd overheard one say enthusiastically.

Money was surely being spent here. Men spun the women, the room's light catching on the sequins of the girls' brightly colored dresses. I touched my belly, my own dress of a similar shade, but theirs was scandalously short, coming to the middle of their shins, nearly touching their tasseled boots, or even to their knees. My lips parted, uncomfortable with their attire, their risqué mannerisms, the fact they acted such a way for money.

On some, their petticoats stuck out beneath their ruffled dresses. On most, their arms and shoulders were bare. On all, their bodices were cut low over their bosoms, the men feeling as if they were free to sink their faces there. One woman threw her head back and laughed, as if she enjoyed it. But I couldn't fathom how.

It was all too much. I held my breath, the smoky room overpowering me. Abruptly, they stopped dancing, and I surmised the seventy-five cents had expired. The saloon girls led their dance partners to the bar. One girl turned, as if she felt my eyes on her, and I startled, my right heel clinking against the rise of the step behind me. The girl smiled, motioning for me to descend the final stairs. There was little chance of that.

When Patricia and I had been caught watching, we retreated, snickering, hands to our mouths, taking tiny, quick steps to climb the stairs.

I experienced none of that merriment now as I fled.

Chapter 5

I WISHED I COULD say morning's light flooded my room, but that wasn't the case. The outside of my room's window was coated in dust and grime, making it difficult to let light in or to adversely see out. The glass's hue certainly had the opposite effect of rose-colored lenses, which would've been a great benefit in my current situation.

I struggled to raise the windowpane. The ladder was gone. Bleary eyed, I watched the bustle and bedlam of the square. The Plaza was louder than I was accustomed to, and not only from the constant hammering, but from voices, animals, wagon wheels, and ship horns. In the distance, masts of ship jutted into the sky. Of course, we had all those things in *La Nouvelle-Orléans*, but it all felt greater here. *Here* I felt like a fish out of water.

My gaze trailed to the floorboards, as if I'd see straight through and witness more debauchery below. But it was quiet. I assumed those responsible for last night's mayhem were still sleeping. I'd be, if sleep ever came to claim me.

As I'd sailed, I also slept little. I was too consumed with listening for footsteps outside my cabin door, the rumble of my stomach, or my tortuous thoughts. In the interlude between guilt and regret, I also had thoughts on my new life, what it could be—what *I* could be. One such notion was that I could own something of my own, like I would've done with Papa's shop if I had stayed. The idea was appealing and—looking out across the Plaza at Clay Street, where it had barely been developed, with plenty of room for buildings to go up—I could see the potential. There was room for such a thing. But the question was, was there room for *me*?

I pictured the hungry glances from the men and the upturned noses of the women from the eatery. I pictured the unruly behavior of the men and women downstairs, and I realized now, with a hint of shame, how I had turned up my nose at those girls.

I spun from the window and sunk to the floor in front of my trunk. I needed to touch the fabrics and mementos of the life I'd left behind. I began to do just that, when annoyance at my melancholy washed over me. I may've left my hometown, but I'd done so because there was no life for me there without my family. I reached for my trunk's lid, prepared to close it, to dust off my skirts, to chase after whatever new existence awaited me, when my eye caught on my playing cards. They'd been Maman's, passed to me. Patricia had been happy to play, but it was me who was entranced by the strategy, the numbers, the allure of Maman's game, *vingt-et-un*.

I took the deck and felt the familiar weight of it in my hands. A rap at the door had me twisting toward the sound, holding the cards against my chest. The door flung open. A girl stood there.

"You're not Elizabeth." She tapped her fingers against the door's frame. The girl laughed. "I'll be damned. She did it. She ran off with the brute. I should've known when she didn't show for work last night."

I remained silent, not sure how to react in such a situation. Once the girl had her moment, she focused on me. "Who are you, then?" She all but slapped the doorframe this time. "I saw you last night. On the stairs."

I recalled her as well. Still unsure of a reaction, I smiled sweetly and stood. *"Bonjour."*

She analyzed me—there was no better way to describe her

scrutiny—with a hint of her own smile. "Oh, the men will love you. May I?" She gestured to the chair at my toilet-table.

"Please," I said, leaning on my well-taught manners. I settled on my bed.

Names were exchanged. Hers, Lydia. She wore the same clothing as last night. Bows, once perched on top of her head, sagged to the side. Her upper arm was bruised.

She nodded toward me. "What do you have there?"

I still held my playing cards. I turned them around.

Lydia said simply, "Never played. Now, Simone, I assume you're here to work?

"I am." It was the truth, but her question had my brain spinning again. I'd chase that new existence, I would. But I'd need to get by in the meantime, until my money arrived. I'd need to find a way to belong. I let my thoughts trail off as I felt the weight of Lydia's scrutiny of me. Then the first woman who spoke to me in Gold Country got down to the particulars, so different from how Sophie would've acted. But I couldn't think of my friend and how I also left her without a word. "If you're going to survive here," Lydia said. "You need to know the rules."

"The rules?" I asked, admittedly amused.

"The rules," she repeated. "The two types of women. The married and the unmarried. The *good* and the *bad*. I could go on. But let me ask you this. Do you have a husband? Is he off in the mines somewhere?"

"I've no husband," I said simply.

"So what is it you intend to do in town? Do you cook?"

"I've never had to."

She snorted. "Laundry? Clean?"

I shook my head.

"I'm not surprised. Your dress has every color of a peacock. Your face is powdered, your cheeks rouged. Those eyes of yours are like saucers. You'll be a natural for downstairs.

Or upstairs if that's more your thing?"

My lips parted in surprise and horror. The rouge and powder I wore didn't denote me a courtesan, but simply a woman.

Lydia laughed. "Not upstairs then. I imagine promiscuity is a falsity given to the French?" She waved her hand. "I like you, Simone. But all those married women. The so-called *good* ones. They won't. They'll see you and think your fine dress is nothing more than you flaunting your profits. They'll see you with their husbands."

The room felt too warm and I fanned myself. There was a new rap on the door. More of a thump, actually. Even with the forceful nature of it, I welcomed the interloper to put an end to Lydia's declarations.

The door opened, as it had with Lydia, before I could cross the room. This time a man stood at the threshold.

"Mr. Sullivan," Lydia said. "Have you come to call on Miss Jules here?"

Lydia's smooth skin and wide grin was a stark contrast to Monsieur Sullivan's weathered face. He wore a hat, a vest, and a moustache. The combination gave off intimidation.

He offered Lydia no more regard then a slight nod of his head. "I'm here for my money," he said. "How long you paying for, Miss Jules?"

I swallowed, all the while keeping a smile on my face. "May I ask your rates?"

His response nearly knocked me off my feet. One month's rent was nearly two grand. In the French Quarter, an entire house, fully owned, had cost only a grand more. I fought for composure, which I shored with my posture. Chest out. Head tilted down. Eyes up. "Very reasonable. I assume you extend credit. Only until my funding arrives, that is."

I'd done this before, many a time. A man would name a price he was willing to pay for jewelry. I'd counter. He'd stare me down. We'd come to an agreement, fair for both sides.

Currently, this man locked eyes with me.

"Monsieur?" I prodded in my silkiest of voices.

He didn't blink, only chewed on some thing or another. I took the slowest of breaths, not wanting to show my unease with the rise and fall of my chest.

Lydia stepped forward. "Elizabeth is gone. Couldn't Simone take her place and work for her room?"

I bit my tongue. I assumed Lydia meant as a saloon girl. But no, that wasn't for me. I waited, feeling certain Monsieur Sullivan would balk at the suggestion. What experience did I have? The man looked me up and down, his one eye squinting.

I never knew five words could cause such alarm. "Bring her to me tonight," he said. And that was that. He was gone.

Lydia clapped. She grabbed both my hands, my deck of cards still in my grasp. "How wonderful! And of course, you're welcome."

My chest pressed hard against the boning of my dress. I questioned how many more breaths I even had in me.

"Simone," Lydia said, dropping her hands. "Aren't you happy? You should be."

I licked my lips and found it hard to meet her eyes. "I appreciate your efforts, but—" I wasn't sure how to continue without offering offense.

"Come now, don't be all judgmental like the *good* women. We sing, we dance, we keep the men drinking. I get half of whatever they spend at the bar. Sometimes I'll do fifty dances a night. Better than washing their whiffy clothes, I daresay. Plus, I get gifts. Jewelry, mostly." She proudly flaunted a glistening wrist.

Despite my unease, I laughed. Lydia was likeable.

"That's better." She smiled, then leaned forward. She inhaled as I stiffened. "Good, you've bathed recently. Now let's get you ready for tonight."

◆

"Tonight" came too quickly. Lydia sat across from me on my bed, touching up my powder. She was *petit*, like me, and had tried to lend me clothing, but I insisted upon remaining in my own, that showed less of me.

I was familiar with my femininity. It was a tool I used, often. But I preferred to use my words and my charms to gain the advantage. How terrifying that these men most likely expected more. That they believed they could touch whatever they wished to touch. That, offering a few coins gave them that right.

I told Lydia as much, as she led me downstairs, where those hungry men awaited us.

"Be easy," she said over her shoulder to me. "There's no need for nerves about all of that. We don't remove our clothing, not in the Bella Union. And, if they get too frisky, take a page from Mary." She nodded across the room at one of the girls. "One fella got too forward with her and she slapped him. The fool knocked her back. Mr. Sullivan had him locked up for the night. Afterward, Mary said, 'I don't mind the black eye, as long as everyone now knows I'm no whore.'"

I gasped at her word choice while my head spun, as if falling down an endless hole, but still possessing the fear of hitting the bottom, where greedy, lustful men awaited me. All my life, Papa had taken care of my sister and me. His money saw to everything. Sheltered us. Protected us. Offered us a future. There was none of that now. It was only me. And Lydia, who took my hand and began dragging me toward Monsieur Sullivan. My throat felt swollen and my bones leaden, but I put one foot in front of the other to follow.

My eyes caught on the men playing cards. During the *soirées* in our parlor, Maman had often played the tables. Sometimes, if she had more than two glasses of champagne, she cackled with laughter as she relieved the croupier of his table. "I'll deal," she'd declared. The others were delighted, their innocent games always more spirited with her behind the deck, but they were also intrigued, as women were never employed as card dealers.

"Mr. Sullivan," I heard Lydia say.

I turned to find the man appraising me, his moustache twitching. He wore the same hat and vest. He wasn't any less intimidating than when I'd met him earlier. "You're like a doll. Why don't you start by sitting on laps." He added, "Encourage them to play, drink, stay a while."

I could never. I stiffened at the thought of their arms around me, their breath on my neck. My gaze returned to the men playing cards. Around another table, men drank. A greasy, dog-eared deck of cards lay in front of them, not having yet begun a game.

But I could do that.

I could begin a game.

Perchance it was Maman's spirit that put the thought in my head. Patricia's influence, too, as the clear-sighted one, helping to guide me. I squared my shoulders to Monsieur Sullivan. "I'd like to propose a different arrangement."

Chapter 6

"I'D LIKE TO BE A CROUPIER in your fine establishment," I finished. With the room's loudness, those words came out as an unladylike shout. Still, as ever the persuasive woman, I'd asked from beneath my lashes.

Monsieur Sullivan guffawed. He towered over me, as most people did. "Why a woman croupier is nothing more than teats on a bull."

Charming, I thought.

"Especially," he added, "when the lady is as fancy and dainty as you. You'd never stand a chance against these men."

"Thank you," I said deliberately. "Surely, my appearance will work to your advantage."

As if proving my point, the gentleman to my right missed the spittoon on account of me standing there. I kept my expression soft, and posed another question, "But if you won't have me, do you think the Parker House would find me a novelty? I hear they also rent rooms."

Monsieur Sullivan narrowed his eyes. Lydia tried not to smirk, but her eyes betrayed her. Fortunately, she was whisked into a dance.

I followed my question with a solution, an old bartering trick from Papa. "I'll rent a table and send the gentlemen to the bar after they lose. I won't even ask for fifty percent, like the other girls. Everything I make will go toward my room until it's paid off."

I smiled, though inside I was nothing more than churning anxiety. Monsieur Sullivan sucked on his own tobacco. A chair to my left opened, its former occupant announcing he had to *have a leak*. The deck of cards lay on the table. I tapped it with my pointer finger, again and again, waiting. Monsieur Sullivan released a grunting noise, and I took it as acceptance and reached for the chair.

"Tonight," he said flatly.

I cocked my head in question.

"You'll earn the entirety tonight. Both your room—a month's worth—and the cost to use this table—say an even five hundred. Or this *arrangement* is off."

It was robbery, the table alone, not withstanding the fact he wanted an entire month's rent instead of a single week. I took a step back from the chair. "I think I'll change my room to the Parker House after all."

"I'm sure they'd be tickled pink to have you"— he grinned, showing blackened teeth—"*if* they had any rooms available. Roof came off earlier today while they build out those rooms. Truth be, lots of men are looking for a room. I wouldn't mind the vacancy."

I clenched my teeth, and then smoothed my face into a smile. "On second thought, seems such a bother to change rooms. May I?" I said, motioning to the table.

The man half curtsied, the mockery.

If I appeared composed, it was only for outward appearances. Inside I boiled over with aggravation, but also uneasiness. I possessed all of three dollars, while I needed twenty-five hundred. There was no time to waste. I turned my attention to the table. "*Bonsoir*, gentlemen." One of the men overturned his seat to pull out the available chair for me. Chivalrous, never mind the bowie knife sheathed on his belt. With a dip of my shoulder, I said, "*Merci*."

Four faces stared back at me. The mention of *gentlemen* was premature. Lydia's mention of *whiffy* was accurate. On their own, my fingers moved to prepare the deck, but uncertainty plagued me. While Maman's male acquaintances accepted her, these unknown men could object to a game with a lady. They could argue women had no place in a man's sport. Then, there was the small detail of how I'd never before played with actual currency. The wagers I placed with Patricia, Sophie, and any others who'd joined us were valueless tokens, for our mere enjoyment. If she were here, what encouragement would my sister offer me?

Petit a petit, l'oiseau fait son nid.

Little by little, the bird makes its nest.

I smiled to myself. Between two of the men's scraggly faces, a mirror hung. I saw my smile. Life's timing was fortuitous, because there, I also saw the comforting likeness of my sister.

"Miss?" a man asked.

I picked only him to focus on. "You will play?"

His smile showed a blackened tooth. "Play with you?"

I wished for gloves as I palmed the deck. "Do you see any-one else sitting here, monsieur, brandishing a set of cards?"

There it was, the temptation in his eyes. I let my gaze wash over the others, wordlessly inviting them to play as well.

One asked, "How'd you get to be sitting here? I've never seen a lady dealer before."

"Well now you have. I daresay your story is more enticing than mine." I added a demure smile. "What game shall it be?"

The man looked to his companions. One puffed from his cigarette. One gulped from his glass of whiskey. Another left the table, mumbling under his breath.

I exhaled; glad they did not have a strong opinion, save for the one who had vacated a moment ago. The other tables played poker and faro, which were not my games of choice. And faro, as I understood it, required two people to run the game, though I was unfamiliar with how. "*Vingt-et-un*, then." I dealt a card face up to each, willing steadiness into my hand. To my delight, I noticed the newness of the word *vingt-et-un*.

I put a card in front of each of them, and myself. I dealt a second round, this time putting my card face down. "See there, your card totals are twelve, seven, and eleven. You could *stand* where you are, or I could give you another card. However many cards you wish. If your total is closer to twenty-one than mine, you win. If my cards are closer, or if you go over twenty-one, your money becomes mine."

"But we can't see your second card."

"That don't seem fair," another said, his voice ringing with distrust.

I hid my unease behind a wink. "That's the fun of it." Then, evoking confidence, I raised my arms, as if asking, *Who's in*?

Slowly, one by one, as if the men needed the approval of the others before they continued, leather purses were opened. Wagers were made—from fifty cents at the lowest to a more eyebrow-raising ten dollars. If that bidder meant to intimidate me, he succeeded. That amount could end me. It could also be my beginning.

The bet at fifty cents took cards until he busted. The biggest mistake a novice made was forgetting about my hand while determining his own. I had also explained my restrictions. If my cards totaled seventeen or greater, the rules dictated I must stand. But, if my cards were less than seventeen, I was forced to take another card. Maybe another, if still below. With only a five in front of me, chances were I'd need to take multiple cards.

The bet for a dollar stood at fifteen. Time would tell if he kept his money or not.

But first, there was the man who bet ten. A seven and a ten sat before him. He wanted another. I pulled from the top of the deck, and, I could've cried with relief; there you had it, it wasn't in the cards for him.

I verbally praised his daring nature as I discreetly moved his money in front of me. He banged his hand on the table, yet he grinned like a fox. Swiftly, I returned my focus to the man who'd stood at fifteen. "Shall we see my card?"

My faced-down card was a queen. We were at a draw at fifteen, except I was still below seventeen. I took another card. An eight. Not as I had hoped, yet I purred, "You win, *mon amie.*"

His chest puffed like a peacock's, which was pleasing as he was the one with the bowie knife sheathed on his belt, and I made a show of sliding a dollar's worth across the table to him. All the while, I put to memory the cards that were played this round and calculated my winnings. Nine dollars and fifty cents, plus the three I brought to the table.

Petit a petit.

In my chair, I readjusted, my dress pulling against the grime of the seat. To pay for my room and for this table, there was two thousand four hundred eighty-seven dollars and fifty cents to go—both daunting yet rousing, as that round took less than a minute. How many more minutes did this evening hold? Three hundred and sixty, perhaps. The potential for over three thousand dollars, should my pace continue and my luck hold, should the men continue to bet in a similar manner. Yes, both daunting and rousing, with only one thing left to say. "Shall we play again?"

The three men agreed. A fourth joined us, and I offered him my finest smile. My table was now full. I learned their names: Issac, Jesse, Stephen, and Frank. And I used their names freely, along with my accent.

Issac bet more when winning, but never more than five dollars. Jesse bet more when losing. His original bet of ten doubled to twenty. Stephen bet steady and often asked my opinion in a flirtatious way. When he reached for my hand, I quickly brushed hair from my face. Frank, untrusting, narrowed his eyes whenever I spoke, as if trying to decide if a woman dealer was the devil's work.

Potentially determining the same, Monsieur Sullivan kept

a close watch over me. Though, more likely, he only had an eye on his money. As it was, there were ebbs and flows to my pile, all depending on the luck of the cards and my ability to entice the men to bet more, to take another card, to indulge in another drink. French and English rolled quickly off my tongue, both to keep the games moving swiftly and also as a result of my nerves.

When I'd played back home, the games stretched over a lazy afternoon, tea and sandwiches arriving at some point. Our winnings mattered little more than bragging rights. This evening, it mattered a great deal more.

I remained keenly aware of my table's movements, especially Frank's. The room was short on tempers. As I thought it, two different men occupied Lydia's hands, each growing more determined to have her full attention. She tittered, turning her head from one to the other, but the muscles in her thin arms were strained. Monsieur Sullivan stepped in. Four drinks were poured, one for each of them. Except, Lydia's, she later told me, was only colored sugar water.

I focused again on my game, where the men were beginning to fidget from their losses. I counted my total, just shy of a grand. "So, Jesse, how long were you in the mines?"

I dealt new cards.

"Four months. Hit some pay dirt. Came back flush."

"You don't say," I poked, considering much of my winnings were his.

He motioned for another card, then, upon seeing it, Jesse leaned back in his chair. "Whore's son." He blew out a breath, while I flinched at his profanity. "But it appears I'll need to go back sooner than later as my money is quickly vanishing."

The table laughed at his expense. I, on the other hand, chuckled at my good fortune that Jesse was at my table this first night. Problem was, I knew the night was nearing to a close. The level of drunkenness had crossed from rowdy to sloppy. Some men were beginning to leave. The girls were beginning to watch Monsieur Sullivan and I assumed he was the one to announce the saloon's closure for the night. Lydia confirmed my assumption, catching my eye and raising her brows in question as to my progress.

I shook my head, ever so slightly.

The hand ended. I added to my total. One thousand and five dollars. I was short. Considerably so. I had achieved only half of what I needed to keep a roof over my head and a door between these men and me as I slept. I licked my dry lips and stole a large swallow of Jesse's whiskey. I felt its warmth slide down my throat. I took another sip, smaller this time, thinking I could very well need its effects to sleep outdoors. I'd need my wits about me, too. I took one last nip, then pushed the glass back. Jesse enjoyed my boldness, chortling at the loss of his drink. "Never seen a woman do that before."

Isaac said, "Never seen a woman with a thousand sitting in front of her before, either."

Frank scoffed.

Stephen announced he was done for the night. He reached for my hand, and I allowed him to kiss it. Jesse tried to delay him. "Just one more round," he insisted. "She's so purty I'd give her another grand."

He had more than that sitting in front of him. It gave me an idea. I tapped my fingers on the shallow deck, enough cards remaining for one final game. Enough perhaps, to pay for my room, leaving the table's fee for later. "Jesse, *mon amie*, what if you and I played a round, just the two of us." He didn't say no, and I went on. "One round for a thousand dollars."

He whistled. They all did. But then Jesse finished his drink in a single swallow. He counted out the sum and moved it forward. "All right then."

Frank called him a god-damn fool. Isaac called over others to watch. Before I knew it, a circle of raucous men surrounded us. Lydia squeezed next to me. She whispered in my ear, "I hope you know what you're doing."

I did, as long as no one here was clever enough to ask me to shuffle, to use a full deck instead of this deck with only six cards remaining.

I was quick to put a card in front of Jesse. An ace. I let out a slow exhalation. It was the last of its kind in this particular deck. All the others had been used in previous rounds. I was pleased to have it out in the open. In general, Jesse was pleased to have it, as its worth could be either one or eleven. And, the only way to achieve a total of twenty-one. He threw up his hands, reaching for the heavens. Those closest to him knocked off his hat, rustled his hair, thumped his back.

I couldn't see Monsieur Sullivan in the mass of men, but I knew he'd be watching the spectacle. I dealt my own card, a seven. The men acknowledged my lesser card with hoots and hollers. I ran the deck's remaining values through my head. A two, three, six, nine, and the jack.

I steeled myself to deal. The jack would ruin me. It'd give Jesse twenty-one and, subsequently, all my money. A man to my right tried to peek at the next card on the deck. Lydia slapped his hand. If so much weren't riding on this next card, I would've playfully chided him. The men seemed to like that. They began chanting, "flip it."

I gave them what they wanted, in regard to a flip. Not the card. They all let out a groan at the two that landed in front of Jesse. It was not the twenty-one he'd been hoping for. His total was now three or thirteen, depending on how he played the ace.

I dealt my second card face down. Jesse quickly motioned for another. The six. That put him at either nine or nineteen, with the three, nine, and the jack still available to potentially play. I ran the outcomes through my head, blocking out the other men's lamentations for Jesse to make the call.

He wanted the twenty-one. And, it was possible. He could add the three and the nine to his existing cards. Or, he could bust with the jack. In agonizing yet mathematical truth, it was likely I'd go over, if he took no more cards. He'd be a "god-damn fool" to take more.

Jesse used his hat to whack the closest man. "Enough. Quiet. If I lose, it's not going to be because I bust. It'll be because this beautiful creature bested me with her own hand."

He nodded toward me. I dipped my head, then revealed my faced-down card. It was the three. A lovely, majestic three— that put my current total at ten. And, there was a nine and the jack remaining. Either, I'd get the jack, and I'd be the gracious winner and a month-long resident of the Bella Union Hotel. Or, I'd show the nine. Jesse and I would tie, which meant money was neither lost, nor paid.

I felt Lydia's weight on my shoulder, leaning against me. I clenched my teeth as I flipped the card. Jesse's head immediately fell to the table. My heart pounded in my chest. Lydia jumped in place. When Jesse raised his head, he was laughing. It wasn't as if I could hear the sound, the room had gone wild.

He began pushing the money toward me, covering my jack of spades. Then, he rounded the table. "It's been an honor to lose to you, miss." He shouted, "Sullivan, I'm going to need another drink."

Someone hollered, "If you can afford it."

I sat there, stunned. But I had the presence of mind to begin squirreling away my winnings. Once the room began to thin, I found Monsieur Sullivan. He was more than a foot taller than I. He stood there, chewing, waiting for me to speak first. "I'd be happy to pay for my room," I said.

His hands were deep in his pockets. He motioned with his elbow. "And what about the table you used all night?"

"I'd like to use it tomorrow night, too. When I'm done, I'll pay you for both nights."

He was slow to speak.

I added. "The men seemed to enjoy me and my game, wouldn't you agree?"

"You intend to create a spectacle like that every night?"

"Only when need be. My guess is tonight will get people talking, though. I, for one, expect a large turnout tomorrow night as a result."

He spit, hitting the spittoon. "If you can make two thousand tonight, you can make it tomorrow. That should cover tonight and tomorrow's tables."

My mouth fell open. "That's four table's worth."

"Consider it interest."

I considered it the second time this man had robbed me. I also considered using the Parker House as a threat again. But it hadn't worked the first time and I now had a roof over my head for a month. A month to figure out how to survive a second month, until my money arrived. Then, I could go anywhere, do anything.

I said, "Tomorrow then."

Chapter 7

BY THE SKIN OF MY TEETH—and to much fanfare—I reached two thousand again, mostly because Jesse returned and the others antagonized him to bet larger and larger amounts. The nights after, the table ran me five hundred. One would think the lesser amount would be easily achieved, but the cards didn't play favorites and my conscience didn't allow me to let the men heckle Jesse any further.

I shooed the spectators away. If they wished for the game to continue—and they did—they'd have to turn their attentions elsewhere—and they did—until a seat opened at my table. Then noses were bloodied and eyes blackened, seemingly enticed by the *femme française* with the doe-like eyes and soothing accent. Like with the saloon girls, the miners were starved for female companionship, even, it appeared, at the card tables.

I overheard one say, "She'll take your money, but you won't mind."

I certainly didn't mind, either. I did, however, learn early on in my first month that having a rental fee hang over my head didn't suit me. I was constantly aware of its extortionate existence, constantly totaling my winnings instead of enjoying the game. And, *vingt-et-un* was a game to be enjoyed, savored. The fee only dampened how I felt alive with a deck of cards in my hand. A croupier was who I wanted to remain. I daresay it was who I was meant to be.

I smiled at the revelation, taking in the faces at my table. It was Jesse's fifth night in a row with me. Each time, he seemed at odds with himself about whether he should return, but he did. He'd play poker or faro at the other tables, watchful for when a chair opened at mine. Tonight, Jesse seemed worse for the wear. There'd been gossip about him, how he made over twenty thousand dollars in the mines. And now he was on his way to losing thirty, spread out between the Bella Union and the other gambling dens in town.

I was reluctant to deal him into the next hand. Papa had always said not to listen to the customers' stories. It'd touch your heart, bend your will, and allow you to accept less for a sale. But Jesse—God bless him—had already allowed me to pay Monsieur Sullivan my rent for this month. The least I could've done was buy him a drink—and get him off the tables.

"Jesse, *mon ami*, would you be so kind to escort me to Monsieur Crocker?"

He looked to the bar. I extended my hand. It was the first I'd let any of the men touch me beyond a hand-kiss, dodging their less gentlemanly attempts at every attempt. Jesse was quick to rise, then to help me from my chair. Standing, I angled my hip toward the remaining men. "William, Daniel, Samuel," I said, reciting the names I learned for this game. "I will return in a mere moment. I expect my winnings to remain the same."

It wasn't spoken as a question, but a statement. Over the past few nights, I'd seen men leave the table to tend to various needs. They left their money where it lay, as if silently daring the other men to pinch it only if they wanted to subsequently resolve who was tougher.

In my case, my only advantage was my femininity. I added the blow of a kiss, then followed Jesse to the bar. "On me," I told him and nodded to Monsieur Crocker. I shifted my attention to the room. Lydia shared the lap of a man, pointing at one of his cards before whispering in his ear. The faces of the other girls had become familiar as well, as Monsieur Sullivan preferred to keep the number of his ducklings small.

"To keep tabs on us," Lydia had told me.

She stood and turned her attention to a new man. Monsieur Sullivan didn't like when a girl focused on the same man for too long. "We may decide we fancy each other," Lydia had explained to me. "Then thoughts of marriage may enter our heads, like it did for Elizabeth. Remember her? Then we'd leave this lovely establishment behind." I hadn't remembered Elizabeth. I'd never met her. But Monsieur Sullivan's concern seemed justified.

Lydia's new man wanted to dance. They began twirling around the room. Jesse was handed a drink. Over his shoulder, the color of two other men was starting to rise. One of the fellows kept tapping the pistol in his waistline. I barely caught his words over the room's volume. "If I get hold of your beggarly carcass just once, I'll use you up so small that God Almighty himself won't be able to see your ghost."

That resulted in a shove.

And a shove in return.

Yes, I thought. You are both very large men. And while I jested, I knew this situation could escalate, very quickly. Monsieur Sullivan hadn't noticed their exchange, conversing with a table across the room.

But if I stepped in and settled them down, it could be what I needed to prove myself with some finality to Monsieur Sullivan. Hadn't he told me I'd be no match for these men? I wasn't one to let opportunity pass me by. Catch when catch can. I cleared my throat and put myself between them. My head came only to their chests, but I put splayed fingers on each.

"Gentlemen." Their foul, whisky-soaked breaths wafted into my face. "There's too much gold to be found not to be alive to find it." I added a line of French, not saying anything of significance, but knowing most men here reacted positively to my tongue. To my relief, I felt the tension under my palms recede. "Now, I've a spot open at my table. I'll make room for two if you'll both behave."

They met eyes, nodded, walked off.

Monsieur Sullivan stopped me before I followed, as I had hoped he would. "Dainty and fancy isn't such a bad thing," I said in greeting.

He said, "You best keep a close eye on them, with them both at your table."

"I plan to. And speaking of that table. I'd like to get back to dealing, as your patrons have taken a shine to me."

"You're the first I've seen play *vingt-et-un*," he acknowledged, mangling the sounds of the *van-tey-un*. "Let alone the first gal to deal it."

I smiled. "It appears I am. However, I'm finding our arrangement tiresome."

His response comprised only a shift of his toothpick from one side of his mouth to another.

I went on, "As such, I'd like to continue on without the fee."

The toothpick wavered in his mouth until finally, "Fine, no fee. Fifty-fifty with the winnings."

I held my smile, despite the unfairness of his offer. "I'll keep sixty—along with a salary of ten dollars a week." The noise at my table began to rise, the men no doubt growing impatient. "I've a table to see to, Monsieur Sullivan. Do tell me, is that table mine or ours?"

He removed his toothpick, flicked it. "Ours."

"How wonderful," I said, and as I did, Monsieur Sullivan's words replayed in my head. *You're the first I've seen play* vingt-et-un. *Let alone the first gal to deal it.*

And now, I was the first person, man or woman, to get paid to play the game.

Chapter 8

ARM IN ARM, huddling beneath a shared umbrella, Lydia and I acted as argonauts, but in search of food rather than gold. Our routine had established quickly. Up all night, sleep all morning, wake at the mid-meal bells with immediate need for victuals. It'd been a few months now. After my first month's rent came to a close, I'd enough to pay for a second month, then a third. It was now the first of November. It was, I realized, All Saints' Day.

I stepped directly into a puddle, distracted by that date, and looked in the direction of *La Nouvelle-Orléans*. If I were still there, it would've been unforgivable not to stand before my family's mausoleum. Not as a way to mourn for my deceased family, but to achieve communion with my parents and sister. Now Texas and the Mexican territory separated us, however many miles that was. It felt far.

"Rain's got you down, don't it?" Lydia said.

I only nodded.

We decided on Delmonico's to eat, mainly because it was a door closer than the Florence Dining Saloon. But also, I admitted, because it was the nicest of many of the eating houses in the city. Inside, Lydia lowered our umbrella and we clicked in our heels toward the buffet, catching the attention of men and women alike, one gender's response adverse to the other. We both chose roast meat before taking our seats. Lydia poked at her meal with a fork. "I miss green vegetables." She sighed, and I raised a brow, knowing she needed no further coaxing.

"I grew up on a farm. I'm sure I've told you that? Vegetable gardens. Wheat fields. Chickens. Pigs."

"How did you end up here?" I asked.

"I saw a playbill promising high wages, easy work, and fine clothing." Her expression was smug. Her clothing was silk, only the fabric covered more skin now than it did during the night. "Daniel's been an added bonus to what was advertised."

"Daniel?"

Like me, Lydia learned the names of her men. Unlike me, she actively thought about them afterward, the next day, right now....

"Daniel," she emphasized. "Dark hair. Tall. That boy's come by every night this week. Gave me this necklace." She touched it, kept her hand there. "He said how he's well on his way to get what he wants for his future, mostly."

"Which is?"

"First, enough of a windfall to start his own mill. He's almost there, so he told me all that was left was finding himself a wife to help him run it and fill it with children."

I chewed slowly, swallowed. "And do you hope it's you?"

"Not sure. Life would surely be a lot different. What are you? In your early twenties?"

"That's fair to assume." And, I left it at that. I never spoke of myself or of my past. I thought on it, plenty. But to speak the words wasn't something I'd done.

Lydia snorted at my evasion. "I'm not far behind you. I should be considering marriage, right? Haven't you been?"

I paused, then shook my head as I chewed, giving her a nonverbal answer that only cracked the surface. As it was, her question further cracked my resolve, all thanks to how the universe kept forcing my past on me—just now with the realization of All Saints' Day but also an improbable two times yesterday.

I'd been at my *vingt-et-un* table, conversing with the men.

I'd perfected a balance of aloofness, elegance, and charm. Laugher. Sprinkling of French. The right tilt of my shoulders. It all encouraged the men to bet more freely. With one of the men, Arthur, it also encouraged him to ask, "*Votre nom*? I'd like to call you something other than miss, like everyone else does."

The trivial question and his use of French caught me by surprise and I instinctively answered with my name.

When he repeated *Simone*, it sent a chill to my very core.

The last man to call me Simone had been David, all those months ago.

At the end of the night, I returned to my room. My head ached from the smoke, noise, and reminiscence. I wanted nothing more than to sink into bed and pray my insomnia gave me a reprieve for the evening. But I had no such luck. I noticed an envelope that'd been slipped beneath my door.

I knew what it was even before opening it. I left it there, the white of the envelope contrasting with the dark floor like a beacon, calling to me. I undressed and dressed for sleep, I splashed water on my face, I turned down my bed. Then I retrieved the letter. Still, I didn't open it until beneath my covers.

Tears sprung to my eyes, stinging them, at the mere sight of my previous address, at the news that my former home had been sold just as I had asked. A considerable amount of money from the estate sale was now at my disposal. Surely, the money would make life easier. I truly could go anywhere, be any-thing—with the exception of who I'd been with my family. It was a great loss, even as I'd become content with who I was now.

I held my breath as I read on, hesitating before I proceeded from one word to the next word. My heart pounded each time a sentence ended and my lawyer's signature drew nearer. His wasn't the name I both hoped for and also despaired to see.

I kept waiting for *David* to appear. For word of his well-being. For an inclination of whether he meant to follow me. I'd admit, to disrupt my life here.

Then, there was his name.

David.

David accepted the transfer of your father's shop.

That was all. Only, I wished I could transport myself through the leaf of paper and see David's acceptance of the store with my own eyes. Had he also accepted how I'd left? Was he still hurting? Had he moved on? Or, could he still come? If a return letter had reached me, enough time had passed for David to do the same. I looked overtop the letter and toward the window, as if expecting to see David standing dead center in the Plaza, with his almond-shaped eyes and a neatly trimmed beard. I had set the letter aside atop a book, closed my eyes, and convinced myself it was best there was nothing more of David.

But now, even while I ate with Lydia, he was still on my mind as she questioned her own future. She said, "It'd be smart of me to figure out marriage and if it's something I want before it gets any colder, right? Daniel mentioned Texas."

I looked up from my roast meat, barely eaten, and nodded, not entirely sure of what I'd just endorsed.

"Do you think you'll stay?" she asked. "Or will you move on, go back to France?"

I smiled coyly at her mention of France, an assumption many made. If Lydia only knew about my past, she'd be asking me a different question. She'd be asking: will you stay and risk being found?

But if I left, I'd be giving up all I'd built here. And I *had* built something in the whirlwind weeks I'd been in San Francisco, beyond a paying job and a roof over my head. The novelty of a pretty woman dealing cards had spread quickly. There was never a free chair at my table. Hats tipped as Lydia and I walked through the crowded plaza. Random belongings accumulated in my rented room. I'd hung curtains. My account at the Miners' Bank had grown, even before yesterday's addition.

"Will I stay?" I repeated. "I'd like to."

Lydia ate, nodding her head. Then asked, "Can you believe that man?" She said *man* in an exaggerated tone. "I can't believe he asked your name last night."

"Arthur?" The question was a non-point as no one else had inquired about my name.

She nodded, eyes large. "Do you think he's free or was he brought here?" Her eyes grew larger still. "Maybe he ran away? Another black man was captured here a few months ago. Shipped back South."

How horrible, to ship a person against one's will like cargo. Truth be told, when Arthur had sat at my table, I didn't question if he was a freeman or even a *gens de couleur libres*. There were many free people of color in Louisiana, who commonly owned businesses, properties, and even slaves. In my own household, we hadn't owned slaves. We had employed Caucasians and Negroes alike. Here, I'd only seen a handful of black men, but I'd heard most either worked to buy their freedom or worked to finance a new business. Either way, it didn't seem like much of my business.

The first black fellow who sat at my table was named Daniel—no relation to the Daniel making eyes at Lydia. He had proclaimed how he'd open a soap factory. I had playfully swept my gaze across all the soiled men at my table and replied, "Sounds profitable."

Lydia went on, "Well, Arthur sure took an interest in you last night. Be careful, Simone."

What she left unsaid was that it'd be criminal if anyone thought us a couple. Unions between whites and blacks were banned. I thought of it as a nonissue. I had no desire for a man in my life, David or otherwise. "Arthur only wanted me to deal him winning cards."

"Correct me if I'm wrong, but you have no control over the cards."

I winked.

♠

After fulfilling our need for nourishment, Lydia and I hurried down Kearny Street toward our rooms. We had a few hours before we were set to begin work. Rain bounced off the backs of steeds and dripped from the brims of hats. We side-stepped puddles, mud, and cattle dung. When I barreled into the Bella Union, I nearly sprang back in surprise.

Arthur stood in the main room. "Simone," his lips moved, lost to the sounds of Monsieur Sullivan sawing a circle into a long table. Lydia's elbow was sharp as it jabbed my side. I ignored her. I also wanted to ignore Arthur's presence, but there was no way around that. I smiled my hello.

"Girls," Monsieur Sullivan said, stopping. He blew the sawdust. "Come look. Your French ways have inspired me, Miss Jules. This is where the wheel will go."

Lydia beat me to the table. I kept my eyes down, feeling Arthur's on me. I still wasn't sure why he was there.

She said, "The wheel for what?"

"Roulette," I answered. It meant *little wheel* in English.

"So you're familiar?" Monsieur Sullivan asked.

"To an extent."

I favored cards, as there was greater skill involved. Roulette was a game of chance. Papa had played from time to time, coming home with tales of lucky winning streaks. Sometimes he came home with his pockets turned out, as well.

Monsieur Sullivan tapped the saw against the table. "Wonderful, after she's ready, you'll act as croupier here, too.

I bit back the response of *Will I now?*

"I've played a handful of times, so I can help if you've forgotten any rules."

The offer came from Arthur, standing with his hands deep in his pockets and a grin wide on his face.

It was odd for him to be here. Last night's men who were too drunk to stumble elsewhere and who slept on benches in the backroom were usually gone by now. Tonight's miners wouldn't show their faces until around eight. I was too polite to ask why Arthur was so early. Lydia was not.

He laughed. "I saw Jack here struggling to get the table inside, so I lent a hand."

The pitch of Lydia's voice was too high. "Well aren't you as sweet as pie."

"I help out when I can." Arthur gestured toward the ceiling. "Painted his sign a few months ago."

Lydia's response was little more than a noise. A breath later I was being drug toward our rooms, Lydia chirping in my ear about how Arthur was sniffing around like I was a dog in heat.

The way Lydia phrased it was off-putting, the crassness of these men obviously rubbing off on her, and the thought of one of those men—any of them—taking interest in me left me uneasy.

Still I was eager to get to my table and deal them cards. I felt in control with a deck in my hand. I felt emboldened when tensions rose and I soothed them down. Plus, my table sat beside the wood-burning stove. I relished the heat and even the slight sheen of sweat that covered my arms beneath my sleeves after hours of dealing.

A few minutes before eight, I headed toward the barroom. Halfway down the stairs, the oil lit in the chandeliers, I spotted him, the only person in the room. Arthur. He already sat at one of the chairs at my table.

Chapter 9

ARTHUR REPLACED THE HAT he'd removed as a greeting. "It was the only way I could ensure a seat, Simone."

It was the two of us in the room. Monsieur Sullivan wasn't here, perhaps in the back room. The bartender had finished setting up and gone elsewhere. Lydia and the rest of Monsieur Sullivan's ducklings hadn't yet come downstairs. Her warning triggered.

"And why is it my table you covet?" I purposely left off his name. Then, purposely took my seat, to downplay the discomfort churning inside of me.

"I find you charming—and curious. There's a story in you."

It wasn't his interest as a black man that offended me. While mixed marriages were forbidden in *La Nouvelle-Orléans's* society, relationships—and subsequent offspring—were common. It was his presence that left me uncomfortable, along with how others would perceive us together, especially alone. I also admitted, it was his interest in who I was that brought me to my feet. "Forgive me, I'll only be a minute."

My heels fired like guns as I returned to the stairs, returned upstairs. I felt bad for my dismissal of him, but Lydia was right that I should be careful. Now that I'd built a life here, I had no intention of jeopardizing that life. And, as it was, I already worried over one man. Only a silly woman would worry over two.

When I took my seat at my table again, it was full. Arthur remained, and as I smiled at each man, greeting them, I held Arthur's gaze a second longer, a silent apology.

Our games were lively. Overturned chairs. Hands in the air. Profanity. Insults. Charming ones, at that.

Bet your mother is quite popular with sailors.

No, but you sure look a lot like my father.

That type of exchange.

I didn't know how I hadn't noticed it last night, but Arthur wasn't like the other men, with their vulgar, guttural tongues. I bit my own tongue on numerous occasions, wanting to chastise them for their ways. Alas, it wasn't my establishment and hence not my place to lecture them. Instead, I sipped on over-priced champagne. Monsieur Sullivan ordered the drink per my request, then he marked up the prices by nearly sixty percent of what I once paid.

The men placed their bets, pushing forward coins and bills. My attention caught on Arthur's hands, the only dark ones. But also, his skin held splashes of color. Blues and greens mostly. Was it paint?

The game continued and I lost myself in the numbers, imprinting on my memory what cards had been played and what were left to deal. By the third or fourth game, the numbers jumbled in my brain. Roulette would be a welcomed reprieve, now that I thought about going from one table to another throughout the night.

The next afternoon brought the opportunity to learn the second game. It brought Arthur, too. Once more, he was with Monsieur Sullivan working on the roulette table when I returned from lunch. This time Lydia wasn't with me, having errands to run.

I steeled myself with a breath. Arthur's presence wasn't altogether unwelcome, especially with Monsieur Sullivan present. In truth, I was unsure how I felt about seeing Arthur again and I wondered how long his respite in town would be before he was off to hunt gold once more. These mountain men sometimes came into town for a day, sometimes a week, before heading back to the foothills and rivers, piling their mules or donkeys with blankets, a frying-pan, a pickax, a shovel, and food. When their flour, salt, pork, and brandy ran out, they'd return for a home-cooked meal and shelter. They'd deposit their earnings in the bank next door or exchange gold dust for bank bills. The men were often lured into the Bella Union afterward—or before they ever made it to the bank, putting their gold-filled jars straight onto the table.

"Grab a brush," Monsieur Sullivan said simply to me.

Arthur glanced up from his work, a paintbrush in his hand and a look in his eye I couldn't quite place. In front of him, he had outlined a number of squares that'd make up the betting section of the table. He now painted them in black and in red.

My hesitation to join them hung in the room. But this was to be my game to run. I picked up a brush and eyed the outlines Arthur had drawn. Then I began on the odd numbers ranging from one to ten and between nineteen to twenty-eight. Those were red. Even numbers were black. Adversely, odd numbers were black for eleven to eighteen and for twenty-nine to thirty-six. Evens were red.

I often had to stop and double check the correct paint was on my brush.

As we painted, Arthur refreshed my memory about how roulette was played. The rules were more complicated than I had recalled, with numerous betting options: single number, two vertically or horizontally adjacent numbers, three consecutive numbers, four numbers that met at one corner, six consecutive numbers that formed two horizontal lines....

I stopped Arthur there, saying, "I need to write this down."

"I haven't even gotten to inside and outside bets."

"Please don't." He laughed, while Monsieur Sullivan's appraisal of me wasn't as kind. It was his money on the line.

I quickly filled the silence. "How do you know how to play?"

Arthur dipped his brush, taking his time to answer.

"Well, I studied at the Academy of Fine Arts in Pennsylvania before—"

I raised a brow.

"They let us free black folk in."

My cheeks heated and I opened my mouth to explain that wasn't the reason for my reaction. Rather, his trade was impressive.

"They let us into Paris, too."

"I—"

"I studied there," Arthur said, "after my schooling in Philadelphia. In France, I played roulette to help pay for lessons."

"What a remarkable history you have." I meant it, but my words felt like an apology. I quickly added, even though I had already heard him speak French, "*Parlez-vous?*"

"*Pas très bien.*"

I smiled. "The language can be difficult to learn I'm told."

I wanted to speak more about his painting—what style, his inspirations—but Monsieur Sullivan preferred we discussed roulette.

My lessons continued the next three afternoons, the table and my understanding slowly coming together. Arthur gambled each night, but wasn't able to get a spot at my table. While I found myself searching for David's untimely arrival with a pit in my stomach, I searched for Arthur amongst the dancing candlelight and the chaos of the room with something else. What that was, I wasn't certain.

He had said there was a story in me. But clearly, there was a story in him, too. I already knew him to be a charming, charismatic man. I'd give him those qualities. But that was all I was prepared to give him.

Still, my traitorous eyes kept turning toward him. At a poker table, Arthur's left hand placed bets, checked his cards, and sipped his whiskey, while in his right hand he held two animal bones on either side of his middle finger. To a beat I couldn't hear he knocked the bones together with flicks of his wrist.

No matter if he folded his cards or if he pulled money toward himself, the movements went on, never altering. I wondered what melody he played. Amused, I watched the faces of his opponents, frustration creasing their brows and tightening their jaws at being unable to read him.

Bones I heard him called.

"*Bonjour*, Bones," I said as Lydia and I entered the Bella Union the next afternoon. The oils and candles were not yet lit, the only light seeping in from the front windows, and dreary light at best with another day of rain. Arthur was fitting the roulette into the table.

Lines appeared on either side of his mouth. "*Bonjour, Mesdames.* Today, we play."

Monsieur Sullivan wasn't there, as he was the past few days. Lydia placed her umbrella to the side then looped her arm through mine. "I'll play, too."

She was proving to be a protective friend.

I stepped behind the wheel.

"I'll start easy on you," Arthur said. "I'll make a straight bet of a thousand dollars."

"Goldseeking has been kind to you, I'd say."

"I'd say that I've got all the money in the world when we're playing for fun. So how much will I win?"

I worked the math in my head. Based on the odds, his stake was cut in half to five hundred. Multiplied by seven. Added a zero. "Thirty-five thousand."

He whistled. "That'll do."

I waggled a brow. "What's your number?"

"Seven. Give her a whirl. Let's see how lucky I am."

I did, sending the wheel in one direction and the ball in another.

The sound rattled in the room until landing on an eight. I won.

Arthur threw his head back, groaning.

Lydia coughed, inserting herself into my back and forth with Arthur. My cheeks heated at concentrating so soundly on him. We included her in the next round, each chiming in about the rules, the odds, and even strategies.

As I bobbled the ball in my hand for another go, they placed their stakes.

"No more bets," I said, ready to spin and drop the ball.

"How would you say it in French?" Monsieur Sullivan stood at the front door.

"*Rien ne va plus.*"

"Yes, say it that way. The men'll like that."

Arthur raised a brow, yet that evening Monsieur Sullivan proved himself to be correct.

I ran roulette for an hour at a time, pausing for hands of *vingt-et-un* in between. The men's eyes went wide with excitement at the roulette table. It was a sea of colors, numbers, and possibilities. With each *rien ne va plus*, then spin of the wheel, they cheered and circled their hats in the air. Their subsequent enthusiasm all depended on which pocket on the wheel the ball landed in.

Arthur stayed by my side, whispering anything forgotten about the game's rules. When he could, he spoke in French, keeping our exchanges private. The other men, caught up in the thrill of gambling, didn't seem to notice our quick exchanges. However, I felt Lydia's eyes on me as she twirled around the room with Daniel.

Our *tête-à-têtes* felt harmless, even with the intimacy of the sleeve of his duster brushing against the silk of my arm. But it was nothing more than a man helping a woman learn a new trade. That was, until he whispered in my ear, "*Marche avec moi?*"

I kept my eyes trained on the spinning wheel. "Walk with you?"

My words were lost in the roar of the room, but I felt Arthur's eyes on my lips, deciphering my response.

He switched to English and said in a hushed whisper, "After closing, meet me at the flag."

With that, he walked away, distancing himself, not allowing me the opportunity to respond. The flagpole was at the corner of the Plaza. Knowing where to go wasn't the problem. It was whether I should.

It was the middle of the night. I didn't know his intentions. They could be ill; though, I already doubted Arthur capable of any indecent behavior.

Then, there was the difference in our complexions. Not that it mattered to me, but it could—and likely would—to others.

I also expected the universe to intervene at that moment, to shove David through the door so my jilted fiancé could claim me as his. In fact, a man by the door resembled David in such a way that I nearly choked on my champagne. I set it aside. There wasn't much a woman could possess in this world. But we could surely keep our wits about us.

Arthur settled at a poker table and began playing his bones. As it did before, his playing gave me pause. Who he was certainly piqued my curiosity. The cadency of his bones was enticing, mysterious even. I imagined the tempo as morse code, as if he was communicating directly with me.

He took that moment to catch my eye. Arthur smirked. It smarted me, getting caught watching him. But his expression said it all: *I know you're going to come.*

Heat rose under the collar of my dress, but I stood tall and swallowed. "*Rien ne va plus,*" I said to the men at my table, then continued the game, forcing my regard not to stray.

At the end of the night, as gamblers stumbled out the

door—others into the backroom because they lacked the facility to leave—I climbed the stairs. Lydia was at my side. Daniel was at hers.

Lydia peeked over her shoulder, no doubt surveying for Monsieur Sullivan, who wouldn't be pleased one of his girls was spending time with a man with a mind for marriage.

I didn't say a word. Then, at my door, "Good night, *chérie*."

She held my gaze a moment longer than usual before smiling and wishing me goodnight.

I slipped into my room, closed the door, and leaned against it. I held my breath, listening for the click of Lydia's door. Decided. Grabbed my cloak. Turning the knob as silently as possible, I slipped back into the hallway.

Downstairs, Monsieur Sullivan worked with his back to me as he pushed the night's grime with a broom. The sound of scraping glass covered the click clack of my low heels.

It wasn't until I was at the door that I realized my oversight of not bringing an umbrella. Though as I emerged outside, the night was pleasantly dry and the skies had finally cleared. Even in the darkness, the sky held a hint of blue, illuminated by the moon, only a sliver away from being full.

The Plaza's flag snapped in the night, its fasteners creating a melody, mixing with a handful of coughs and deep voices from men who lingered in the square. Arthur's silhouette stood by the tall pole. With his dark clothing and hat, his eyes stood out. I walked toward them, training my own eyes on him, remembering his smirk and assurance.

When I stood before him, he said. "You came."

My heart thudded. "I've come this far."

He said, "For me."

Chapter 10

ARTHUR HELD OUT HIS HAND, for me to put mine in his. I questioned if this scenario—him and me standing here, alone— could've issued me a penalty or fine. I didn't know. Only David had courted me. I'd only ever walked on his arm. Only ever stolen moments with him.

Yet here were Arthur and I, forbidden to be together, in the midst of the witching hour, no less. Maman had always warned about being outdoors in the middle of the night, as women who didn't have a good reason for being out of their beds were often accused of practicing witchcraft. Truly, I didn't think anyone would've named me a witch in these parts. A prostitute was more likely, disappointingly.

I looked back at the Bella Union's door. Then, to Arthur. He didn't speak a word. He waited, his hand open to mine. Perhaps it was his earlier confidence, followed by his current passivity. Whatever it was, I wanted to unravel more of this French speaking, bones playing, painter-of-some-sort man.

I placed my hand in his. It was smooth, not what I had expected of a gold seeker.

We hurried down Kearny Street. That alone was exhilarating, as I rarely did more than a brisk walk to avoid the rain. I found myself grinning.

Since my arrival in town, the Palmer House had been completed and more buildings had been erected. Never mind that some appeared to be held together with paste.

Soon, there was nothing but a large hill and a footpath ahead of us.

"The Spaniards called this hill Loma Alta. Now it goes by Telegraph Hill. There's a burial ground on the far side, so some call it Dead Man's Hill." He shrugged.

Sure, yes, shrug at that, but I supposed more importantly: "Are there any coyotes, bears..." I paused, feeling shame at saying, "Indians?"

I hadn't left the Plaza since my arrival, but I had heard about the dangers of the frontier and the wilderness.

Arthur whispered, "The animals won't bother us and the natives have been chased far from here. Not all the miners think this way, but some miners see the natives as competition. They kill the men, rape their women, burn their villages. Those who survive flee and don't return."

I was stunned into silence. Men—except the ones who sat at my table—rarely used such words in the company of a lady. The air felt colder than only a moment ago. As an afterthought I realized Arthur spoke of the miners as if they weren't one and the same. Arthur's hand tightened on mine. I concentrated on us, here, this moment. "Where are we going?"

"You'll see."

My breath grew ragged, along with the terrain. The slope of the footpath increased, the effort quickly heating my calves, the burn intensified with each pull of my foot from the mud. Arthur clearly hadn't considered my footwear. "How high until I see?"

"The top."

I craned my head back, and saw a windmill there. The distance looked far and I released a groan, as ladylike as possible. Arthur reacted beside me. I said, "That better not be a giggle out of you."

"I assure you it was no such thing." He helped me over a log of sorts. "Men don't giggle."

A bellowing noise came from our left, saving Arthur from my retort. "What was that?"

"There's a dairy ranch on the west side of the hill. My guess is a mother and her calf were separated. They cry like that, at first."

If I allowed the thoughts to build, they could've—about separation, about family—even though we spoke only of animals. But I often quashed any mushrooming emotions, when Lydia spoke of her sibling, when a miner mentioned going home, when a man coughed in such a manner that it resembled my Papa's. It was uncanny how men had such distinctive coughs. For women, I'd concluded it was their sneeze. The derailment of my contemplations brought me back to the muddy footpaths and Arthur's presence at my side. I asked him, "How is it that you know so much?"

I regretted the wording immediately. A simple compliment, not constructed as a question, would've done just as well. To my relief, Arthur didn't show any signs of being insulted. "I make it my business to know things," he said. "Otherwise, how will I know how to see the world?" Illuminated by the moonlight, he must've noticed the confusion on my face. "How will I know in which manner to paint it? Here, let me show you."

Our pace quickened. At the merciful hilltop, what I'd believed to be a windmill was not actually such a structure. I felt a challenge to reason what it was on my own. Atop the cylinder-shaped base, a pole held two arms, of sort. I supposed the arms could catch the wind, but they didn't appear to spin. However, cords attached to the arms indicated they could be moved. I twisted my lips.

"A semaphore," Arthur said.

"Of course."

He laughed at my obvious lie.

But knowing the name, and the meaning of *sémaphore* in French—a bearer of signals—I made an educated guess. "A lookout for the approaching ships."

"Yes, are you afraid of heights?"

I couldn't say I was ever at such a height to know. However, I could fairly say I suffered from seasickness easily. And, the sight of blood left me queasy. At my silence, he led me through a small door. I held my breath while my eyes adjusted to the darker inside.

"Also," he said, "can you climb?"

A ladder, almost comical with how it seemingly stretched into nothingness, snaked up the inner wall of the semaphore. I said gruffly, "Let's find out."

Arthur went first, to open the hatch. Light filled the tower, as if the moon directed all its efforts onto us. Before I began, I was surprised to see Arthur descending. At each rung, he used the inside of his jacket to wipe clean the mud, a true gentleman.

His smirk from the Bella Union appeared once more. "I'll catch you if you fall, but I rather you didn't."

I shook my head in amusement. "Me as well."

Climbing thankfully came easily to me. I was at the top in no time, feeling prideful that I didn't stumble in front of Arthur. There was a crow's nest at the top, though I felt certain that that wasn't its proper name. Gallery? Watch room? The walls came only to my chest. I held onto the brick and marveled at our elevation. Here I was, above all of the Plaza, the wharf, and the budding San Francisco.

Arthur came to stand beside me, wiping his palms discreetly on his dark trousers. He was silent, and I took the time to let my eyes roam and explore. I'd never seen the Plaza motionless before. The darkness was like a blanket, tucking the miners in at night.

The darkness stilled the water, too. Outlines of ships speckled the bay.

Nothing moved.

Arthur spoke softly. "It's remarkable seeing everything so quiet."

I nodded.

"Perspectives can change like the wind. The last time I was here, the city's energy could be felt, even here. This spot is almost magical. There"—he pointed toward the water—"is where the crafts enter the bay. Only, the fog gathers so thickly there in the warmer months, it's as if the ships appear from another world."

I pictured them, though the night stole any true renderings of the harbor from my bird's-eye view.

He said, "That's where the semaphore is of use. You see, the two arms are arranged in varying patterns to communicate to the people on land if an approaching vessel is friend or foe, or in distress, or most excitably the type of vessel carrying goods. The town comes alive with that telegraph, hence the hill's name."

"I can see it."

"Can you now? My guess is you're normally asleep during the signals because of the hours you keep," he said playfully, and he nudged me softly with his arm. It caught me off guard, both the bump and that he'd so casually touch me. Off balance, I sidestepped, not noticing until that moment how cold my feet had become in the cooler November air. They prickled at the sudden movement.

I composed myself, asked, "Why is there such excitement over a merchant ship?"

"The price of goods here is high, yeah?"

I thought of my champagne. "Oh yes."

Arthur smiled. "But when a vessel comes in with a belly-full of commerce, the merchants need to react, restocking but also lowering their prices. They don't want to be the over-priced man. The Pacific Mail Steamship creates frenzy, too, bringing news from the east coast. Ships leave, of course, as well. Some return to charter more passengers. Others distribute the gold. To France, for example." He pulled on a cord, then another, shifting the semaphore's arms.

Entertained, I waited for him to finish, then, "What signal did you arrange?"

His smile was that of a child. "I haven't a clue."

"Ah, so there are things you do not know. Curious, though, you said you'd been here before. Why is that?"

"So I could commit it to my mind's eye to paint the view."

"That is right. I am standing in the presence of a worldly artist. I must insist to see this work of yours sometime."

My comment was cheeky. His was earnest: "How about now?"

"Now?"

"Unless you're too fatigued."

Why was it that sounded like a challenge? Further accented by the playful look in his eyes.

I raised my brows. "By all means, lead the way."

The way down the ladder and the grand hill proved more challenging than the way up, as I tried to maintain control of my body. It allowed for numerous occasions for Arthur to grasp me, steady me, increase my comfortableness with him. I wondered if I'd feel the same comfort if we weren't seen by only the moon.

I hadn't thought to ask where his paintings were kept until we stood outside a boarding house. At that point, I longed for the warmth of inside, greater than my uncertainty at being alone in his room. The rules here were night and day from my previous life—in that there were so few of them.

Then, only as Arthur seemed capable of doing, he surprised me and had me laughing an *excusez moi* after he asked me to climb upon his back.

"Simone," he whispered. "I'd hate for someone to hear the sound of your heels, then investigate which shady lady was walking their halls."

My mouth dropped open.

I could've left. But tonight's stolen time with Arthur felt intoxicating, and I wanted to steal more. I climbed onto his back, albeit awkwardly with my skirts. The last time I'd done such a thing was as a child with Papa. Fortunately, I hadn't grown much larger than a child and Arthur was a tall man, with muscled, broad shoulders. I now had undeniable proof of that.

We made it to his room without any attention, though the way we snuck through the main room, up the stairs, and to his room left me giddy. It was funny how sneakiness aroused that childhood emotion of glee. I was almost sorry to drop from his back to his bed.

Until, sitting there, in the darkness, unnerve set in. Arthur's footsteps sounded and I tracked his movements with my ears. One candle was lit, then another. As soon as I saw his face again, my nerves melted away. This was a man— dare I say a heart-stoppingly handsome man—who wanted to share something special with me, who put his own self at risk to be nearer to me.

And now, his early confidence and bravado seemed to go missing with how he wrung his hands. "Of course," he said, "others have seen my work. But never have I personally shown them to anyone."

"I'll be gentle."

His lips curled. In the small room, his canvases were stacked against a wall. He brought the first to me. Truthfully, I knew little of paintings. I appreciated the arts, but I'd always been drawn to the theatrics of stage performances. Yet as my eyes drank in Arthur's painting, I saw the theatrics he'd worked into this piece.

The painting captured the wharf. Its liveliness, commotion, crowdedness, and somehow its noise. Birds seemingly chirped. Dogs barked, their heads tilted in a howl. Arthur depicted the abandoned boats, sails either missing or torn. Crewmembers fled their vessels, one with a head turned over his shoulder. I recognized a porter, and thought warmly of the young boy who'd helped me.

Another painting so vividly showed the Plaza from above. Yet another captured a boat's prow and figurehead emerging from the mist at the harbor's mouth. I smiled, knowing I'd stood in the exact spot Arthur had while committing those sights to memory to later paint.

A third canvas was of the miners. Even more remained stacked against his wall.

"Is this why you go to the country? Not to pan, but to paint?"

He nodded. "Back home, my work centered on bringing to life the life around me. I saw the opportunity to do the same out west. I paint what I see. Though, I'll admit, this painting"— he referenced the one he held of the miners—"isn't wholly accurate. The miners pan in the rivers, their fires smoke from the previous evening—those portions are true—but the natives don't lurk on the outskirts how I've depicted them."

"Why did you paint them that way, then?"

"It'd be simple for the natives to be erased from history. But I couldn't look at the miners on this land without thinking about those who inhabited it hitherto. Or, how the Indians were gold seekers, too, before being chased off, enslaved, diseased...."

His voice trailed off, and I wasn't sure how to continue our conversation. I absently picked at dirt on my skirt, my eyes trained on his artwork. Despite the sadness in his brushstrokes, there was beauty, too. Even with the bad, I recognized the good of gold discovery. Years ago, when gold was unearthed in North Carolina and later Georgia, it had done wonders and created so many new opportunities, even benefitting Papa's business, states away.

Selfishly, the discovery of gold was a way for me to reconstruct my own life, too.

"I can tell you're thinking," Arthur said. "But if I were a betting man"—he grinned—"my guess is you won't tell me what that is."

"You win."

His laugh was deep, yet quiet, kept in his chest.

"If you won't tell me, then you can at least allow me to paint you."

I physically recoiled. "Paint me?"

"Yes, I'd like you to see how I see you."

I licked my lips, all the while shaking my head. "You're clearly talented, but I don't think that's necessary. It's late."

He began gathering brushes and ink, a clean canvas, an easel.

Between my teeth I said, "Arthur...."

I wasn't mad, but uncomfortable—and nostalgic. The last time I'd been painted had been a family portrait. We'd worn our finest clothes, the collars of our dresses hugging our necks. Papa wore a suit, vest, and tie. He sat in a chair, with Maman beside him. Patricia and I stood behind, each with a hand on their chairs. I'd been happy.

In my haste to flee my home, I hadn't thought to remove the portrait from the wall.

"I'm ready," Arthur whispered, perched on a stool, his canvas between us. "Just sit as you are; I plan to transport you to another setting and—well—not on my bed. But I won't begin unless you say it's all right."

My breath was prolonged. Arthur's brown eyes already moved over me, and I grew hot at being the object of his attention. How was it that he saw me—and in what setting—I did wonder.

"Who else will see this?"

He shrugged, but his words were clear. "I don't plan to sell this one."

I heated further. "All right."

His back straightened. "I'll sketch quickly, and complete the painting later."

I nodded. "Please don't show the exhaustion in my eyes."

His smile held, slowly slipping away as he concentrated on his work, on me. I wasn't sure where to look, so I chose a knot in the planking of his wall. Still, I felt his gaze on my face, on my arms, on the entirety of my body. I circled my watch on my wrist and let my lips curl ever so slightly. I hadn't smiled in my family portrait. Maman had warned Patricia and me to wear an expression we could hold. But this was to be quick, and within minutes, I heard the scratch of his brush slowing, as if he was performing final touches.

I brought my gaze back to him. As he worked, he had leaned closer to me, a glow on his cheeks. He straightened again, then stood.

"Well?"

He finessed one spot more, then turned the canvas around.

I laughed, even while my forehead creased and I fought the urge to run from embarrassment. "You've removed all my underclothes?"

"But not the outer! I wanted to show you unrestrained. I see you more freely."

I covered my eyes with my hand, feeling my cheeks burn. In his rendition of me, nothing supported my breasts, with the uppermost potions exposed behind a sheer cloth that draped around me. "How can it be that you see me without a corset or camisole when you've never seen me that way? What is it that I *am* wearing?"

"I'm not familiar with the word *corset*, so I can't claim to know a name for the garment I sketched. Are you insulted?"

"Insulted?" I pondered. "No, you haven't shown me indecently, I suppose. Rather, differently..." I paused, laughed. "You've drawn me as if I'm going to bed."

He shrugged again, this time wholly playfully. "It is late."

I widened my eyes. "I won't be sleeping here."

He held up his palms, amusement in his eyes. "What about the rest of my sketch? Do you like it?"

All that remained from my actual appearance seemed to be my hair—piled atop my head in a voluminous twist, and my wristwatch. I swallowed, mindful of Arthur having had no way of knowing its importance to me.

"Besides my near nudity, the painting is charming." Arthur had positioned me behind a table, I assumed in a gambling den, as I rolled dice out of a cup. "However, I've never before used dice to play."

He shrugged. "A few days ago you'd have said you had never played roulette. So maybe one day you will. I'd like to be there to see it. Beside you. Whispering French in your ear." He reached to touch his drawing, stopping short as not to smear it. "Here you look alive and unburdened, Simone."

I did. And for the first time, I saw myself as solely me and not as Patricia. I came here because I was no longer *sister* or *daughter*, and I'd yearned to assign myself a new identity. Now, here I was. Simply me.

"I look happy. Like I once was in *La Nouvelle-Orléans*."

"Oh?"

With his response, I startled at the realization of my admission. I buried my past as not to remember it aloud. Then along came Arthur, with his familiar French tongue, who showed himself and myself to me. "I'm nothing more than an orphan. I came here after my parents and sister died in a fire," I said. "My whole life was decided, and not in a way I resisted. I was eager to take over my Papa's shop. But how could I carry out that life without them? So I boarded the first ship I saw."

"To start over," he finished.

I agreed, "*Tout à fait.*"

"Well, Simone Jules, I'm glad you did."

"Me, too."

Chapter 11

I WOKE TO THE SOUND of knocking, hard and sharp. Exhaustion was a heavy blanket, and all I wanted was to sink deeper into it, only surfacing tonight to find Arthur at a table playing his bones to an unbroken, unheard melody.

"Simone!"

Lydia.

I kicked my limbs free, saving my torso for last to meet the day's chill. The room was bright, the burgundy fabric I'd hung over the window losing to the sun.

On unsteady feet, I wobbled toward the door. I almost laughed at how my muscles strained from last night's exertion. My eyes tracked over clumps of mud, now dried, leading to the shoes and clothing I discarded as if in a drunken stupor.

But of course, it was my stolen evening and not the bottle that intoxicated me.

I longed to go back and experience the night again, every moment of it, ending with Arthur releasing my hand at the Bella Union's door as the rising sun kissed the Plaza.

Our time together had been innocent enough, nothing more than a stroll and a marvel of the arts. I smiled. But I couldn't help thinking it was the beginning of two people who were unpermitted to be together.

Lydia's impatience sparked again and I opened the door, crossing my arms over my thin chemise.

"There you are. Was about to come in." She shook her head. "I thought we lost you to death."

I kept my body angled to block my dirtied clothing and floor. "Only tired."

Her response delayed a few beats, as if considering me. "My guess is that Daniel," she said, whispering his name, "didn't look much better than you. He was up with the sun. All the men were from the sounds of it. The rain finally stopped and it was a mass exodus to the goldfields."

To think, the whole of town would've caught Arthur and me in our rendezvous had I not paused from describing Papa's shop, and how I kept the books, to notice the sky growing pink outside Arthur's small window.

"You speak of it all with such zest," Arthur had whispered as we dashed from his room toward mine. "You'll work for yourself one day."

I had laughed and also enjoyed the notion. Creating my own space, my own rules, free to do as I wished. Perhaps there'd be a French-speaking, bones-playing, painter-of-a-man at my side.

Lydia busied her hands, smoothing her dress. "Now all I've to do is wait and hope cholera, consumption, dysentery, bears, Indians... why are there so many ways to kill the man I love?"

"Love?" I asked.

"It's moving in that direction, anyhow. Been considering his idea of marriage, but I'll be honest I'm not ready to take on his life instead of my own. Alas, there's no marrying a dead man, so he best come back to me." She shrugged, and I marveled at her practicality. "It'll be slower here tonight with many of the men gone, but we'll have enough to keep busy. Funny how there's never a shortage of thirsty, rowdy men. Now, get yourself dressed. Food bell is about to sound."

On the way to the eatery, a child planted himself directly in front of me, only long enough to shove a note into my hand. With Lydia's eyes on me, I had no choice but to unfold the paper while standing in front of her.

Back Soon it said.

"Ohh," Lydia said. "One of the men has taken a liking to you."

I let out a small laugh.

Lydia looped her arm through mine. "Don't keep a girl in suspense. Who is he?"

I folded the note, adding a shrug when I was done. "Couldn't say."

But I could, and it made my belly tighten.

♠

That night at my table, I dealt cards to Frank, Robert, Willie, and Oscar. But my mind kept wandering to Arthur. Was he sitting around a campfire with those bones of his? Or was he asleep—he was probably asleep—after being up all night with me then going off with the men. The conditions out there had never bothered me much before, but now I thought of Arthur hungry and cold, or falling victim to the list of dangers Lydia so blatantly recited.

I recalled a tale from a miner who had braved the monsoon season. He slept in a rubber cap, raincoat, and boots. He, however, was one of the lucky ones with an umbrella to prop over his head. It was no wonder many reached for the bottle as a first consolation as they warmed their bodies around small brush fires, darkening their pork on sticks, and heating water to stir with flour.

I was relieved the rain had called a truce with the miners. Under tomorrow's sun's rays, I wondered what moments in time Arthur would capture.

"*Zut alors*," I mumbled the cuss, realizing I hadn't been tracking the cards I'd dealt. By the time this deck was spent, I'd have lost money. Monsieur Sullivan would've lost money. I considered reshuffling, but Papa always taught me to be fair.

Lips pressed together, I smiled at my table of men. On the other hand, Maman always taught me to be savvy. I asked, "Who needs some whiskey to help the next round go down?"

Drinks were served. The men's brains and tongues became looser. We played on, night after night, one new table of men after another, November turning to December.

Arthur hadn't yet returned.

David hadn't yet barreled into my newfound life.

One of those made me happier than the other.

One day, another *femme française* arrived in town. With so many foreign arrivals, my French-ness had become un-spectacular, but Isidore Boudin's gender raised quite a few eyebrows. Women were still far and few between. In a moment of self-consciousness, I envisioned Arthur's reaction to her. Hadn't our shared French language initially drawn him to me?

Within days, Madame Boudin had opened a bakery. That surely helped her popularity, men demanding her sourdough with each meal.

I decided to pleasantly make introductions while purchas-ing my own loaf, and perhaps I scrutinized her. Yes, she'd turn heads. I kept my distance, as it felt unhealthy to compare myself to her. But I told myself it was because I was in no hurry to trade backgrounds with her. Of course, all of the town thought we knew each other from our French and the country they assumed we both sailed from. Each time someone remarked on our likeness, I thought more of Arthur, the one soul who knew my truth.

It was early December and, although San Francisco didn't show signs of the approaching holiday, I couldn't help thinking of Christmastime. Without my family, it was a holiday I would've been happy to bypass, but now, in my free time, telling Lydia I wished to nap, I found myself knitting socks, as a gift for Arthur. That was, if he returned by the holiday.

Then, as if he'd been there all along, he suddenly appeared

at my side at the roulette table, swirling the whiskey in his glass. He wore that smirk of his. But as my regard traveled up his face, I found his skin darker around his eye. A small gasp slipped out, one I quickly played off with a head tilt toward a man who'd made a sizable bet.

"*Qu'est qui s'est passé?*" I said, adding, "*Rien ne va plus.*"

The men were clueless to my question of what had happened to Arthur's eye, only recognizing the second half where I announced *no more bets*. The first half was for Arthur. But instead of answering me, he elbowed a man, James, beside him. "Sold one of my pieces. Plan to mail it tomorrow after I sleep off tonight."

James slapped him on the back, but his care was on the roulette wheel I was about to spin. Another man, Reuben, scowled in Arthur's direction, clearly not a friend who was pleased to hear of Arthur's good fortune. I already didn't like him. That feeling grew when Reuben abruptly took my hand. He kissed it, his lips pressing down hard, too long, in a way that felt possessive. A right he did not have. I freed my hand and spun the wheel, delighted to take Reuben's bet when he lost.

Lydia, on the other hand, was not delighted the next day when I mentioned I'd be a few minutes late to our meal. I had an errand at the post office to see to first.

"I make no promises I won't start without you," she said.

"By all means," I said, tapping an envelope against my palm. Inside, I'd placed a folded blank sheet of paper to give the envelope more shape.

From what I was told, the mornings proved to be the busiest time at the post office, with separate lines for Spanish-speaking patrons, general deliveries, parcel deliveries, and for picking up newspapers.

In the early afternoon, there were fewer men and the lines combined to one. In it, Arthur was a head taller than the others waiting for service. I spotted him right off and my stomach fluttered in response. He shifted and I saw he held a canvas wrapped in brown paper. Arthur had truly sold a painting. For a moment, I doubted his announcement of a trip to the post office was for my benefit. Then, he looked over his shoulder, found me, smiled.

That set free butterflies.

At a writing table, feigning the act of writing, I watched him slowly move forward until it was his turn. He tipped his hat to the worker and accepted a written confirmation of their exchange. Whistling an upbeat tune, he approached my table and began feigning his own writing on the receipt.

Arthur's back was to the room, his body blocking me from view. I whispered, "Your eye?" I ached to touch his skin, as if his story and pain would transfer with the act.

Head down, he tapped his pen against the paper.

"Arthur."

"My pal James asked me if I wanted a try at panning. All it took was one fellow thinking James owned me to cause an uproar. It appears some men don't take kindly to slaves mining."

"But you're free."

He shrugged. "They thought I was mining for James and, out in the mines, there's a law that the gold belongs to whoever finds it. Having your slave find it for you violates that law. Folks got angry and tried to chase us off. James can be hot mouthed."

"Yet you have the busted eye." James didn't have a visible mark on him last night. "You should press charges."

"Against a white man? I'm black, Simone. The law prohibits me from testifying against a man like him."

"How is that fair?"

"It's funny, really."

"Funny?"

"When I paint, all skin color starts the same, equal parts

red, yellow, blue and white. A brown shade."

My left hand had held my paper flat while I feigned writing. I shifted my palm to brush my fingertips against his hand. "We all start brown?"

Arthur nodded. "For you, I'd add more white and yellow. Until I had a smooth, soft ivory color."

I felt my cheeks fill with heat.

"And a hint of red," he teased.

I playfully slapped his hand, then clenched mine together at my belly. "Congratulations on selling a painting. Sounds like you know what you're doing."

He chuckled. "I think I'll stick to that."

"Which one did you sell?"

"The wharf."

"So you'll need to do another one, then."

"Guess so. I should probably hit the hay early. Get a good night's rest."

I narrowed my eyes and began to fold the paper in front of me. "Is that so?"

"Unless there's somewhere else I should be."

I returned my pen to its holder. "I'll see you tonight, then. At my table?"

"If you insist."

"I do."

"Then I will."

And he did. Arthur found a way to one of my coveted seats. Arthur also discreetly told me, as he pulled out my chair, how he had new paint to purchase and clothes to launder the next day.

I happened to drop off my own clothing at the same time. Lydia, too, which limited our exchange to how do you dos. But it still felt thrilling and clandestine to see him during the daylight. However, the nighttime hours were ours. He came in to the Bella Union, as usual. That evening proved to be a lively one. My feet were dragging up the steps by the night's end, from equal parts exhaustion and for the opportunity to take a *coup d'oeil* of Arthur before he left the Bella Union. His smile was suggestive, one side of his mouth higher than the other. But suggestive of what, I hadn't a clue.

I stopped short after opening my door. An envelope had been slipped beneath. From Arthur? With giddiness, I flipped the envelope over. My stomach promptly dropped. It wasn't from Arthur. I recognized the seal. The sender was my lawyer.

I tore into the envelope and shook the paper straight. When I completed reading, I simply held the correspondence at my side, my mind rolling with questions.

My lawyer had said David had asked for an address at which to contact me.

For questions relating to my father's store, my lawyer assumed.

He had provided my address, and then realized his absolute oversight.

He was writing to inform me.

I checked the date, did the math. The math didn't work to my favor. All along, I'd known there was the potential for David to discover my whereabouts and follow me west. I'd been mindful, scanning faces, but hopeful I'd never actually spot him in my new town. This letter put that mindset into question. David's interest, by asking where I'd gone, made the possibility of seeing him here all too plausible. This very moment, he truly could be standing in the middle of the Plaza.

I blindly stepped backward until my legs hit my bed. I sat. A sound rapped at my window. My heart jumped into my throat and I didn't dare move a muscle. I was on edge, was all, and the sound was an errant one. My window was on the second floor. The curtains were pulled shut. It was well beyond the witching hour.

The noise occurred again—a persistent, yet dull-sounding knock.

"Simone," I heard.

I stood, hands to my chest. The letter drifted toward the floor. There was the voice once more and this time I released a breath, as I recognized the deep tones. When I tore aside the curtains, Arthur stared back at me, perched outside my window like an oversized nightingale.

I heaved the glass open and he tumbled inside. We both laughed, while hushing each other, causing an even greater amount of noise.

"Are you mad?" I whispered.

"Undetermined."

"How did you get up here?"

His scheme was explained. Arthur had propped a ladder against the Bella Union's side, out of sight. Then he scaled and dangled his way to my window. He needed more than *How do you do*s and a brush of my hand.

"I needed this." He intertwined our fingers. "And this." Arthur swooped me off my feet. My legs hung over his arm. My back cradled against his other. And he circled, his boots clanking against the hardwoods. The letter from my lawyer crinkled beneath his steps.

He stopped, his eyes on mine. I thought he'd kiss me, but he didn't. Instead he whispered, "I needed to see you," and carefully deposited me back onto my feet.

"Me, too, but…" I looked over my shoulder at my door. "Your being here is unsafe."

"Only if we're caught." He dipped to my considerably shorter height. "We won't be. Don't look so concerned."

I licked my lips. I was concerned about the here and now, but it went beyond this moment. It went to the correspondence on the ground and the potential ramifications of that news. I bent to retrieve the letter.

"Come sit with me," I said to Arthur. He took my chair. I sat on my bed. And, I told him about David. Arthur had known about my reasons for coming here. I'd been orphaned, my life derailed. But I hadn't mentioned how I'd been promised to another man. How Patricia and I were planning a shared wedding or how my future with my fiancé felt so intertwined with my sister's. "Surely, though," I concluded, while also admitting out loud, "if, deep down, I wanted to create a new life with David I would've stayed and dealt with my emotions. Instead I built this new life out west. Do you find me horrible, cold?"

"Never," Arthur said. He shifted his chair closer, our knees touching.

"It seems that life yanked me off that path with David and put me here—on yours."

"My apologies to David, but I can't say I'm unhappy you're here."

I held up the letter. "But now what's to happen? He could be coming. This very moment."

"We could go."

Those three short words dripped with meaning. The *we*. The fact he'd be willing to leave San Francisco, where he'd created a livelihood for himself.

He added, "Right now. We could disappear into the night."

It felt so sudden. I'd fought to create a livelihood for myself here, too. And there was the gamble that David may never come.

Arthur ran a thumb over my hand. "Or we could leave when you're ready. I'll be painting down at the docks tomorrow."

"You would really leave? For me?"

"For us."

Chapter 12

ARTHUR'S WORDS SANG in my head, along with a slew of questions of what would we do—deal cards and paint as the obvious solutions—and where we'd go if we actually left San Francisco. The latter question posed a slew more. Where we'd live, being the foremost of uncertainties. But also, how we'd live. Would we do so safely and separately or would we cohabitate together? Dare I suggest as man and wife? If Lydia only heard my thoughts now. But they were private, inside my head, and she was none the wiser across from me as we dined, distracted by her own uncertainties considering her Daniel hadn't yet returned from the gold fields.

Of course, thoughts of matrimony with Arthur were dangerous fantasies to allow myself to have. The law wouldn't permit our union. But what was to stop a mixed-race couple from living as husband and wife in secret, without the consent of the state? There had to be others taking such a risk. We couldn't be the only two unpermitted souls drawn to one another.

I was surely drawn to him now, and I'd do something about it, determined to set my eyes upon my French speaking, bones playing, painter-of-a-man. I suggested to Lydia that we stretch our limbs and we headed toward the docks. The wharf was much changed since my summertime arrival. The hotel on top of the ship had been completed and named the Niantic Hotel. More saloons and restaurants had sprouted up as well.

I couldn't help my regard as it jumped to the docks and the many boats, one of which was unloading passengers, any of which who could be David. It continually felt cruel to think his arrival would disrupt my hard-won existence here, when I'd thoroughly disrupted his life back home. It was equally cruel to fear that David would jeopardize what was growing with Arthur. If I had allowed my heart to heal in *La Nouvelle-Orléans*, there never would've been an Arthur. I wondered over what that life with David would've been. Safe, predictable, neither of which were unfortunate circumstances. But I'd seen the passion and wonderment in how Arthur approached life. And, it was a life with him I wanted. How obvious it now seemed—that we should leave before anything unsettled us. I'd accept his offer and off we'd go.

Arthur and I caught each other's eye. With Lydia at my side, I hadn't intended to do more than set my gaze upon him, maybe a hello as we walked by. But now that a decision had been made that I'd run away with him, I had to talk to him, tell him, be near him, touch him. I tilted my head toward a storefront. *Meet me* I hoped the gesture communicated.

"Lydia," I said. "I think I'll bathe before work, but I'm out of soap. I won't keep you, so I'll just see you downstairs for work, yeah?"

She opened her mouth, her eyes narrowed, before her mouth morphed into a grin. "Daniel!"

Bless that man, his return from the mines coming at the most opportune time. He walked down the hill from the Plaza, his head on a swivel. Upon seeing Lydia, his arms spread, ready to swoop her into his embrace.

Lydia didn't say good-bye, nor did I. She let out the squeak of a mouse and ran for him. I took the moment of divine intervention to quicken my pace toward the storefront. Once inside, aromas hit me, filling my head with a sweet dizziness. The store was a maze of shelves. I disappeared into them, needing to stand on my tiptoes to see over. I felt Arthur come in. I felt that he was near. Almost giddy, lost in the romance of Lydia and Daniel's reunion and the knowledge that I was about to steal a moment with the man I was going to run away with, I twisted through the shelving. Their moment was public. Ours would be private.

Come find me, I thought.

"*Excusez-moi*," I said, brushing past a woman in my haste.

The store wasn't large, but it felt vast. Until, footsteps sounded behind me. A laugh bubbled up my throat, releasing as a squeak as Arthur caught my arm. I spun around, facing him, with his chestnut eyes, his sharp cheekbones, a dash of blue along his jawline. Was he painting the sky, the sea?

I laughed. What did that matter? Not a thing. Not when my thoughts narrowed on his lips. Last night, I wanted him to kiss me, but the moment had passed. This moment wouldn't, society and the laws be damned.

I kissed him.

I lost myself in his lips, in him. His arms wrapped around me, creating our own world; there, between two seemingly sky-high shelves, in the corner of the soap shop, the smell of lavender soaps enveloping us.

We parted too soon. My insides panicked with the separation. The first kiss was reckless. A second kiss would be doubly so, but I wanted more. My eyes flicked to the right, to ensure we were still alone. Arthur's gaze never left me, his eyes jumping to the various delicate features of my face, immune to the danger around us. Or, maybe it was that he was accustomed to it. Perhaps, he simply didn't care.

In that moment, I didn't care either. I kissed him a second time.

And I thought about what this could become. How easily it could become.

I told him, "My answer is yes."

❤

Lydia stood at the bottom of the stairs waiting for me. "Don't you look fresh? How was your bath?"

"Invigorating."

In our corner, Arthur and I had decided we'd leave after the Bella Union closed that evening. My trunks were packed and I had managed a quick bath, not knowing when I'd come upon a tub again. Tonight, he'd come for me. I only had to wait in my room, until a ladder appeared at my window. Until then, we'd carry on as usual. As if the pitter-patter of my heart would allow for that.

"I assume your reunion with Daniel was equally invigorating?"

Lydia waggled her brows. At the stair's bottom, she linked her arm with mine and leaned close. "Don't think that I didn't realize why you wanted to go to that store alone, or what you've been up to. I won't say a word, but you'd better hope others don't notice."

I pulled my sleeves to touch my wrists, this side of the country proving to be colder than I anticipated, and the stove not yet heating the room. "Notice what?"

Her concern wasn't unwelcomed, only unnecessary, as Arthur and I would be on our way in a few hours' time. Lydia shook her head. "Remember that man who dug out over twenty grand then gambled away over thirty?"

I wracked my brain for his name. "Jesse."

"Sure. Well, he took his own life."

"That's horrible," I said, meaning it. I had grown fond of Jesse.

"Yeah, but *c'est la vie*. There's some French for you."

"I'm sorry, Lydia, but I'm not sure I'm understanding how Jesse relates—"

"All I'm saying is that these men don't always make sound decisions. They're impulsive. Competitive. The gold makes them do crazy things."

"And you think, what?"

"That someone is bound to notice what you're doing. Someone other than me."

"Has someone?"

"Listen, I just don't want you testing your luck, Simone. All right?"

As a croupier, I tested luck every night. I'd test it tonight, and I'd test it wherever I set up my table next. However, most men around my table were deluded. They thought because the roulette ball landed on red six times in a row, it had to hit black next. But that was a fallacy. The odds of hitting red or black remained the same, no matter how overdue the wheel was to hit black. As the saying went, the wheel has no memory.

That night, I would learn that a wheel may not, but men do.

Chapter 13

ARTHUR WAS ON EDGE. Lydia's warning replayed in my head. Had she warned Arthur, too? Around the poker table, he showed his tension in how he played his bones. He broke his rhythm while thinking over his hand, or while his eyes dashed over the room as if looking for someone other than me.

There'd only been a few hours since Arthur and I had schemed in our corner of the soap shop. But something had changed since then. Arthur's gaze was unreadable and my stomach formed knots. I spun the roulette, dropped the ball. Anticipation built around me. Unease built within me.

Arthur glanced at the door, the fading bruise on his right side catching the light. I looked, too, yet again aware that my past could walk through it at any moment. Was that all? Did Arthur fear the second coming of my jilted fiancé now that we'd cemented a plan for our joint escape? The element that made the theory implausible, however, was that Arthur didn't know anything of David's physical appearance. It couldn't be my past lover Arthur was searching for. Perhaps it was the conflict from the minefields. Had that man returned? I still didn't know who he was.

Lydia walked her most recent dance partner to the bar. Daniel watched on, jaw tight. Arthur stood and nodded toward his pal James. My guess: to keep an eye on his winnings. He sauntered to the bar, where he sidled next to Lydia. His lips moved. Her head cocked toward him. My unease piqued further.

The roulette ball landed in a pocket.

Red seven.

Whoops and curses.

I struggled to calculate the payouts, the numbers sticking in my brain. Arthur returned to his cards with a glass of whiskey.

I spun the wheel, dropped the ball. Howard, Joe, Earl, and Peter awaited the outcome. Or was it Howard, Joe, Earl, and Reuben? Peter had gone broke and left. The air felt combustible.

Red eighteen.

Whoops and curses, always with the profanity.

Red was on a streak. Half the men stuck with red. The others insisted black was overdue.

Arthur sipped from his glass, his bones put aside. He peeked at his cards. His eyes flicked to me. With my own, I tried to portray the question of why he seemed bothered. He concentrated again on his game.

Lydia sat in Daniel's lap. Her eyes also flicked toward me. I widened mine. Nothing further from her. I longed to ask Lydia what she knew.

Men quarreled. Men died. Men disappeared. Tensions were generally high. But for some reason, tonight felt different, like one strike of a match could end us all.

The roulette hit red again.

One of the men, Reuben, slammed down his glass, breaking it.

Monsieur Sullivan stepped in. "Let's give the wheel a break, boys." That was met with groans from the ones who'd bet red. "Miss Jules." Monsieur Sullivan directed me toward a table and I began a game of *vingt-et-un*, Reuben and Earl joining me. The others paid their seventy-five cents for a spin with the saloon girls.

Arthur remained at his poker table. He finished his drink.

It was odd he didn't take a seat at my table. It was odd he hadn't stood next to me at the roulette table, speaking French into my ear.

"Got any pointers for me, sweetie?" Reuben asked.

I forced a honeyed smile, also including the other men: "Get as close to twenty-one as you can, *messieurs*."

They laughed, all except Reuben. His moustache twitched, his eyes shaded by his hat's brim. Then, "I didn't mean pointers on how to play cards."

That caused an uptick of laughter.

Reuben had been coming around the past couple days. He must've been hunting gold before that, though I heard mention of him being a mercantile. He'd been at my tables, always a roughness to him, a crudeness to his flirtation. I kept my distance, along with a chip on my shoulder, on account of him scowling at Arthur the other night. I'd handled Reuben's type before with a playful pet on the back of his hand and a smattering of French. What I said mattered little, as long as it was breathy and melodic.

L'oie porte une perruque.

The goose wears a wig.

In the past, it had worked like a charm. But before I spoke to Reuben about geese, I'd see how he mannered as the evening progressed; I'd rather simply ignore his larks altogether. I was pleased to see Reuben didn't overturn a chair any more times than another man. However, I wasn't pleased, each time I looked at Arthur, to find a drink so frequently at his mouth. Unfortunately, I looked plenty. However, he had stopped looking at me.

Closing time finally ticked near, and my unease was mounting. I was supposed to be jittery and hopeful. In mere moments, I was supposed to return to my room and wait for Arthur to call on me. Except, in the flurry of disbanding men, I spotted Arthur on wobbling legs. Legs that'd barely carry him from this room let alone the city of San Francisco. Had he changed his mind about fleeing with me?

On my way to the stairs, I rounded an extra table so our paths would cross. I let my shoulder brush his arm, saying, "Pardon," loudly, then asking in French if he still planned to come for me.

I felt him tick toward the sound of my voice, but he didn't respond. I walked on, not looking back until clicking up the stairs. James, equally spent from spirits, had an arm slung around Arthur's waist. Together, they tripped over each other toward the back room, where the men too intoxicated to make it to their rooms sweated out their liquor.

Arthur's head twisted toward me, his eyes finding mine for a breath. Then, his head drooped.

In my rented room, I sat on my trunk, my toe tapping, staring at the window and waiting for the ladder to appear. Arthur would come, despite his mood and his level of intoxication. I closed my eyes, envisioning where we'd go. It wasn't a conversation we had shared. But to deal my cards, we'd need gambling men. Somewhere remote, where trees shot into the sky and gold glistened across the ground. The west didn't seem short of that.

A noise startled my eyes open. I straightened. Voices carried from below, loud and angry. Arthur had told me to wait in my room. But tonight seemed off, in every way possible. I ran to the hallway and into Lydia.

"Simone," she gasped.

"What is happening?" I asked her.

"Nothing, I'm sure. Go back to your room and slide a chair beneath your doorknob."

"But why?"

The shouting continued, and I ran toward the stairs.

Lydia caught my arm at the top of the stairs, pulling me hard into a sitting position. The Bella Union's door was wide open. Voices flowed in. I craned my neck to see into the back-room where Arthur had gone, but I saw no shadows. The downstairs was empty.

"Where'd they all go?" I asked, mostly to myself.

"Simone," Lydia said. "You shouldn't be here."

Her use of *you* struck me. Not *we*, but *you*. I clenched her hands. "Lydia, right now, tell me what is happening."

More people emerged from their rooms, also creeping toward the stairway. I ignored them. "Lydia?"

She whispered, "Reuben made comments."

I widened my eyes, stuck out my neck, all but screaming, *go on.*

"About you."

"Me? What did Reuben say?"

As if speaking his name caused him to actualize, he rushed from outside to inside. Arthur and James were on his heels.

"Stay away from her," Arthur growled.

I shivered, goose flecks erupting on my skin. Lydia pulled me back and around the corner, a notch in the flooring tearing my nightgown and scratching my calf. I reached for the cut, squeezed. "Arthur means me? For Reuben to stay away from me?"

"Shh," Lydia said. Then, she spoke quickly, hushed, vehe-mently. "Who do you think gave Arthur that black eye? Then Reuben comes back to town and sees the two of you together."

"When?"

Lydia's eyes jumped to those around us, then back to me. She spoke between her teeth, not to be cruel, but for discretion. "Does it matter? Arthur told me about you two, sneaking around. A black man and a white woman. A black man taking one of the *few* white women here, when it's not even allowed. God, Simone, Reuben's enraged. Then there's the gambling. There's money at play. He accused Arthur and you of card sharping."

Lydia shook me with each word. The hallway spun around me.

"Simone," she said more slowly. "He told Arthur he was going to get back what's his. His money and his women. That's why Arthur camped out downstairs."

Instead of climbing through my window, I thought.

Lydia let out a breath. "Arthur's not drunk, Simone. I served him colored sugar water all night."

I snapped my head toward her. "And you didn't think to tell me any of this? When you warned me earlier, you knew."

"That's not what's important right now."

I shot her a glare, all the while knowing she was right. Arthur was what was important, along with our future together. I crawled to the corner, where someone else also watched, and peered around. Lydia held onto my ankle, a tether keeping me from going any farther.

Arthur, James, and Reuben stood in a triangle, Arthur and James closest to the stairs, as if a barrier.

Reuben demanded, "Out of my way."

He followed it with an offensive slur I wasn't keen on ever hearing again. I flinched. Arthur stood taller. "As long as she's upstairs, I'm not going anywhere."

This wasn't happening. I had to get downstairs. Arthur hadn't put the ladder up yet, but perhaps there was a way for me to jump. What could it be, maybe ten feet to the ground? I could hang, cutting the drop to less than five feet.

James ripped free his coat, his movements erratic; proving his drinking hadn't been pretended. "I'm not leaving either. What right do you have to make me leave?"

Reuben said, "Stay out of this. It's none of your business, you hear? It's only between me and the dame upstairs."

"James," Arthur tried. "It's all right. I can handle this."

"The hell you can," James said. "Last time you took a beating."

Lydia still gripped my ankle. Her face was white. I was about to tell her I'd return to my room when I heard James's shouts. "Whoa. Whoa."

I turned to find Reuben waving around a pistol. He cocked it, pointed it at James's chest. "You sure you don't want to go anywhere?"

I couldn't see Arthur's face. James's either. Only Reuben's with anger etched into every line and crease of his skin. My fingernails dug into the wooden floor.

"Go on," Arthur said to James. "Get out. No one's getting hurt here."

James raised his hands. "All right, man. All right. But I'll be right outside that there door."

He left, leaving Arthur and Reuben alone. But, I realized, giving me the opportunity to get outside and talk to James. James could go back in, let Arthur know I'd escaped.

"Your turn," Reuben said in a cocksure voice. I paused.

"That won't be happening," Arthur said. "And I advise you to take the next boat, wagon, mule, whatever will take you out of town. Go back to New York. Your kind isn't wanted here."

"Think you should be saying all of that when I'm the one with a gun?"

He aimed it at Arthur, as if to prove his point. "Either you leave or I'll kill you. Either way, I'll be attending to the lady tonight."

Arthur's fists tightened.

I hadn't seen Monsieur Sullivan come in, on account of every fiber in my body being focused on the gun pointed at Arthur, but he appeared, pulling the gun down, telling Reuben he didn't want to go and kill nobody.

"No?" Reuben said. He fired the gun at the floor.

Lydia and I screamed. Tears wet my cheeks. Arthur had ducked, his hands over his head. Slowly, he straightened. James was back, along with two other men. I'd seen the men before, but my mind couldn't take the energy to place them. They scuffled, trying to restrain Reuben.

Reuben pulled a knife with his free land. A gun was in the other.

I fought for breath. My body pulsed, feeling each beat of my heart in my ears.

Monsieur Sullivan threw his hat, seemingly more irate than anything else that there was a hole in his floor and that this was happening in his establishment. He cursed and announced he was going to get the sheriff.

Before he was even out the door, another shot was fired.

The sound hitched my already shallow intake. But Arthur was still standing. He wasn't shot.

James whacked Reuben with a chair. Twice. When Reuben stood again, Arthur seized him from behind and pinioned his arms. They scrambled, a dance of changed positions, until hitting the bar. Their efforts sounded like ones from an animal. I myself felt like a trapped animal, kneeling on all fours, watching from afar.

The men stilled.

Arthur's arms dropped.

Shaking out his arms, Reuben distanced himself from Arthur. The dagger caught the light, glistening.

Seconds passed. Five. Ten. A dozen. Still, my mind couldn't comprehend what had happened. The others didn't move. Only Reuben, pacing, shaking his arms and head. Until, Arthur sunk to his knees, his back to me. His hands found his chest, before he fell forward. Before, he was gone.

Chapter 14

ARTHUR HAD BEEN STABBED. James, Reuben, the two unnamed men, they all vanished from my mind's eye. Only Arthur remained. Lying there, his face against the floor, twisted away from me.

I started toward him. Lydia's fingers tightened around my ankle.

A pool of darkness puddled next to his torso. The sight of blood turned my stomach and a wave of nausea rolled through me. I clamped a hand over my mouth as my forehead touched the cold floor.

I couldn't look.

But I couldn't lose my sight of him either, as if Reuben would do something more to cause Arthur harm. Only there was nothing more for Reuben to do. He fled, his abrupt motion bringing the entirety of the room back into my focus.

Lydia whispered a string of profanities and prayers.

James crept toward Arthur. One man ran out of the Bella Union. To chase Reuben? To go in search of futile help? The remaining man stood watching, his words similar to Lydia's.

I was in disbelief. That couldn't be Arthur, the man who always seemed to be planning his next wink, who saw life with such vibrancy but also realism, who orchestrated this whole evening to protect me, who in mere minutes I was supposed to continue a life with.

Monsieur Sullivan burst into the building, the sheriff on his heels.

Lydia startled. Her grip tightened on me still. "They shouldn't see us," she whispered. "They shouldn't know we saw anything."

Her words made no sense. I planned to be the first person to finger Reuben.

"Especially you," Lydia added. "Your feelings for Arthur are written all over your face. The sheriff will ask questions... about tonight, about the past few weeks. I warned you it wasn't allowed." She cursed, then said more softly. "Simone, the sheriff can't speak with you. Or me. We don't have the same rights as a man."

She began to pull me away. I slapped her, broke free. She was on me within a second, pinning me against the floor. "No," she said, such anger in her voice. "He's gone. You can't help him. But if you talk, you'll be arrested right alongside Reuben."

I didn't know if that were true. But when Lydia lifted her body weight I didn't run. I let her pull me away. *But not for me,* I told myself. I retreated to safety for Arthur, because he wouldn't want me in shackles. When he'd sketched me, he'd seen me free and unrestrained.

In my room, Lydia deposited me into my bed, removing my outer clothing as if I were a rag doll. The thoughts that happen upon us in times of grief were strange; at once I felt a relief that while Arthur had snuck into my room, he'd never been within my sheets. I didn't smell traces of him upon my pillow. But at the same time, the loss at knowing I never would was paralyzing.

I lay there, stiff, only tears tracking down my face. Lydia paced, mumbling thoughts and decisions. She stopped at a noise, men's voices below. "Stay," she told me.

♠

I couldn't move. Where would I even go? I couldn't go to Arthur. I had damned him the instant I told him my name. It

didn't matter he was the one to ask. I answered. I met him
outside. I took his hand. I let him paint me. I kissed him. I
kissed him again. I told him yes. All the while, the threat to
him had always been more heightened. I sincerely didn't know
my outcome if we'd been caught together. A fine, a short stint
in prison? For Arthur, I should've known it was death. A white
woman's integrity was always the one protected.

He knew that, and still, he asked, he painted, he kissed
me back. He suggested that we could go. I squeezed my eyes
shut, fisted my hands.

Lydia returned with a glass and a bottle of whiskey. I took
only the bottle. I rarely sipped whiskey. That night, I gulped,
relishing the burn in my throat, the heaviness of my limbs,
until every voice below became muted and my eyelids closed
on Lydia's haunted face.

I woke, squinting against the late-day sun. My head
pounded. A stale, sour taste lingered in my mouth. Those sen-
sations paled in comparison to knowing Arthur and I would
never leave San Francisco, hand in hand, eyes forward, a new
adventure awaiting us. We had only just begun.

My breath came out hitched—at the same moment as a
cough not belonging to me, one that came from across the
small room. I sat up, the brown of my paneled walls spinning,
the sunlight creating bursts in my vision. The whole of it took
only seconds, but panic set in at my vulnerability. When my
head came back to me, it was Monsieur Sullivan I saw.

The man sat at the chair from my toilet-table, where
Arthur had sat the night he snuck into my room. Such a small
realization, but it widened the hole in my heart.

"About time," Monsieur Sullivan mumbled. His expression
was stone cold, with a tobacco lump in his bottom lip.

I pulled my quilt higher. "What are you doing in my room?"

"I own the building, along with the room."

"That doesn't give you the right—"

"The moment you caused a brawl that left one of my patrons dead, I had the right to do as I damn well please."

I didn't follow his logic, but I'd be a fool to say as much. Nor did I care to discuss his being in my room any further when I wanted to know something else. "Has Reuben been caught?"

Monsieur Sullivan shook his head.

"But they are looking for him?"

Next came a shrug.

"Where is Arthur?"

"A deadhouse."

I flinched. I'd been expecting a mortuary, where his body would be cared for, like my family's had been. But a deadhouse? It was nothing more than a holding room until he could be buried, with no ceremony, no prayers, no recognition of the great man he had been.

My nails bit into my palms at Monsieur Sullivan's next words, as if he read my thoughts. "Though he's likely to already be in the ground."

In the ground with all the others on the far side of Telegraph Hill. I knew it wasn't realistic to return him to family across the country in Philadelphia. If his family did, indeed, live there? There was so much undiscovered between us. My eyes pricked with tears and I rubbed my collarbone, stopping short when Monsieur Sullivan's eyes traced my movement. I nodded to his answer. I didn't want to prolong his time in my room, not when a thin chemise and a quilt was all that separated us.

He stood.

I bunched the quilt.

"Miss Wilson is gone."

"Lydia's gone?"

His voice was angry. "She took off last night with another of my patrons."

Daniel. Off to Texas—just like that—without a good-bye. Though, I'd done the same to friends back home. Worse, I'd done it to David. I glanced in the direction of Lydia's room and my insides twisted at another loss. At least I'd seen this one coming. And Lydia was safe. She'd be cared for.

"That's two patrons," Monsieur Sullivan went on, "a rented room, and a saloon girl you've cost me, Miss Jules. I should have you arrested. Instead"—he spat tobacco juice onto the floor—"I'm changing our deal. I'll be the one keeping sixty of the profits. And you'll be getting no salary."

I bit my lip; those terms were criminal. But, currently, I wasn't in a position of power. "Fine."

Monsieur Sullivan stepped closer, his thumb rubbing circles over his belt buckle. "Good."

I sat straighter. "I'll see you downstairs, then."

"We're closed tonight."

"Tomorrow, then."

He leaned closer, his face only inches from mine. "Sheriff doesn't know about you and the Negro. Keep it that way and keep your hands off anybody else. You got lucky this time, Miss Jules." He said my name like it was dirty.

I hadn't thought to ask after my own welfare. Nor did it matter right now. He had reduced Arthur to nothing more than *the Negro*. He knew his name. Arthur called him Jack. Arthur helped around the Bella Union. I spoke through my teeth. "I'm in your debt."

Monsieur Sullivan nodded toward his spat tobacco on the ground. "Clean that up." Then, he left.

I fell back onto my pillow, exhausted by our exchange and relieved he was gone. The half-empty bottle of whiskey still sat by my bedside. I lifted it to my lips and took a long swig. Another. My throat burned like someone had taken a branding iron to it. I kept at it until the bottle was empty—until I was certain I wouldn't have to face a world without Arthur, at least for a few hours more.

♣

The second time I woke after Arthur's murder, darkness filled my room. In my current state, I was grateful for that. The stillness allowed me time to slowly grip reality, even if the actuality of Arthur being gone wasn't one I wanted to hold as truth.

But it was, and all of Arthur that remained lay in a dead-house ... or already with the other unclaimed souls at the far side of Telegraph Hill. There was nothing I could do about that, as much as it pained me. But I could see to his belongings before the mountain men scavenged them for their own gains.

I eased out of bed, my body fighting each movement I made. On my feet, I swayed from too much alcohol and too little sustenance. I managed to dress—reaching for my mourning clothing I'd arrived here in—and made my way outside, pressing my eyelids tight as I walked through the lower room where Arthur had been killed. The boarding house Arthur had stayed in was only a few buildings down the road. Under the cover of night and rainfall, I let myself in through the front door, kept unlocked.

My soles caused an echo in the room. I tiptoed past prone bodies who had snuck in for a dry place to sleep. My throat felt swollen at the memory of climbing upon Arthur's back only weeks ago. This time, I removed my shoes. I could've done the same before, I realized now, but that Arthur was a crafty man. He had orchestrated a way for my arms to wrap around him.

I longed to do that now.

I padded inside his room, only enough to close the door. There I stood, my hair dripping. I remembered Arthur sketching me in this room, his eyes roaming my body. His sketch was more than lines and curves. It felt like a suggestion, a proposition that I'd roll dice one day, and he'd be beside me, whispering French in my ear. The fumes of his paint lingered, and I closed my eyes, breathing it in.

I wasn't certain how long I stood there before my mind winded to the present, and the fact that Arthur needed me. I wiped hair from my face and stepped farther into his dark room, fumbling until I found and lit an oil lantern. Ever so slowly, I touched his bed, his pillow. My eyes blurred.

Forcing resolve, I opened a desk drawer. I snorted at the orderliness of it. I had expected a free-for-all of sketches, letters, receipts, and newspapers, even. They were all there, but in neat piles, the newspapers folded in halves. Twine bound a stack of letters.

The first envelope was posted from the Pennsylvania Academy of the Fine Arts. Curious, I reopened it, then felt immediate pride at the words I grasped between my hands, informing Arthur of the purchase of his painting. A newspaper clipping from the *Freedom's Journal*, announcing the news to the African community, accompanied the letter.

I shook my head, in equal parts awe at his accomplishment and sadness that he was gone, never able to receive another letter remarking on his talent. And, what a talent that had been, his remaining canvases stacked against the wall. Was my portrait amongst them?

I bit my lip as I crossed the room, then revealed each landscape and setting. But none of my face. Surely, it had to be in this room. Arthur had said he didn't plan to sell it. It was for him.

I found our portrait beneath his bed, wrapped in a cotton shirt. With care, I revealed myself, the light of the lantern bringing me to life. What was once a quick sketch was now complete.

He'd added a tint of red to my hair, along with my cheeks. Otherwise, my skin was ivory. The little clothing I wore was finished in a pale blue. I couldn't help blushing, even now, at how the mounds of my breasts were shown. Crafty, indeed.

My watch and earrings both gleamed. And then my eyes caught on something else Arthur had fabricated, something that had me holding my breath and clenching my teeth, or else I'd fall to the ground in tears.

Arthur had placed a ring upon my finger.

He had claimed me as his own, like I had done to him in my daydreams. I imagined what witty, sure-footed remark he would've made when eventually showing the portrait to me.

"Notice anything new?" he'd ask.

"Yes," I'd say. "My answer is yes." I'd wait a beat, sly smile on my face, then continue, "I do notice something new. The dice are complete and a number one is facing up on them all. What luck."

Then, he would've grabbed me, twirled me around, and said, "A jokester, are you now? Well, you are the lucky one, I daresay. To have a life with me."

There'd be blue paint along his jawline, from completing my dress. I'd touch my forehead to his. "I do think you're right. Yes, I do."

I set the portrait down, held a ringless hand to my chest, and let my head hang. Sadness rose in my throat, a scratching sensation. I swallowed it down and looked at Arthur's vision of me again.

He'd drawn me beautiful.

Free, unrestrained.

I'd take it with me.

I couldn't leave behind any of his belongings, to be pillaged or thrown away, as if he never existed here. Though, there wasn't much he owned. I explored Arthur's room, biting back the feeling that I was invading his privacy, and found his art supplies, the contents of his desk drawer, and a trunk. Inside, there was a week's worth of clothing, a Bible, and a smaller stack of letters, as if he'd begun packing but was interrupted before he finished the task.

I picked up the top letter. Walnut Street in Philadelphia was listed within the return address. I debated not reading the letter, this one most likely personal, then fingered open the envelope. My eyes immediately jumped to the closing.

Your loving sister.

I smiled, just as the first of today's sun hit my face through the small window. I had found family. I had an address in which to return his belongings. Most of his personal items, anyway. I'd keep our portrait and the shirt he so carefully wrapped it in. With a bob of my head, I decided his other paintings should be donated to his art school. Those were meant for many eyes to see. I gathered his remaining belongings into his trunk, touching each item a final time before closing the lid.

With a plan in place, I held the scent of Arthur in my lungs as long as possible, then left, hugging our wrapped portrait to my chest. Outside, it took a mere moment to pinpoint a young boy to do my bidding. He ran across the courtyard, energy from a rejuvenating night of sleep falling off of him like dust.

"Boy," I called to him.

His eyes were like saucers as he skidded to a stop.

I flashed the two envelopes with the two addresses. "How'd you like to make a few coins?"

His eyes grew larger still.

I explained my instructions to him about what should be mailed where. It was all to be billed to my account at the bank. The boy nodded, eager to comply, and raced into the boarding house. He soon emerged, his arms full of canvases.

I perched on the edge of a bench in the courtyard, where I had a view of the postal office. My concealed portrait leaned beside me. Funny, but I hadn't noticed the advancement of the Plaza since moving here. Walkways were being laid, trees planted, a fence was being built.

The boy ran from the postal office and back to the boarding house, his arms now empty of Arthur's paintings. His canvases would go out with the next batch of parcels aboard the Pacific Mail Steamship. It was a little thing, but I knew it was what Arthur would've wanted.

I relaxed my posture, allowing myself to lean back against the bench. The wind tousled my hair, but it was an otherwise pleasant day, save for the mud and puddles from the prior night's rain. It wasn't long before the boy appeared from the boarding house, heaving Arthur's trunk. A man stopped to help him, the duo bringing it to the back of one of the lines.

The post office was a big building, with an overhang supported by four pillars. It was as busy as I'd been told, with its three lines—one for Spanish-speaking patrons, another for deliveries, and the last for newspaper pickups. Lines, for each, naturally formed between each pillar; although there was nothing orderly about the lines themselves, with how the men seemed in constant motion, shaking hands, slapping backs, shifting their weight from one foot to another.

To think, this happened every morning while I slept. But I was glad I had seen it this way, even if just this once.

Soon, the boy returned, a triumphant smile on his face.

"All done, ma'am," he said.

With his polite address and the fact that he didn't press for his reward, it was clear his maman had taught him well. I gave him an extra coin, and then he was on his way, skipping every third step, aiming for puddles whenever he could.

In all, the task took an hour. What a heavy feeling; an hour to erase a man's existence from a room. It'd be weeks, maybe months, before his possessions arrived on the doorstep of Walnut Street. Within the trunk, I had scribbled a note for his sister, and any other family at the residence.

I hadn't allowed myself to dawdle over what to say, simply writing *Arthur's life was taken too soon on December 14, 1849.*

He will be greatly missed.

I didn't sign it. *Simone Jules* would mean nothing to them.

To me, my name was starting to associate with nothing but heartbreak.

The post office's chaos was beginning to calm after the morning's rush. People would straggle in throughout the day, but it was as if the office could exhale, relax.

I, too, felt exhausted. I wanted nothing more than to sleep. I never dreamed, but I hoped Arthur would find a way to visit me. That was when an idea came to me, rejuvenating me. While I'd only just witnessed the commotion of the early-morning post office for the first time, Arthur had seen it plenty of times. He also had seen the morning ships come in. He'd seen the town react. I wanted to see San Francisco the way Arthur had. To stand where he'd stood and to look where he'd looked.

At once, I was on my feet, my toes pinching in my heels, the first footwear I saw upon waking. Satin slippers would prove easier. I glanced toward Telegraph Hill before quickening my pace toward the Bella Union to swap my shoes and store my painting.

The pathways scaling Telegraph Hill were as unkind to satin slippers as they were to the heels I'd worn before. I felt every root and rock beneath my sole. But I forged on. I was a woman on a mission, which was likely to raise eyebrows if I were spotted. I was alone, roaming beyond the Plaza, eyes trained on the semaphore.

It seemed farther in the light of day.

There were no brays. Had the calf and its mother been reunited? No, I knew, but I chose to believe they were together again.

There was no man beside me, guiding my way, offering me his hand, spouting off bouts of wisdom. I wouldn't allow myself to look toward the hill's far side where it crested.

Not that I'd have been able to see the freshly disturbed earth, but there was no reason to test that theory.

And, this endeavor was meant to be a hopeful one. In that moment of a-ha upon the bench, I had decided I'd see San Francisco's morning in the same ways Arthur had. Though, how he had managed to be seemingly nocturnal and diurnal escaped me. I never had the chance to become familiar with the intricacies of his daily life to know.

That aspect—that realization—was what made mourning Arthur so unalike to mourning my family. Patricia and my parents had been woven into every memory. They were my past, my present, and my future, leaving me hollow and adrift after their deaths.

But, with Arthur, I had only dipped a toe into what we were becoming. Our future had been an exhilarating blank canvas, and I felt as if I'd be forever grasping at what that future could've been.

I arrived at the top of Telegraph Hill with labored lungs.

A man stood at the top of the high semaphore. Instead of announcing my presence to him, I simply went inside. It was dark, the hatch closed. I climbed the ladder and knocked my fist against the hatch's underside.

The face that appeared was nothing short of confused.

I extended him a smile and my hand. "Monsieur."

Once I was safely atop the semaphore, he leaned over the hatch to see if anyone else was there before closing it. "Miss, is there something I can help you with?"

"No, I'm here only to see the ships, the city."

I had said it in a dreamlike voice, and the man's forehead furrowed further. He thought me to be mad, I was sure. That was fine. It felt a touch wild to be here again. I ran a hand over the brick half-wall, sliding to the northwestern side of the lookout until, I decided, this was where Arthur must've stood. From here, I had a view of Golden Gate, the strait at the mouth of the bay. In Arthur's painting, it had been shrouded in fog. Today's colder air left the water clear.

Over my shoulder, I said, "I'll be out of your hair as soon as I see a ship's arrival."

It would've been poetic if a ship had come on my demand. But no, that wasn't how it happened. I waited, then shifted to the lookout's south side to observe the movements of the Plaza below. Cattle lumbered, pulling carts. Children scurried like ants. Patrons came and went from rectangular-shaped stalls. From up here, the canvas coverings nearly blended with the ground.

Despite the air's coolness, the sun beat down on the semaphore man and me. Was there a name for his role? He wore a wide-brimmed hat, but for me, there was no escaping the sun's effort. I'd be freckled by the time a boat came.

"Miss?" the semaphore man said. "We got a ship coming."

I rushed to his side.

He held a binocular telescope to his eyes.

"Do you know the kind of vessel? What *are* the kinds of vessels?"

"Various warships, barques, steamships, brigantines. That last one usually means trouble."

"How—"

"I want to see either a barque or a steamer. And," he said, slowing his words, "we've got ourselves a barque."

"What's that mean?"

"Most likely, supplies. See here," he said, passing me the telescope, "she's small yet sturdy. Takes less men to tame her and she can carry a lot."

It looked no different than any other ship I've seen. "Can I signal?"

He laughed.

"Go on," I said, "Tell me how."

He stopped laughing. "Well, all right. Pull here." He gripped a rope. "And then here. You want it to look like a backwards K."

The two arms pivoted on either side of the mast. I did as he said, watching the lower arm tilt down, then began to tilt the upper arm toward the sky.

"Higher, higher," he instructed, motioning to the top arm. "Otherwise, you'll signal a brig-of-war."

I gave a final tug on the rope, then wiped my palms against my skirt. "Crisis averted."

Just like that, I had telegraphed to everyone below that San Francisco was about to be resupplied. How exciting.

My semaphore man said something more, but the rustling of my skirt and the thud of my hurried feet drowned him out. I was at the lookout's south side in a handful of heartbeats. I don't know why I expected the signal to be instantaneous in the Plaza, but my mouth hung open in anticipation of a smile.

Finally, it formed. Like a wave, hoards of people from the square headed toward the wharf. Arthur was right; the energy could be felt all the way up here. In a way, it was mesmerizing, watching the commotion. And if it weren't for Arthur's enthusiasm, I never would've made the effort to witness this phenomenon.

Silently, I thanked him. I swore he responded. I felt a teasing nudge against my arm, like he'd done the last time we'd stood here side by side. I refused to believe it was simply the wind.

Chapter 15

I SAT ON MY BED, where only my windswept hair could be seen in the mirror. It was best that way. I wagered a guess at the remainder of my appearance. Unsightly. I leaned to rub my ankle. Lydia had left bruises there.

I had noticed the discoloration while descending Telegraph Hill. My foot had caught on undergrowth and I stumbled. I felt the tear in my stocking as it happened. When I'd gathered my skirt to do a visual check, there was the outline of Lydia's grip—from when she had held me in place during Arthur's murder.

On the hillside, I had collapsed into a sitting position, my knees pointing to the heavens in the most unladylike of ways. How foolish of me, but I had slung a curse at the underbrush not only for tripping me, but also for ripping away the magic that lingered from atop the semaphore.

Now, in my room, I rubbed my skin, as if I could erase the effects of that evening and bring Arthur back. But I knew I couldn't. All that was left was justice for Arthur.

Reuben was still out there; it was why I still remained in this city, because I knew the miners gossiped more than a parlor-full of women. With tonight being the Bella Union's first night since Arthur's murder, there'd be a lot to say. Their fraternizing was my sole motivation for dressing, adding extra rouge to liven my cheeks, and dragging my tired mind and body downstairs at eight.

I took to my table at once, wanting to sit instead of standing behind the roulette table. Also, the roulette was nearer to the bar, where Arthur's death had happened. I looked, breath held. Between the boots, there were no bloodstains. At least, I saw none beneath a layer of sawdust.

The first man arrived at my table. I softened my jaw and forced a smile. "*Bienvenue*, monsieur."

More men filled my table. I asked their names. I dealt. My routine continued, with the exception of the tick of my head at every mention of *Bones* or *Reuben*.

The miners recounted the night with vigor, as if they witnessed it with their own eyes: the wagging of a gun, the whacking of a chair, the shouting, the shoving, then, ultimately, the stabbing.

I swallowed hard, all the while trying to give off the semblance of being unaffected. But I had to listen. The last I saw or heard of Reuben was when he fled, nothing more than a murderous coward.

The conversation picked up at my table. "James got him good with the chair," one of my players, Richard, said. "Cut Reuben's side and messed up his leg. Someone said he can barely walk."

I shuffled the cards for a new round, my mind replaying the events. I didn't recall Reuben limping, but I hoped I'd simply missed it. He couldn't have gotten far with a bum leg, and someone had seen him. When? Or was it one of the witnesses from that night?

"From what I hear," Richard went on, "Reuben went to his boarding house, cleaned out his wounds, and went to bed."

"Went to bed?" I blurted.

Fortunately, the other incredulous responses were just as lively.

I didn't want to show too forward an interest, heeding the warnings of both Monsieur Sullivan and Lydia, but I couldn't help asking as I dealt, "Is he still in town? Has he been seen since?"

"Nah, the fool's long gone now."

I asked, "The sheriff didn't think to look for him at his lodging?"

The man made a noncommittal noise.

And again, "Or continue to look for him?"

"He's another town's problem now."

My smile was tight. "Well, what excitement. Would you like another card?"

He did, even though he sat at nineteen. It appeared he was too caught up in his storytelling to give his cards much mind.

He busted.

"Aw," I said, "*tu auras plus de chance la prochaine fois.*"

Though, I didn't truly wish him better luck next time. I wished for this man and the cavalier way in which he spoke of Arthur's death to be out of my earshot.

I stood, explaining to the men it was time to spin the wheel. As I walked to my second table, I avoided the bullet hole from Reuben's stray shots as if they were chasms that could've pulled me to the earth's core.

As my game of roulette began, I noticed two things.

The first, without Arthur by my side, whispering French into my ear, I was the only one who sprinkled the language into my diction. The significance, nearly doubling me over, was that, before Arthur, the last French I had heard came from my family. Arthur had filled a void created by my family's absence. Each time he spoke the language, it was like going home. Or perhaps it was like a piece of my past was kept alive.

I felt the loss of him so greatly, which led to my second noticing. It was only me who mourned Arthur. While the room had spoken about Bones and Reuben with such animation at the evening's onset, the conversations had moved on. Just like that. Now they spoke of how a grizzly ransacked a camp. How a hooker—his verbiage, not mine—took a young man to town charging him twice the normal rate. It was his first time. And how new mining bars were popping up all over the foothills.

I had envisioned Arthur and me in one of those mining settlements, amidst the sky-high trees and glistening ground. He would've painted. I would've dealt. No one would've minded us there. It was remote. Removed. The setting, I realized, was perfect for star-crossed lovers—but also for a fugitive. Had Reuben gone to hide in the foothills?

At my table, I spun the wheel, dropped the ball. The men's eyes stalked the spinning combination, fortunes dependent on the ball coming to a stop in their chosen pocket. They were risk takers, driven by wealth. Their proclivity gave me an idea. They may not know Reuben's whereabouts now, but they could find out, with the right motivation.

♦

I stood at the counter of Miners' Bank, deliberating. That word sounded cold. *Considering* may've been better. But that also felt insincere. No matter the word choice, I was here to withdraw money to offer as a reward for Reuben's capture.

But how could I attach a monetary amount to Arthur's worth?

"Miss," the teller prodded. While there was no line behind me, his impatience was evident with how he leered over his eyeglasses at me.

I cleared my throat, licked my lips. I should've determined the amount before I had rung the bell at his counter, but I couldn't; so I had come, hoping the answer would reveal itself.

It hadn't. I couldn't attach a number to Arthur, so I wouldn't. I'd decide an amount that'd be alluring to the gold diggers. Lots of them wanted a windfall to open their own business or farms. Last I heard the average acre cost five dollars. A man named Freddie said he had his eye on two hundred.

He'd made only a little over eleven dollars the other day digging.

A grand. I'd anonymously offer a thousand dollars for whoever found Reuben.

I opened my mouth, about to give the teller the sum, when I thought better of asking for the specific reward amount. "Two thousand," I said, adding artfully, "for rent."

Over his eyeglasses, the teller looked at me again. But this time it was as if he was questioning why I was withdrawing additional money when I'd already withdrawn for this month's lodging. I had also charged the shipping costs for Arthur's belongings to my account. It was more activity than usual.

Thankfully, people rarely asked questions around here.

He counted out the bills.

With discretion, I put a thousand in an envelope and pocketed the remainder. On the envelope's outside, I instructed the sheriff to use the amount as a reward for the capture and delivery of Reuben Withers for the December 14, 1849 murder of Arthur C.M. Reynolds.

Unsigned, I slipped it under the sheriff's door.

That night at the Bella Union, I listened, I watched. I was tempted to start the grapevine about the reward myself, but then the chatter began. The sheriff must've told one man, who then told another.

"I'm heading back out tomorrow," one man said. "I plan to keep my eyes peeled for the fool."

Another said, "Plan was to leave for Sacramento next week, but I'll ride out at first sign of light. Reuben was from a city. Makes sense he'd hide out in another."

One man elbowed a companion, asking in a whisper if he'd go down to the docks and search the ships with him. They finished their spirits in gulps, agreeing the search was worth a couple hours.

Each comment and assertion drove my heart rate higher.

It'd been three days since Arthur's death. I was hopeful Reuben would be delivered to the sheriff in a week's time.

I spent those days working, sleeping, and wandering the Plaza, studying each moustached face, as if Reuben would be foolish enough to walk straight through town.

He wasn't, and the wandering only left me feeling utterly alone. There were no more habitual food outings with Lydia. There were no secret rendezvouses with Arthur.

There was only me—and whatever gaggle of men chose to patronize my tables in the evenings. I'd never become close with any of the other saloon girls. I avoided Monsieur Sullivan as much as possible.

In my desperation to feel more than desperation, I even prayed David would come strolling into the Bella Union. It'd give me something to react to. As it was, the week in which I had hoped to hear of Reuben was now at an end. Travel time was slow, especially so with the onslaught of rain most days and snow in the mountains, but voices moved like the wind. If one of the hunting parties had spotted Reuben, I'd have heard. Alas, the men's interest had once again expired. It'd only been ten days since Arthur's death.

In my room, I reluctantly dressed for a night of gambling, longing for 1849 to end. But, first, I had to survive Christmas Eve and the false utterings of Happy Christmas.

In *La Nouvelle-Orléans*, Papa always had an evergreen delivered by stagecoach. It was a grand affair. We'd decorate, sing carols, exchange gifts. On Christmas Day, we feasted on turkey with oyster sauce; a pair of roast geese with apple sauce; roasted ham; chicken pie; stewed beets; cold-slaw; turnips; winter squash; Plum pudding; lemon custards, and of course the *Bûche de Noël*, our Yule Log cake.

I anticipated the season all year.

I'd known this Christmas would be a challenge, even this far removed from my past. Or maybe *because* I was far removed.

But then Arthur had come along. I'd begun knitting those socks, excited by the idea of gifting them to him. They'd been nearly complete before I abandoned them. I had used white yarn and tried to create the impression of paint splatter. Truly, it would've been easier to splatter actual paint on them. I'd never been a good knitter. That was a skill only Patricia's fingers had inherited.

I wondered… had Arthur planned a gift for me?

The portrait. It had to have been his painting of me, and his intentions of a future together. I resisted the urge to pull it from beneath my bed. The men were arriving downstairs, their joyful voices rising through the floorboards.

"Thank you," I said aloud to Arthur. It was the first time I spoke to him in this way. It wouldn't be the last.

Downstairs, the mountain men were boisterous, more so than usual. Dancing, drinking, singing. All at once, the town had realized tomorrow's holiday.

Even here, Monsieur Sullivan had cleaned the floors and trimmed the bar with *guirlande*. Upon seeing me in my dark clothing, he asked me to change.

My feet felt rooted to his clean floors. I raised my chin, but said, "As you wish." While I went from my mourning clothes to the more vibrant burgundy, I tossed my dress, I stomped around, I let myself feel my mounting frustration toward Monsieur Sullivan's ownership of me. *You'll work for yourself one day*, Arthur had told me.

At my table, a man—Herald, I believe was his name—thumped a bottle of champagne in front of my person.

I asked, "No glass?"

"Not tonight." He grinned, multiple teeth missing, before he sloppily kissed my cheek. There was no need for a glass after that.

Throughout the evening, the men regaled each other with Christmases of the past. One man spoke of his own feast of a gobbler, roasted with a score of fat hens, pound cakes, and pies. He noticeably left out green vegetables, and I invariably thought of Lydia. How far had she made it by now? It wasn't as if she could simply head south and east to Texas, unless she and James decided to blaze their own path. I'd seen a map once, laid out across my *vingt-et-un* table. The El Camino Real trail would lead them down the coast of California. I couldn't recall what trail they'd take from there.

Nevertheless, it was exhilarating. More so than my table of drunkards, who'd likely drown in alcohol before the sun rose, which surely couldn't be long now. I sipped on my own champagne, straight from the bottle. I dealt new cards. Then, sighed. Their eyes wobbled like teetotums, and I wanted nothing more than to retire to my room.

So I did, without informing Monsieur Sullivan. My departure consisted solely of a sugared smile in the general direction of the revelers before I planted each foot firmly on the stairs.

In front of my toilet-table, I removed the watch Papa had given me, my jewelry, then sat for some time. How long, I couldn't be certain. With the noise downstairs and my room darkened, each minute was like the next. Later, I'd think in earnest how fortunate it was I had chosen that spot to sit instead of lying in bed. While I habitually chased the onset of sleep tirelessly, I would eventually succumb, sleeping like the dead. On that night, that surely would've been the death of me.

It was the frantic uproar of voices that first alerted me to the goings-on. I cocked my head, listened. The sounds—not ones of excitement, but alarm, as there was a clear delineation in the pitches and urgency of the two—reached me not from downstairs, but from outside. I scurried to my window, jerking aside the curtains.

The square was dark, save for the flickering of oranges and reds halfway down Kearny Street. I recognized all too well how the flames danced and taunted. The shadows of men darted in and out of its glow. I hurried downstairs and joined them, stopping at the outskirt of nervous hooves, hurried footfalls, calls for water, screams for help.

Passing men jostled my body. I was in the way, the men racing to save crates of wine and goods from the Dennison Exchange, but I was too mesmerized and too lush with alcohol to move. Mother nature was a paradox. Fire was deadly, a painful truth I knew in the flesh, but it was also hypnotizing, with how it moved. A tendril flicked, until it caught something new. Then flicked again, and again.

Hand to my mouth, swaying from one foot to the other, I watched as the flames ate the building, once a gambling house. It spread, remarkably fast, the wind seeming to offer suggestions as to what to devour next. The Parker House, which adjoined the Dennison Exchange, was an easy next course. The flames reached its tar roof, a foul smell plunging into the night air.

Men attacked the buildings, not with water, but with axes, trying to strip away the burning wood before the flickering claimed more. Glass shattered. Smoke, as thick as waterfalls, poured from windows and doorways. Voices, thousands of them it seemed, were everywhere. One man's raised to the top, joined by others, their alarm palpable. Parker House stored gunpowder. Men raced inside, while I held my breath, wondering how long they could hold theirs. The building spit them out, the men coughing, wheezing, their darkened faces nearly lost to the night. With them, they brought countless barrels, and not a moment too soon. The fire was tireless, seeking more to consume to its south, left, and right.

There, the United States Restaurant, where I'd had my first meal, was rapidly kindling. The fire, a storm of crackling heat, inched closer to the grocery store on its other side.

The Exchange came down, similar to an old man lowering

himself to a chair, sighing and creaking with the movement. There was little acknowledgement, save for quickened paces. Ladders were propped against the El Dorado, a new four-story building at the street's end, and windows crashed in.

I covered my ears, fearful that I'd hear a popping sound that'd bring me once more to my knees.

At the other end of the block, two men, atop the adjoining Delmonico's Dining Saloon and the Florence Saloon began laying blankets on their flat rooftops. Blankets already hung from their glassless windows. The men meant to soak the wool, a feeble attempt to create a water barrier against the flames.

I twisted, hands still on my ears, in search of water. Of course, on this evening, there was no rain, even while it had showered the past five of six nights. A line of men stretched to a well and buckets passed from one body to the next. I meant to help; I had moved a step in that direction, but then the collapse of the grocery released a pop that went straight through my hands, as if they weren't over my ears. My knees buckled and I fought with my thoughts to keep them in the here and now and not let them drift back to the opera house.

"Stand back!" voices chimed. "Back! Back!" they demanded. The instructions came from behind me. When I initially rushed outside, I had crossed Washington Street into the Plaza, where, for all intents and purposes, I was safe with Kearney Street between the flames and me. It was on that block where the fire spread from one building to the next. Now I turned, toward the Bella Union. Its second story was on fire. The fire had traversed a dirt road, most likely carried by the wind.

The men screamed for explosives, their attention on the Louisiana that flanked the Bella Union Hotel. It hadn't yet sparked flames. Did they mean to deliberately bring down the building? An attempt to separate the burning Miners' Bank and the Bella Union from the restaurants, printer, medicine store, and laundry on this block?

With how the fire roared on Kearny Street, leaving nothing but charred wood and the false front of the United States Restaurant, it seemed a practical decision, a *dernier ressort*. But would it also bring down the Bella Union, and all that was inside?

The question, I realized, was dimwitted, as the fire would take what the explosives hadn't. That notion was paralyzing, as I didn't possess much, but what I did have was everything. Arthur's painting. The watch from my Papa.

The irreplaceable.

My feet carried me toward the building, having to angle my way through a sea of vacated bodies. Once my brain caught up, it was at my window, I saw, that dark smoke seeped through a crack in the casing. No one stopped me. Or within the commotion, no one noticed the child-sized woman entering the building. The barroom was a tease, untouched by the fire. I sucked as much of the clean air into my lungs as I could, even pausing at the base of the stairs, circling my arms to guide the unsullied air to my mouth. I gulped it, my heart pounding, and then I ran. The heat grew with each step higher. Flames had taken up residence down the hallway, Lydia's former room lost to it.

I'd left my door open in my earlier haste. Smoke funneled through the doorway. I did the same. My room was dark, made darker with the smoke. The breath I held wouldn't last long, but I also had little to grab. Blindly, I patted the toilet-table for my watch. Cologne bottles were knocked and shattered. But I found it, just as the last of my breath depleted. The first inhale of smoke-filled air burned. From my skirt, I ripped a strip to hold over my mouth.

My hands found Arthur's portrait on their own. I'd pulled the canvas from beneath my bed on so many occasions, unwrapping Arthur's shirt like a present, that I knew exactly where to find it. I should've left after that; it was foolish of me to think of money at such a time, but I had and I took precious seconds to retrieve the thousand dollars in bills from my writing desk. When I turned to leave, the smoke was too dense to see the way out.

I thought I was acting with intelligence when I threw a chair against my window to release the smoke. But I didn't realize it'd also let cooler air in, and that, to my greatest despair, the fire was drawn to it. Flames flicked at the open doorway, my original mistake not to close the door behind me.

A fit of coughing brought me to my knees, the air not as hazardous closer to the floor. It was there I saw the basin of water I kept in my room. Hurriedly, I splashed water on the backside of the canvas, where it was still wrapped in Arthur's shirt. Without wasting a moment more, I ran toward the flames, using Arthur's gift as a shield against the advancing flames.

I burst free and plunged down the stairs, missing my footing on the final step as the Bella Union shook fiercely. An explosion had been set off. The far wall fell in, taking with it the nude portraits. I held tight to Arthur's painting and, once outside, I immediately stripped the shirt from the canvas, angling it toward the fire's glow to see the damage. I waved away the effects of the explosion. The painting had been unmarred, only the backside held discoloration, mostly where the canvas had been stretched over the frame. The relief I felt was immeasurable.

Hands lifted me up, the men faceless. They led me into the square and asked me if I was mad, if I was well. I nodded to each. When their hands left me, I kept walking. Where, I hadn't a clue. But I held the canvas to my chest, too large for my arms, and I walked.

Fire was common—here, anywhere, so easily begun—but still, it had followed me to San Francisco. It felt like a personal assault or perhaps a sign from the universe and I wished to be anywhere else but in this burning town.

The thought of climbing aboard a departing ship and suffering from endless bouts of seasickness was fleeting. Instead, I went to the stables, as I had assumed Arthur and I would've done together. In the glow of controlled firelight, a man was readying a wagon.

"Where are you off to?" I asked him.

"Foothills."

His accent suggested he spoke Spanish. I said simply, "Me, too."

Chapter 16

THE MAN COCKED HIS HEAD AT ME. I believed my original response to be clear enough, but with a smattering of gestures and with my limited Spanish vocabulary I informed him I'd be going with him to the foothills. While I spoke various languages fluently, Spanish was not one of them. Not that I needed to decipher his response to understand the shake of his head and arms. I wasn't a welcomed addition. That was, until I put money into his palm.

I patted my chest. "Simone."

He responded. "Bruno."

Bruno used the word *loca* no short of three times as he mumbled to himself, readying us to leave. By the time he was complete, the sun was rising.

I didn't look back at what had become of the Plaza.

With my money tucked securely within my corset, my watch on my wrist, and my canvas beside me in the wagon, I rode out of San Francisco.

There was much I left behind. I recalled neither the trinkets nor the fine clothing—those were of no concern right now—but I left behind the opportunity to hear if Reuben was ever captured. That was, unless this path I was setting out on was the same course Reuben had followed. The rattle lulled me to an ease I hadn't felt in some time. It settled me. Sitting and waiting for the miners to do my bidding was of no help. Now I had the potential to spot Reuben with my own eyes.

The wagon was full of crates and barrels. I myself sat on a

crate. My left ankle and shin were exposed, where I'd torn my dress. What a mess I must've looked.

Bruno walked alongside, silent save for an occasional whistled tune, as if he was alerting any wolves, grizzlies, or rattlers of our presence. Fortunately, only the fowls responded, creating their own duets.

We followed the packed road, spooking deer along the way. They'd go still, only their ears twitching, before they darted deeper into the California oaks and pines. The countryside was remarkable. Arthur would've had much to paint here. Far-off mountains, forests, rivers, and prairies, and even broad open plains covered only in low shrubs. The plants were most peculiar, leafless and barkless, resembling the antlers of the deer we'd chased off. I told Arthur so, out loud.

Bruno turned his head. I shook mine and looked to the sky.

When night fell, Bruno fashioned us a camp and fire. He offered me water and motioned toward his face, then mine. I touched my cheek, my fingertips blackened from our kicked-up dirt. I washed, the best I could, pouring out handfuls of water from a canteen.

I paused, noticing how wasteful I'd been, but Bruno only nodded, as if saying, it was fine. He seemed content in his silence and I tried to find the same contentment in my own and in the scenery. But my surroundings only drove a wedge of regret into my thoughts. Had Arthur lived, there would've been a plentitude of earth for him to paint.

When day broke, Bruno handed me a biscuit and salted ham and, after we separately saw to our needs behind a bush, our journey began once more. We continued in this same pattern for three long days. Christmas passed, I realized after it had. I felt relieved. Along the path, we came upon only a handful of other travelers. Some on foot. Others on mules, horses, or within wagons. Some men were solitary, while others traveled in groups. Would Reuben? Would he hide himself among many? I studied each face we passed, leaning over the wagon's edge and straining to see a resemblance to Reuben, but there never was one.

At some point, the earth changed from flat to inclined and the earth shifted from mud-covered to snow-covered. It was then that I first regretted my impulse to climb aboard the wagon. On my crate, I huddled in several blankets Bruno had unearthed for me, and I squinted at the vast whiteness. It shined. Truly, it was the first snow I'd ever seen, but it seemed more an inconvenience than anything else once I eliminated its beauty, a problem that seemed all too common in this world.

At first, I wondered why Bruno didn't ride in the wagon. Instead, both he and the mules took exaggerated steps to overcome the snow's height, their breaths coming out in puffs. Then, I saw how often the snow clumped around our large wheels or clung to the wagon's belly, rendering us stuck. Bruno was constantly using a stick to free us and speaking to the mules in soft tones to encourage them forward again.

I'd be honest; I had no urge to help, for that'd mean unraveling myself from the little warmth I had created in my blanket-cocoon high in the mountains. Then, in the same moment we began to descend the great hill, the sun sprung from behind the clouds. The earth reverted back to mud and the wagon rattled my bones more steadily once again.

Finally, we arrived at our destination, which turned out to be a small town. I knew it as our destination only because Bruno lumbered away. He left us—meaning the mules, wagon, and me—in the middle of a wide street. A street, it must be clarified, that was full of no less than four hundred mules. They stood facing me, an impenetrable wall, their hooves stamping as if from impatience. I had little idea what to make of it.

On either side of the dirt road, a row of buildings made up the town, soaking up the sun's final efforts. There was life beyond their windows, but the street seemed to belong to only the mules and me. I stood, shaking free of my blankets. From behind, a voice startled me, sending me abruptly onto my backside once more. "Looks like we have ourselves a stowaway."

I smiled at his English. I hadn't heard it in days, save for the caveman-like words I exchanged with Bruno. Though, when I turned to face this new man, I was surprised to find myself in the presence of a native, another first for me. His face was weathered, appearing twice my own age, with two long braids dangling over his chest. He held a pipe between his teeth, staring at me, until he removed the device to say, "Encounter any Indians on the way here?"

In the time it took to stand again, I'd formulated a response to his ironic question. "Only you, it appears."

He nodded, his weathered face hidden by the cupped hand over his eyes. "If you did run into any, I'd imagine you'd have nothing to pull you or ride on."

"Is that so?" The casualness of my question was merely a ruse.

"Couple weeks back some travelers weren't as lucky. Never made it here."

I extended my hand, by which he helped me to the same level. While I had his hand, I introduced myself.

He replied, "William," and puffed again on his pipe.

The name hadn't been one I was expecting. "Well, William, may I ask where *here* is?"

"You don't know?"

"The foothills, I know that much. Though I didn't fathom I'd be in the company of a sea of livestock."

Plump ones, at that. I'd never seen beasts with such rounded sides.

"They're headed out at first light. Every few months the

muleteers bring supplies to the settlements. We almost didn't make the rounds this season on account of the weather up in those parts."

"So you go as well?"

"I do, daughter. I talk with other Indians should we encounter any."

"Yes, I can see why." I surveyed the fat mules, the thin town. The wind blew a strand of hair across my face and I batted it away impatiently. "Tell me, do you get a lot of people passing through this town?"

"Can't say I've been here long enough to know, but the faces change everywhere I go."

Reuben's, perhaps. I described him.

William said, "Most men have moustaches."

"You don't."

A hint of a smile broke his lips. I saw his eyes take me in, including my torn clothing, my overall disheveled appearance. "I take it you have business with this man?"

"I'd like to find him, yes. In fact, I'd like to go along." I nodded to the mules. "The mines, you said?"

"Those settlements are no place for a lady."

Neither was a gambling den. I held his gaze.

William shook his head. "Only way I could bring you is in a straitjacket."

"Well then, I'll wrap myself tightly in blankets." It wasn't the first time and it surely wouldn't be the last that I'd be called mad.

William missed my put-on. "It's not the cold that worries me, Miss Jules."

"Surely," I said, "anything I face in the mountains can't be worse than what I've already endured."

We shared a moment, and perchance he was remembering his own memories, as I was mine, for his face appeared lost in another time and place. "Very well."

❤

And very well it was, for the first few hours of our trip, at least. At daybreak, William perched me atop a mule, fashioning a blanket behind a saddle. There I sat, with both my limbs to one side. The mules—the coloring of one unlike another, with markings of sorrel, brown, black, white, gray, cream—were positioned, head to rump, and we set out, a string of animals I'd estimate to be half a mile in length.

The approach was most interesting. The first mule, which a man walked beside even while his mule wore a saddle, jingled with each step. Behind him, nine mules, heavy with supplies, followed the sounds of his bell. This arrangement of ten animals was repeated, again and again, with a muleteer walking beside each set. To encourage the docile beasts to follow, the men spoke sharp yet endearing sounds in their native tongue, rarely having to tug on their ropes. My mule, with the markings of a cow, led its own grouping, with William urging him on in the language of the muleteers.

We stopped at a picturesque stream to water the animals. William lifted me down and I scooped water straight from the stream, a novelty for this newfangled pioneer woman, a title I coined for myself as a result of the endless wilderness enveloping me. Our journey thus far had been similar to what I'd encountered from my wagon, save for the blessed omission of snow. One could even call those first few hours enjoyable, except for the cloud of dust the animals kicked up, which did its darndest to fill my eyes, nose, ears, and hair. I accepted it; I was moving forward, toward the opportunity of laying my strained eyes upon Reuben. I'd restrain him, in some way. Rope, perhaps. William would be of help there. And I'd return Reuben to San Francisco. With no need for my own reward money, I'd send it to Arthur's sister in Philadelphia. Justice would be served. Warmth filled me as the future unfolded in my mind's eye.

However, my mood shifted as William deposited me back atop my makeshift pillion pad and reached for Arthur's canvas. I had secured it to the empty saddle beside me.

"What are you doing?" I snapped.

His brows furrowed. "I plan to ride."

All the other men had climbed upon their lead mules.

"But," I said, not caring in the least my argument was uncaring, "there's nowhere else for my canvas to go."

William considered me, then pulled a knife. I startled, and my pulse, while already antagonized, quickened further with fear. He aimed the knife, not at me, but at my canvas. With careful, swift movements, he cut my portrait from its mount. William rolled it, presented it to me.

I thanked him, despite my churning emotions, one of which was apprehension over damage to Arthur's work. Alas, there was little time for worry because we were off yet again, William on the saddle, my shoulder brushing against his back. Once more, I concentrated my effort and muscles on staying squarely on my blanket as the mule trod on.

Over time, the pathway thinned. It steepened. Jagged rocks, extending seemingly into the clouds, formed a wall to our left. The mules slowed their pace. To my great horror, my side-by-side feet soon pointed at nothing but emptiness. My reaction to the abrupt drop-off caught in my throat. All that kept us from plummeting to the vein-like river below was the irrationally small feet of our mules. Ahead, dirt and gravel trailed over the edge from a misplaced step quickly corrected. With how I already jostled, a similar misstep was likely to slip me forward, just as Patricia and I had wiggled atop our stair's landing until our bodies took us over the edge, riding down within our linens, much to our governess's displeasure.

Etiquette could be damned in this moment, too. I pulled at my skirts until I had the facility to put a limb on either side of my animal. I hesitated only a moment more before I clenched the fabric of William's coat, holding my blanket tight in the other.

We trotted on.

Toward the end of our first day, our troop reached a height where snow regrettably covered the ground. Down once more, we camped in a valley, rain pinging against the tarpaulin strung between two trees. I spent more time watching the dark rivulets of rainwater creeping toward me than sleeping.

Our second day was more of the same, climbing and descending. We stopped only for water, and only momentarily. When the trail became too perilous, muddy, or thin for human feet, William and the muleteers rode in their saddles. I closed my eyes during the stretches where there was nothing to see but the rear of the next animal, a cliff face, and plunging nothingness.

"¡*Barras adelante!*"

I leaned to the side, attempting to see the lead rider. He often called out commands. I often asked William to translate. "What'd he say?"

"The first bar is ahead."

With snowflakes licking at my face, the mining settlement couldn't have come a breath sooner. The mules winded down a final hill, stepping neatly here and there in a path carved through the snow.

What awaited me were little more than a dozen tents and a few log cabins, all blanketed in snow. With the fresh snowfall, the encampment was undisturbed, the perfect place to never be found. There was a machine of sorts, hulking in size, but it sat idle, also covered in white.

I asked William, "Do they not mine in the winter?"

"Would you?"

"But they stay?"

"Some do. Others go into the valleys were the snow melts plenty quick." I looked over my shoulder, as if the valley awaited me there. William's hand waited for me when I turned back. For a moment, I hesitated, only because I knew my body would protest. Never before had my thighs been so sore, stretched over the wide belly of a mule. My feet hit the ground and my limbs buckled. For the first time, I was glad for the snow, which hadn't been shoveled or packed down and its height came to my chest. It took only a slight stretch of my arm to balance myself against the snowbank.

William added, "The rest will be back in the spring. For now, we'll deliver food to those who lack sense in their *aashúuas*."

As he touched his head, I figured that was the inferred Indian word. I wouldn't argue his point. I also better understood his *bon mot* about my wearing of a straitjacket.

Anyone who chose to live in such a fashion was mad or desperate. I hoped Reuben was the latter, for I was desperate, too.

Chapter 17

WAS REUBEN HERE? At our arrival, more men than seemed possible to dwell within the cabins and tents emerged like foxes from their holes. My heart hammered a quickened beat, faster still as they approached us, eager for their supplies.

I was eager, too. My eyes danced from one face to the next, too quickly to even decipher their features, to know if Reuben was amongst them.

The muleteers lined themselves shoulder-to-shoulder, becoming conveyors, and began unloading the potatoes, onions, dark ham, and butter. The miners joined them. After nothing but canned sardines for weeks their fervor was palpable.

Could my own enthusiasm be felt? Did my desire to find Reuben pulse from my body? I calmed myself and saw the opportunity to walk the line, to stand in front of these men as they unloaded the food and to more slowly search for Reuben's resemblance amongst their faces. Would Reuben recognize mine? Would his mouth part in disbelief at seeing me? At knowing vengeance had come for him? Would he try to run? Would he move with a limp? Before such a deformity would reveal itself, I'd slap him, hard enough to cause his teeth to rattle. I already felt the sting in my hand.

But no, I didn't think Reuben would realize who was before him. He wouldn't know the reds, yellows, blues, and whites that made up my skin. I knew who I was to him. A woman he wanted to possess from another man. A man who he felt was beneath him. That was all Arthur and I were to him.

I licked my lips and stood in front of the first grizzly man. His moustache and beard intertwined. He looked twice at me, as if surprised a female was here. I saw no other females. And this man—this man was not Reuben.

I sidestepped in front of another man. Another man who wasn't Reuben. I felt William's eyes on me, watching as I searched. He stood by, with a threatening-looking spear, to ensure the men took no more than this settlement's designated rations. When the muleteers began unpacking the claret, the mountain men cheered. They'd drink it as if it were water, I was certain.

The next man made a suggestive comment toward me. I let out a disgusted noise and moved on. And on. I found myself procrastinating my next step, studying each face longer than necessary, in an attempt to reason that the man was, indeed, Reuben. I imagined him, but with a blink, a different man always stood in front of me, a perplexed expression on his face at why I examined him with such intensity and disappointment.

Soon, the end of the line was before me. There was no Reuben, not at this mining bar. But perhaps at another the muleteers would resupply. Or perhaps in the springtime. William had said many men camped elsewhere until the snow had melted and the ice had thawed.

I expelled my disappointment, my breath lingering in the cold air. William was at my side. All he said was, "Come, daughter," and he led me toward the largest of the cabins, which turned out to be their saloon. As with any drinking den, it was no place for a lady, but at this point I didn't reason myself a normal woman. Piano music filled the room, lively and cheerful. I was surprised to hear the instrument, all the way out in the wilderness, where something as simple as coffee didn't exist, but the sound was very much welcomed. There was no dancing, as there were no other women.

That left much of the enthusiasm and attention to fall on me. Here, I was an even greater novelty. As if I were a wind-up toy, they plied me with claret and asked me to amuse them with my French. I was happy to oblige for the wine soothed my aching body and also the tangible disappointment that Reuben was not here. But when they began to reach and grab and take hold of me, my skin began to prickle. William wasn't there to intervene. What I needed was a table between them and me.

"Who has cards?" I asked, adding a melody to my voice. Since Arthur's death, I'd only truly felt like myself with a deck of cards in my hand.

A deck was set in front of me. "What parlor trick do you have for us, sweetie?"

Another asked, "Are you going to tell us our fortunes?"

I settled into a seat and arched a brow. In my mind, it was as if I pulled on a costume. I was the mysterious card-playing mademoiselle. "*Non*," I said. "No tricks here. Only *vingt-et-un*. Will you play?"

I turned my back to remove betting money from my corset, then promptly took great enjoyment from their intrigued expressions and loose jaws.

They were hesitant, but no one objected. Who would pass up the chance to play with the only woman in the room, even without ever hearing of my game? Soon, they were enamored with it. And I was all too eager to revive my role as a croupier, it reminding me fondly of the people I once loved.

One fellow asked, "How'd a lady come to deal such a game?"

I tilted my head, speaking to the table, as I didn't care to learn their names for only a night. Tomorrow we'd begin our journey to a new mining bar, where a new opportunity to find Reuben awaited me. Until then, I'd play. "A lady never reveals her secrets. You enjoy, yes?"

They did, while winning. One man aimed a fist at another when he lucked out with the card he needed. That same man had the audacity to take my hand at the night's end and speak so closely I felt his breath. "It'd be my honor to keep you warm."

I replied, "A blanket will do just fine."

In truth, it did marginally fine. With over forty of us newcomers, many of the muleteers lined up like sardines on the saloon's sawdust floor. I was fortunate to obtain a straw mattress and a space within a cabin, even if the roof, comprising mostly of sticks and moss, leaked more heat than it retained from the stone and mud fireplace. William constructed a tipi for himself, but I caught him throughout the night moving aside the sheet that'd been strung for my privacy to check on me. During one of those trips, he brought me a gift, a knife.

He said, "I'd like you to wear this."

I cocked my head. "I wouldn't know how to use such a thing."

"I'll show you how to hold it."

I cringed. "It looks dangerous."

He whispered. "That's the point. Watch. Watch. Miss Jules, are you watching?"

I nodded to appease him.

"Put it here." He touched his inner thigh, not looking once at my upper leg in the firelight's glow. "I've made you a sheath and belt. It may rub at first, but it'd put me at ease for you to wear it in this environment. Should you need it, it's merely an extension of your hand. You'd pull it out. Like this."

He looked up to ensure I had watched. Satisfied, he handed the weapon to me.

The idea of using a knife frightened me more than the idea of wearing it. For if I needed it, well, I hoped I never would, but should a man ever try to lift my skirts and assert himself on me, he'd only be revealing my weapon, giving me direct access to it. I realized now it was nothing but a practical gift.

"Thank you. You're very thoughtful, William."

I wondered how he ended up here, a guide of sorts, a man who took it upon himself to protect me, and also a peacemaker between the white skinned—as I've heard him say—and the Indians. At some point, he must've left his tribe.

After we departed the mining bar, we moved on to another. There, I stood before each man again, my disappointment growing as I moved from one to the next. Then, we moved on to another. In total, we resupplied seven bars within the Mexican territory, going so far north to nearly cross into the Oregon territory. In total, I scrutinized the faces of over fifty men who dared to live at a mining bar during the winter months, soon finding myself the unluckiest of hunters.

It took a month. Along the way, I watched the bellies of the mules grow thinner from their exertion. Five mules succumbed to the elements and their efforts. The men were quick to prepare and salt the meat. I was less quick to partake but found the lost animals to taste similar to veal.

Once our saddlebacks were empty, we retired at a *rancho*. My Spanish had progressed beyond that singular word, though not significantly. I found it harder to pick up a language in my twenties than I had in my earlier years. At night, William and handfuls of men sat around a fire exchanging grand-sounding stories. The fire lit up William's animated face in such a way that the glow gathered in his many creases. I caught a sentence here and there, but it was through his expressions and gestures I surmised his storytelling often told of skirmishes and conflicts. I also recognized the word *esposa*, mostly because the muleteers and gold seekers so often asked me if I was somebody's wife, to which I'd raise my chin and respond *non*. Their faces reacted with attraction, confusion, or distaste. To those who scrunched their noses, I was quick to correct their assessment of me as a lady of the night. Perhaps that was why William continued to check on me during the nighttime hours. Truly,

I feared a man soliciting me: not for my own safety but for William's. A man I deeply cared for had already lost his life trying to protect my honor. And, I'd grown fond of William in a fatherly way.

Within two months, the muleteers began their process over, journeying to Marysville—the town in which I originally arrived from San Francisco—then to each small mining settlement along their route. I continued my hunt, praying the springtime months, as the men returned to their mines, would bring me different results. They did not.

Still, I stayed on with William and the muleteers for over a year, taking on the familiar routine of the arrival at a new bar, the scouring of faces, soup at noon, supper at six, *vingt-et-un* until blurry eyed, then off again with the sun. This was my limited existence.

There were no concerts or theaters, no recently printed books, no storefronts, no afternoon tea, no parties or picnics, no latest fashions, no ministers. No carriage rides, no milk, no eggs, no banks, most men having to bury their gold and money in foxholes for safekeeping. Mail came only once a month with an expressman. Never anything for me, but why would there be. No one knew I was here. If I perished to some ill fate, there was no one to write of the news. In a way, my life felt as if it was on hold, surrounded only by these mountain men, each from various walks of life.

I became familiar with their dialects. The Spanish had a melodious nature to their words. The Italian possessed a clearness, the German a harshness, the Hawaiians a pleasantness, and the East Indian men a tranquility.

I realized, too, I became familiar with their faces. That realization came to me earlier this morning, after we'd arrived. It was my fourth time resupplying this particular mining bar. It was springtime again, the number of miners at their greatest. I'd walked the line, as was my routine, but I also greeted more than three-fourths of the men by name. It left me feeling unsettled. It left me doubting my assertion that Reuben would appear within these foothills, when the roster of men altered so slightly. My theory had been nothing more than a delusion, built upon the hope that the foothills were where a man could hide. Or where a man and woman, unpermitted to be together, could've done the same. Truth of that matter is that if Arthur and I had attempted the remote, clandestine life that I had imagined for us, we would've stood out like sore thumbs.

I needed to busy my mind. I took leave to the river. There, I counted my steps from north to south: nine hundred and sixty from one side of this mining bar to the other. Then, from east to west: thirty. I knew little what I'd do with such calculations, beyond further torturing myself with the tininess of a place I had conjured to be my salvation.

I lowered myself onto a moss-covered stump, the trees all around me, sloping down a hill. A small valley was below me, with all its mining activity underway. Never before had I seen the hierarchy of a mine so clearly. The richer white men ruled as the owners and managers of the claims. Some would dirty their hands with the panning, digging, sluicing, and excavating, but mostly it was the Mexicans and the Chinese Americans who were within the streambeds or the ones using steam shovels to create terrifyingly deep holes where richer dirt was believed to be. Those holes were formed everywhere and anywhere, sometimes only feet from where they ate, slept, and cavorted. What they unearthed went into a Long Tom, a ten-foot trough meant to separate the heavier gold from the dirt and rocks. This was operated by a poorer white man. Then there were the black men, only ever one or two on a claim. They used hoes to keep the dirt in motion within the Long Tom. Or, the black men were ordered to work the makeshift outdoor kitchens. I saw now a dark-skinned man peeling the potatoes we'd delivered that morning. Save for William, tending to the mules tied to various trees beyond the settlement, there wasn't a native on these lands. But a Mestizo, who was the offspring of a Mexican and an Indian, worked alongside one of the black men to feed the trough with soil.

My mechanical-minded Papa would've held unfailing interest in the *tout ensemble* of the machine and its various parts: the riddle, the riffle-box, and sluices. But, their names were as far as my understanding went. In a past life, I would've enjoyed how the pieces fit together and the logic behind it all, but I was too downtrodden and was, instead, content to loaf until night fell when the men had a mind for gambling.

A small brown lizard ran by my ankles, drawing my attention from the raucous activity below. It truly was beautiful here, though the beauty was lost to me most days, hidden under snow or overshadowed by the mine's primitiveness or its noisiness. A dog barked, incessantly. A flume, which diverted water to bare a portion of streambed, moaned and shrieked. Then, there was the constant sawing and felling of trees, a dangerous undertaking, no less. Before our arrival, a log had gotten loose and took a tumble down the hill. It hadn't stopped until it leveled two tents and one side of a log cabin. Fortunately, no one had been inside any.

A burst of voices started me to my feet. My head swayed from the quickness, and I searched, blurry eyed, amongst the endless oaks and firs for any trees that'd gotten away from the fellers. The woods were still. But in the valley, the men in their dark flannelled shirts and black hats flooded toward a mining pit like a plug had been pulled from a muddy basin.

With my skirt bunched in my hands, I did the same. I stepped carefully, mimicking the daintiness of my mules, to avoid the now-empty oyster cans, sardine boxes, brandied-fruit jars, and also to evade the other holes the men had abandoned to create new holes. For the life of me, I never understood why they didn't fill them in; great mounds of excavated dirt sat right there. But the death traps were left open.

And now, the men gathered around one of those pits I'd seen the men mining during our last resupply mission. At that point, they'd dug sixty feet down, celebrating with the clinks of bottles how they had finally struck the richer bedrock. From there, they created tunnels, stretching beneath the hillside, in search of gold, only stopping when the flames they carried extinguished, designating the air too impure for even the deadliest of nature's wonders.

I stopped short of the hole. I had no desire to stretch my neck and see the man's broken body at the pit's base, but I also felt drawn to stand amongst the whitened faces aghast with sadness and also fear. Two miners descended the ladder painstakingly slowly, rising even more slowly with the weight of their friend.

As the sandy crop of hair appeared, I turned away. I found the back of a wagon, where a stream of sunlight cut through the trees, and I soaked up every particle of its warmth. I didn't witness but I heard the proceedings. The fallen miner—Uwe—was settled into a box. There was always a coffin at the ready, a new one crafted as soon as the previous one had been claimed.

I jolted at the first thud of a hammer, my palm scraping against the wagon bed's coarse wood. I quickly checked for a splinter, my dealing hands a large part of my livelihood, and was relieved to find my skin clear. I closed my eyes and turned again to the sun, aching for its warmth once more. The remaining whacks were chilling. Next came the shuffling of feet and the clinking of empty bottles that were toed aside. Uwe wouldn't be alone in the hillside graveyard. This gold bar was only two years old, but many had already been lost to sickness, carelessness, and hot tempers. One man, I was told, was hung by his neck after being accused of theft. It all seemed so uncivilized.

Hours later, I felt more myself once I was behind a table in their makeshift saloon with a mason jar of claret in my hands. On account of this hardened life, I'd taken to drinking more. It made wearing the same Garibaldi blouse and skirt for weeks more bearable. I carried a single change of clothing I had purchased in Marysville before I originally set out. The only extravagance I acquired upon my return trip to the town was lotion. At night, I coated my face and hands with the balm, not fully rubbing it in. These assets were most important to me, my livelihood, what I showed to the men who graced my tables.

I shuffled the cards, preparing to deal. More than ever, the miners needed the distraction of gambling. Their faces were long, but their tongues became looser with spirits, and the tales of Uwe began. I sat behind a makeshift table, one the men had erected for me using a board atop two barrels, and dealt out the cards. For lighting, I'd taken to putting two jars at the middle, flames dancing inside. The light caught on wet lips and perspiring brows.

I lowered my shoulder to banter, my weight tilting, and the three legs my chair rested on, due to the uneven floor, shifted me closer to a face than I cared to be. "Another card?"

The man was quick to say yes, when he should've said no. But that was a gold miner in a nutshell. He busted, and I casually tried to shift my chair to three of its other legs to collect his money. Of course, the chair is all or nothing, and it once again stole my grace. How maddening. Really, how silly of a focus, but how silly this mode of living was in general. And more, how little it cared for human life. I'd taken on the role of muleteer to search for Arthur's killer but also, I realized now, to distance myself from the death that seemed to follow me from *La Nouvelle-Orléans* to San Francisco. Only, it didn't stop there. Death was all around me. Sometimes, in the moments I'd been overwhelmed with the noise, the commotion, and my failure at not unearthing Reuben, I'd think about the safety of home. In *La Nouvelle-Orléans*, perhaps I should've buttered my paws. After taking the time to lick them clean, I would've raised my head and saw my heart had mended. I could've married David. I'd be working at Papa's shop, only it'd belong to David and me. I'd own something of my own, more than a second skirt and a bottle of balm. While it was once hard to envision that life, it wasn't as difficult now.

The only saving grace of leaving home was undoubtedly Arthur. Meeting him, learning from him, beginning to love him, imagining a future with him, seeing myself through his eyes. I, too, had his portrait, my most prized possession.

I continued on with my cards, once again finding solace in the game. The men had turned melancholy, their stories now shifting to their own lives prior to coming here. "Tell me," I said, joining into their conversation, "what were your occupations before hunting gold?"

One was a quarryman, his presence here making perfect sense. Then, a sailor, a farmer, a lawyer. More men joined our dialogue. A former steamboat-clerk, a physician, a shoe-peg maker.

They all spoke fondly of their old lives, but all had been swayed by the prospect of gold. I'd admit, despite my growing abhorrence of this primitive lifestyle, there was an undeniable allure to those specks of gold. I myself experienced it first-hand.

I can't recall which bar we were resupplying, but I'd already examined all the men unloading the new provisions, none of which were Reuben. There was a rare quietness so I wished to experience it with a walk along the river. I'd only taken a handful of steps when William gripped my arm. "It's not safe for you to be unescorted, Miss Jules."

I smiled at his thoughtfulness, but, "I have my knife," I said simply, then to lighten the mood, "And surely the bears will protect me from any grizzly men."

The blankness of his face meant one thing: he didn't share in my witticism, but William released his grip, nevertheless. He'd returned to the unloading of supplies.

The river had been blue, oh so blue, until I reached the portion that'd been flumed to reveal snake-like indentations and rocks. A discarded pan lay on its banks and I had a surge of gold lust.

I'd taken a handful of dirt, scooped water from further downstream, and set to swishing both within the pan as I'd seen the men do. My inexperience showed, having to bend and squat for a considerable amount of time. Back-breaking work. Yet I found myself smiling as the muddy water ran over the sides. "Would you look at that?" I said to myself, standing.

"You've got some color."

I jumped at the deep voice, dropping my pan and new-found gold dust. "William," I breathed. "There you are again. I *had* some color."

One side of his mouth curled.

I wiped my hands clean, satisfied with my gold-mining efforts, but content to never do it again. "See, there was no need to worry over my safety, not with you appearing like an apparition."

His smile fully formed.

The memory had stuck with me, and I often thought of my exhilaration at spotting a few specks of gold when thinking of how these men had left their families and former occupations behind for such a gamble.

"And what about you?" I asked a man at my makeshift table who'd taken the care to shave. "What was your prior occupation?"

"A mercantile."

In an instant, thoughts of Reuben's one-time job sprung to mind. Though, to be fair, thoughts of Arthur—and by default,

Reuben—were never far. I said, "How charming. What town allowed for that? Was it nearby?"

The miner gave me a name, Fort Benton, and I thought on it. I could go there, a new prospect to continue my search. I tapped my finger atop my cards, the men awaiting a new round.

I heard, "Miss?" I stirred from my reverie to a man, a newcomer, in fact. He motioned to an errant chair. "May I join?"

The other men grumbled, but even as they protested, they made room.

"*Bienvenue*," I said in greeting.

"So it's true?" the newcomer said. "You're the French women who travels with the muleteers and deals venty-one?" He had awe in his voice as he addressed the other miners. "She's the French woman."

My lower lip trembled from a rush of emotions. What was it ... satisfaction? Humbleness? Pride? A combination of all three, I concluded. "It is me. *Vingt-et-un* is my game." I took care in the pronunciation, as he hadn't gotten the diction quite right. However, the intonation sounded much like its meaning of twenty-one. *Van-tey-un.* And, *why yes, it was my game*, I thought again. I said, "Will you play?"

"Hell yes. Silly as it sounds, I came purposefully, to sit at your table."

I paused. "Purposefully?"

He nodded. "To play you in cards."

"Oh," I said simply. I was at a loss for words. I was touched to an even greater degree, which I hadn't known possible. This man had traversed literal mountains to sit before me. "Then let us play."

I placed a card in front of his companions and then him. An eight. I dealt myself a two. I whispered to the newcomer, "You'll want to hit, *chérie*."

He did, and, in the end, he won, taking my money that hand. But that was fine; he'd given me something far greater.

Chapter 18

I SWAYED ON MY MULE'S BACK, his trot now second nature. The throbbing stiffness of my limbs and derrière had long subsided. I glanced at William walking beside me, same as I'd done ten times over throughout our ride toward the next mining bar. We were in the midst of our springtime rotation.

His head remained straight and he spoke around his pipe. "Miss Jules."

"Simone," I insisted, as I'd done many times before during our growing time together.

A puff of tobacco escaped the side of his mouth before he slowly removed his pipe. "Simone, have I ever told you I can sense a herd of bison half a mile away?"

I rocked left, right, left with the mule's steps. "I suppose that's never come up in conversation. But how good to know."

He looked at me now. "I mean it to say my instincts aren't lacking, so out with whatever it is you have to say."

I twisted my lips, recalling how one of the miners spoke of a merchant town. Reuben was a merchant before coming west. "I'm considering a new destination."

"Still searching for the moustached man I see, daughter."

"Your instincts are once again correct." I studied him. I'd found William to be a private man, much like myself, but his eyes often pinched as his mind worked. "My instincts also aren't lacking," I said, "so out with whatever it is *you* have to say."

He smoked from his pipe. We must've gone another hundred steps, and still, he did nothing more than smoke and lead our mules. Then he said, "Who is this man you search for?"

I was quick to say, "Why should that matter?"

"It's a long time to search for a lover who left you behind."

I breathed deeply. "I am not a scorned woman, William, out to reclaim some lost love. I have no lover."

"Then who are you, Simone?"

"I ..." I *was* a scorned woman because of a lost love. But not in the way he intended. "I am looking for a man who killed my lover." Or so I had fantasized of him as such. Arthur's lips going places beyond my lips. His large hands gripping me. It'd be so easy to close my eyes, think of Arthur as my husband, and go to that place in my mind.

But no, I was here with William, who scrutinized me, those eyes of his squinting once more. "And what will be accomplished after you find this moustached man?"

"Justice."

He nodded. "But at what cost? We've lived together, but we don't know each other. Not really. But still, I know you are lost."

I bristled. "I do believe I know where I am."

"But not who you're meant to be."

"So says the man who wanders with Mexicans and mules and this sorry excuse of a mademoiselle."

"I chose all those things."

"Well, I chose, too. I didn't wear that straitjacket, after all."

He considered me. "Yes, but I've found my purpose, helping those like you, after suffering my own tragedy. I once lived with my people. I was content, married. We had a son. In my tribe, women hold significant roles. It's the wife's mother's home where the husband resides. That's where I resided. Sickness took the entire household, sparing only me. In the aftermath, I realized I no longer had a purpose there, so I sought one as William. It means *protector*, and that was what I meant to be, after failing with my family."

"Why haven't you ever told me this?"

He countered, "Why have you never told me the name of the man you loved? Or the one you were searching for?"

Because, it hurt too badly to utter either name.

"So," I said instead, "William isn't your given name?" I suspected as much, but it's not something I would've asked unless he mentioned it, like now.

"No, different tribes have different naming traditions. In mine, a name evolves with the person, depending on the season of life and what that season means."

How profound.

"For now," he said, "as I choose to interact with the white-skinned, I am William. I overheard the man from your table yesterday, the one who came to play your game. How did that make you feel?"

The answer was easy. "Humbled. Proud."

He said, "Awakened. It awakened you, Simone. Don't chase your past. Find your purpose. Create your future."

Create my future. While my conversation with William had been brief, it lingered in my mind, recounted so many times that it was as if William and I had spoken for hours. As if he hammered an alternative into my head, other than traveling to some random merchant town and crossing my fingers that Reuben was there. That I'd find him. That I'd return him to San Francisco. That justice would be served.

William had asked me who I was.

I wanted to be more than a woman scorned, even if my motivations weren't of a typical scorned woman. I knew what I wanted. I wanted to pronounce myself as the French woman who dealt *vingt-et-un*. And, I wanted to do so at my very own gambling den, where I made the rules.

Arthur would want it for me.

I stayed on with my muleteers, but out of practicality. In the winter months, they'd journey to Marysville for supplies to begin a renewed year. And—I would simply begin again.

During those long springtime, summer, and fall months of waiting, each evening with the unruly men at my tables allowed a conception to gather, like particles of gold accumulating in a jar. My gambling den would be different. Proper ambiance. Proper behavior. Proper dress.

My preparations began as soon as my feet touched ground in Marysville. I began by posting a letter to the Miners' Bank in San Francisco, requesting the sum of my savings there. I'd heard San Francisco had been rebuilt after the fire. When I'd fled, I'd only taken a thousand dollars with me, and it'd been enough to live as a muleteer for two years. I'd even been profitable against the mountain men during our *vingt-et-un* games. But now I'd need my full resources. My theoretical jar of gold was filling and, soon, I'd pour the dust and nugget into shiny gold bars.

While the muleteer lifestyle didn't particularly agree with me, it was hard to see my beloved muleteers leave, exceptionally William. They were only in Marysville for a handful of days. With their four hundred mules plump, and their supplies overflowing, they set off. I waited to see if William, my protector, would give me a backwards glance. And he did. Tears filled my eyes as I waved. With that wave, I said much, including *au revoir* to my muleteer lifestyle—and to my hunt for Reuben.

My new destination would be the California town of Nevada, a two-night trek. I was told gold had been found there. I was also told there'd be snow in the nearby mountains, but that it rarely fell in town, nothing like the human-height snow banks of the mining bars. And Nevada was to be more than a settlement, with an actual newspaper, a theater, and—coming soon—a gambling house. My very own. I'd be more than *miss* or *mademoiselle* or *the French woman*. I would better establish my game, but I'd also establish myself.

Most travelers waited until springtime until the grass had regrown for the draft animals to forage along the way. I did the same. By then, I had accumulated a greater wardrobe and other necessities for my journey. Two trunks worth. On a particularly warm morning, I climbed into a stagecoach, ready to take another step into my new life. While the majority of my belongings were piled atop the coach, the portrait Arthur had done of me went beside me. It was never far, still rolled. To maintain its integrity, I'd tried to keep it bound, but today I took care to unroll the canvas and see myself as Arthur had seen me. I felt as if I was on my way to his vision of me—once I traversed the California Trail.

I'd heard of the trails that cut west across the vast plains. For those who didn't take to the seas, like I had done, they took to wagons. Some took the trails as far as the Oregon territory. The ones set on gold country eventually connected to the California Trail. Trails, really, as they branched to all the gold strikes. I'd take one of those pathways, except I'd be going east, against the grain, but only for a short while. Not the weeks and months it took those travelling west.

After so much time spent wobbling on the backside of a mule, I felt fortunate to be enclosed within a coach. When I peeked out the tiny window, a great plume of dirt stretched on and on, winding through the valley. Through the dust storm, I saw many wagons, pulled by great oxen, creating a great chain. I counted twenty-eight wagons in total. It reminded me of my quarter mile of mules. Except the wagon chain kicked up a considerably larger amount of dust. I wondered how the beasts breathed while within all that muck and in this heat. Those travelling within the wagon chain rode horses right outside the plume as not to choke; though a canvas covered each wagon, so it was likely people hid inside. Children would've been my guess.

My driver remained toward the outskirts. We weren't the only ones beyond the main trail where the sun scorched the trampled grass and wagon wheel tracks hardened in the earth. Travelers spread out, vastly so. The greener valley and hilly landscape was speckled with people and horses. Some in motion, others resting, many watering their animals. We remained close to the river, riding in and out of the oak's shadows.

While my driver maneuvered around most debris, our wheels sometimes jostled over discarded supplies. Anything no longer of use—empty food barrels, broken wagon parts, books that had been read, clothing—became junk heaped here and there. I'd quickly avert my gaze when I saw a deceased animal or a white cross, stuck crookedly in the ground.

I lost track of time. At the end of the first day, we stopped to camp. My driver said we'd gone twenty miles. In the morning, I plucked a stray book from the ground to busy my mind for the second day of our journey. It was written by a Captain Johnson and appeared to be stories of pirates, though he spelled it *pyrates*. The tales were grand, Anne Bonny emerging as my favorite, a woman who had taken on the role of a man to fulfill her goals. The book held my attention much of the day, the sun lowering with each page turned. Finally, we stopped. We'd camp one more night, then complete the final few miles in the morning. I wanted to arrive in my new town fresh.

My driver helped me from the coach. My backside ached from sitting for so long, but I reminded myself my mode of transportation was better than most. I scanned the terrain, spotting wagons, tents, and travelers. The camp was considerably larger than last night's.

I turned, to feel the sun on my face. It was setting, right atop a massive boulder. Surely the boulder was over a hundred feet tall and just as wide. Wider. I had little to judge its actual size, but it was almighty. Its isolation as the only outcropping made it doubly so. All that stood around it was dirt and brush—and people.

I asked my driver. "What are they doing over there?"

"It's a register of sorts, miss. There are a few popular ones along the trails."

I used my hand to shadow my eyes. "So their names go on it?"

"That's correct."

I started toward it.

William didn't know it, but he'd given me one last gift: the knowledge that one's name could be altered. As I entered this new season of life, I could enter it as whomever I liked. And I would. Simone Jules would be kept for me, as I was certain William kept his prior name or names in his own memories.

I thought on it. A name was of importance. But my goodness, how did one decide? While William chose the name for its meaning, I didn't know the meaning of any names besides mine and Patricia's. Maman chose them to complement each other. Patricia would see what I could not and I would hear what Patricia could not. Without my twin, perhaps that was why I'd wandered the way I had, lacking her sure sightedness.

But as I was given the designation of *one who hears*, I'd use that proficiency now to determine who I'd become. So, I asked the names of those around me. I asked every soul at the camp their name and its derivation. If only Bruno could've seen me now. *Loca*, he would've said.

But then I heard a meaning that put tears in my eyes.

"Shining one," a woman had said.

"Eleanor," I repeated her name.

Maman had called Patricia and I her shining jewels. And

just like that, I had a name, one that enveloped both my sister and me. In time, I hoped it didn't cause my chest to constrict with a mixture of hope and pain. But for now, there was the task of a surname. I could've kept Jules, but as Eleanor would honor my family, I wanted the same for Arthur.

I continued to ask for names, people offering even before I approached them with word traveling of my quest.

"Dumont!"

I turned toward the shout.

"It's French. Means *of the mount*." He gestured to the great rock.

I smiled, but not due to his interpretation. Hadn't Arthur taken me up a great hill? It was on that night that he first imprinted himself on my heart. And it was Telegraph Hill where I went again when I wanted to see the harbor and the town as Arthur had.

"Shall I carve for you?" a man said. "It'd only be a few coins."

"It's what you do? Carve?"

He nodded. "A stonecutter."

I handed him a few coins. "Would you show me the technique? This I must do myself." I set to carving my new name, the process more grueling than I had imagined. Night had fallen by the time I added the date. Others had also included their hometowns, but Eleanor Dumont had none.

I ran my hand over the inscription.

Eleanor Dumont.

Yes. *Ça c'est bon.* That was who I was meant to be now.

PART 2

Eleanor Dumont

1852
Nevada, California

Chapter 19

MY STAGECOACH STOPPED, the boomtown of Nevada before me. I had arrived; ready to start anew, in style, no less. At the very least, I hoped to appear bright-eyed and refreshed. No one would be the wiser that I'd tumbled left and right in the back of my covered coach to tie, button, and lace the layers of my clothing. My face was put on. My anticipation added a natural glow to my skin. I wore pearls around my neck and a hat of notice upon my head. This was a new beginning for me. In my short twenty-five years of living, there was much I'd endured, but I'd press on.

Two men eagerly greeted me. To be fair, only one said hello. The other appeared tongue-tied. Call it vain, but I was as pleased as Punch that my vanity had survived the wooliness of the foothills.

"*Bonjour, messieurs.*"

With one hand in each of theirs, they helped me to the ground. Beyond me stretched the town of Nevada. Perhaps *sat* was a more accurate description. This place was a middle ground, not the maturing metropolis of San Francisco, but it also didn't possess the rusticism of a mining bar. This was more than a settlement. This was a town, a budding one. Need I remind myself of the theater? It possessed a church, too, the white steeple a focal point against the dark evergreens and the changing leaves of the hillside.

I saw the two men take me in, my jewels, my hat, my neck-lace. I do wish I held a parasol to complete the look. Truly though, I think their brains were still catching up to my use of *messieurs*. What was it with men and *femmes françaises*?

The one gentleman looked to be a miner, a bit rougher around the edges than the second man, who was well groomed and wore dress shoes opposed to boots. They escorted me down an access road, three-rung fences lining the way, and into town.

"Do tell," I said, "how many people live here?"

"Census was done only last year after a fire."

"A fire?" How a single word sent my pulse soaring higher than the surrounding oak trees.

"Yes, ma'am, but we've rebuilt. Larger than before. Ten thousand of us."

I composed myself. "And, I see you've used brick this time."

"Quite the eye you have," the non-miner said. He was doing all the talking.

I smiled. "I should like to rest."

"Of course, of course. I'm sure you've traveled far." He said *far* as if in question. Like so many others, people weren't certain where to place me. If this gold rush continued, I was certain that reaction would become less common. Emigration and migration showed no signs of slowing.

"The Fepp's Hotel is mighty nice," he said.

"Yes," the miner chimed in. "We'd be happy to bring your trunks to your room."

I was much obliged, but insisted on carrying my rolled portrait myself. The accommodations were indeed nice. The town had taken care in rebuilding after the fire, with buildings of multi-levels, balconies, columns, gabled roofs, and thick wooden signs, advertising what they had to offer. Upon setting the tip of my pen on the guest book, I paused. While painstakingly carving my new name, I'd created each letter in block shapes, for simplicity. But now I could let the letters flourish, new ones at that. I chose to join the letters in cursive, beginning with a large and swooping *E*. By the swipe of the *T*, I was feeling satisfied.

I left my pen on the ledger and smiled at the proprietor. I myself was to be one. I was to be more than the *French woman*. I'd have a bona fide identity. For that, I wanted to give off the airs of a respected woman, to dissuade any salaciousness from this new lot of mountain men. I said, "Please, do call me Madame Dumont."

◆

In the morning, I took to the main street, well rested. I walked, up, down, up again. My pace was slow, unhurried. I was eager to begin, to find a spot of perfection for my new venture, but I knew the process would take some time as I began my own gambling den—no, a parlor. Or better yet, I'd call it an emporium.

I purchased a parasol for the task, as much to complete my look as to protect my skin from the California sun. While I didn't want to invite advances, I did want to seem approachable. There was a balance to it, but hadn't I been perfecting that dance since the tender age of thirteen when my breasts sprouted and I stood on a soapbox behind Papa's counter?

So now, I intertwined my English and my French, ever so slightly dipping my head and parasol in tandem. "How do you do?" "*Comment allez-vous*?" "Good day." "*Ça va*?"

I heard no one else speaking French. In general, the populace of this town seemed mainly English in language and background. The town of Nevada didn't possess the blending of the smaller mining settlements or the larger San Francisco. The latter felt like the nerve center of the gold rush, with people coming and going, the spot where it all began for those of all walks of life arriving by ship. The mining bars were like the beating heart, encompassing every aspect of the mining life: digging, sluicing, eating, entertaining, and sleeping. And here, with their mining efforts happening beyond the town, but whereas the men returned to the same beds each night, this felt like any neighborhood where people of likeness came together. Arthur's skin color would've been obvious here.

I stood out as different, too: properly dressed, multilingual, a woman. There was a small number of other women here, but there were some, more than I'd encountered since my arrival out west. I'd happened across one or two at the mining bars, but I rarely interacted with them. They either worked the night like myself, but in their brothel tents, or slept while I worked, after tending to a full day of their husband's needs. I realized how little I slept during those days, thanks to my muleteer and croupier efforts.

But this life was to be different; it'd more resemble how I lived while in San Francisco, except—and most importantly—I was to be in charge. There was no Monsieur Sullivan. I had *carte blanche* to do as I pleased.

I smiled, and promenaded down the road. The town was built on a slight incline, so I truly enjoyed my time going down rather than up. Along the way, I'd stop, palming my hands against vacant shop windows to better see inside—to envision where my bar would go, my tables, and my couches for lounging.

Of course, I heard the other women, those miner wives. Women had that uncanny ability of convincing themselves they were being discreet while they spoke just loud enough to be heard. I'd been guilty of it with Patricia and Sophie back home.

"There's got to be some bad in a girl, with all her charms, who has nothing better to do but strut up and down Broad Street."

But oh, I did have a purpose. After a full three days of surveying, the final day mostly to keep those women talking, because surely they'd mention me to their husbands, and surely the mystique about me would continue to grow, and then surely their husbands' backsides would end up in my chairs, I'd decided which of the four vacant properties I'd make my own.

It was a complicated decision. A greater distance from the church would work in my favor. Close proximity to Fepp's and the other hotels was ideal. I didn't want to be adjacent to a restaurant that closed the earliest nor the latest. But I'd found my location, with a small apartment overtop for me. It was a place all my own, where I could be unrestrained and free.

"For you," I whispered.

With my looping *E* and swift cross of my *T*, I signed the papers, deciding to outright purchase rather than sign a lease of the building. I had the money. Those women knew it, acting like flibbertigibbets about how that could possibly be.

From there, much work was to be done. And while I took my time surveying, I needed haste in acquiring the decorum, so the town's intrigue didn't become tired. As it was, I knew it'd take a season for orders to be made and shipments to arrive from San Francisco, Chicago, Galveston, and *La Nouvelle-Orléans*. I flipped the pages of the mail-order catalogs with vigor and excitement.

The carpets and crystal gas chandeliers arrived first. With great huffing and puffing, I arranged each Persian rug. The enormous chandeliers were too great an ordeal for a woman small enough to have used them as a swing. They were gold plated with strings of dangling crystals. I hired a young man to hang them, three in all. When the carpenter was complete with the tables, they'd be centered underneath. For now, the mahogany bar was delivered. I considered only serving champagne and wine, certainly no beer. Perhaps whiskey. And then, that decision of whether or not I'd serve whiskey was solved *par défaut*, when an angel of a man delivered the bar fully stocked, as a welcome gift.

As for the matter of a bartender, I had no patience to root around town or interview for the position. At dinner, I indulged in a glass of champagne, watching with great interest how the bartender poured the drink. It was well done.

"Monsieur," I said. "Whatever pay you make here, I'd like to double it—should you decide to come to work for me?"

He asked no questions. He only said yes. John, his name was.

It was all coming together.

Soon, the table and chairs were in place. Sofas lined a wall. The ceiling was coated in gold squares, pulling out the hue of the rugs.

I paused, scanning the room, thinking of anything I may've missed. The walls. They were stark, and needed adornment—not in the form of naked women. My emporium would not be that type of place. The art needed more refinement. Arthur's talent would've lent itself perfectly. My chest restricted; in my mind's eye, I saw him behind a canvas, completing one before diving into another, until no less than twenty hung on my walls.

When I commissioned a local artist, he suggested landscapes.

"No," I said, too quickly, too sharply. Landscapes reminded me too greatly of Arthur's work. I swallowed. "Flowers, please. Roses, poppies, lilies, any additional botanicals you'd like to capture."

I wanted for my walls to feel alive and for their scents to seemingly fill the room.

Lastly, I needed a name. I'd thought on it. What made my emporium unique was my game, *vingt-et-un*, the one the miner had once asked for. The men enjoyed the word, often repeating it, reciting how fancy they felt. And, it was, of course, the only name for my fanciful establishment.

I was lugging a great slab of wood, meant to become my signage, indoors when the artist came by with my completed portraits. He offered to paint the name on the sign for me. But no, I wished to paint it myself, thinking of Arthur with each stroke. Oh how he would've enjoyed seeing me now. I did allow the artist to hang it for me, though.

Still, no one knew why I was in town or what my store was to be. They soon would. And, I nearly skipped toward the *Nevada Journal* offices.

Inside, a *secretaire* pointed me down a long hall. I tapped lightly on an open door before stepping across the threshold.

The man stood at once.

"Ah, Madame Dumont." I was pleased to see my reputation preceded me. "It's a pleasure to see you again."

Again? I quickly scanned, found a placard with his name, his role listed as Editor. "And you, Monsieur Waite."

"Ernest, please."

I smiled, and it dawned on me. This gentleman was one of the men who greeted me at the coach, the more talkative of the two. "Ernest, I'd be appreciative of your help, again. You were already so helpful getting me settled at Fepp's Hotel."

He gestured toward his guest chair. "Anything."

I sat. "Well, it's rather simple. I'd like to purchase space in your next installment."

His head cocked, intrigued, and he reached for paper and a writing utensil. "Yes, yes, of course."

"You see, I'm opening an establishment. One of a kind, really. And, I'd like to attract a certain clientele. It'll be no doggery."

"Oh?"

"That's right. It's to be the best gambling emporium in northern California. The *crème de la crè*, with *vingt-et-un* as my specialty."

His eyebrows rose at the term, but I couldn't tell if it was from recognition or confusion at the details of my game. If it were mystique, that suited me just fine.

I said, "My doors will be open to gentlemen, such as yourself, who know how to dress and properly conduct themselves."

Ernest suddenly grew by an inch.

"I'd like the advertisement to be an invitation. *You're invited,* it should say."

Ernest began to write.

"Rather"—I nibbled on my bottom lip—"we should be specific. Only men, well-dressed men at that, will be allowed inside."

"So, no women?" His cheeks reddened. "Of any kind?"

"Only me." I smiled sweetly. "And, I assure you, I am nothing but a proper lady."

"Of course."

If he held any dissatisfaction that my Vingt-et-un would be missing womanly entertainment, he needed only go to various other saloons in town, each teeming with saloon girls. If he were the kind of man who wanted more than that—though that'd be a disappointment, as he did seem like a handsome man with manners—I suspected those women were available in town as well. But *not* at my emporium.

I didn't bar women for my own gain. I had no interest in their husbands or even the available men. But I also wasn't blind to the persuasion of my kind. Men fought over us. And, at Vingt-et-un, there were to be no brawls.

Additionally, no chewing, no cussing, and only cigarettes rolled and distributed by my own hand, to ensure the room didn't overfill with smoke.

But none of that needed to go within the invitation. It'd be clear enough upon their arrival. However, "There is to be champagne," I said. "Free of charge on my opening night." I saw it as *lagniapp*. Something extra. Something that'll entice them through my doors. I'll leave out how I held no intentions of serving beer, to avoid the room taking on the odors of a brewery.

To conclude, I provided Ernest the date of my opening. I rose, extending him my hand. "Will I see you there?"

He smiled. "With bells on."

I returned it. "Not too noisy of ones, I hope."

But he did give me a thought. We'd need music. I'd hire a violinist at once. And though my funds were dwindling at this point, I'd purchase a piano as well.

I'd spare no expense for Vingt-et-un. Madame Dumont had a reputation to create and uphold.

Chapter 20

ERNEST WORE NO LITERAL BELLS, but he was the first in line and reminded me fondly of the lead mule of the muleteers, with a quarter-mile of animals behind.

But these were no animals, not in appearance at least. Much to my delight, the mountain men upheld to the details on my invitation: well groomed and well dressed.

I eyed my wristwatch, sitting casually on one of the mismatched sofas. I'd chosen an eclectic look, no table, sofa, or chair the same. It was time to open, but I'd let their eagerness grow. My own heart pounded in anticipation. They could see me through the large storefront windows, but I didn't acknowledge them, only slowly sipping the bubbly liquid from my flute. I wanted this moment for myself, to think how my life twisted and turned to get here on this particular sofa. I had been very specific when I placed the order. "Walnut," I had told the merchant, "the frame curved and carved in the shape of flowers, upholstered in a deep red velvet. Can you find one like it?"

He had, but it was delivered only yesterday, getting delayed in the Sierra's human-height snow. Though winter was upon us, snow didn't fall in town, as I was promised when accepting the recommendation of this boomtown. The sofa wasn't an exact match, yet it was close—so close to the one Maman had purchased for Papa's workroom at the shop. It had been the only touch of elegance in Papa's room that'd been cluttered with the necessities of a watchmaker and merchant. But that sofa, he'd always kept it clear.

I ran my hand over the smooth fabric. I had thought about putting my replica in my office. But this room would be my workroom. I wanted to glimpse it while I dealt cards, walked the room, chatted with my patrons. In my office, I put something else of importance. Over my desk, I'd hung Arthur's portrait of me. I'd taken the canvas to a carpenter. He had looked between the portrait and me, where I was captured with so little clothing. I'd cleared my throat. "Well, can you put it back together?"

His head shook, wood clippings clung to his beard, shaking along with him. "There's not enough canvas. Should've removed the nails instead of cutting it from the stretchings."

"I wasn't the one to do that."

"Then you shouldn't have let someone cut it. It's a ... striking portrait of you."

His compliment softened me. "Thank you. I'm a croupier, you see, and I'm opening an emporium in town. You are welcome, with the removal of the wood chips, of course."

He smiled a crooked grin.

"Now," I'd said, "what solution do you have for me?"

The man simply framed the canvas.

With a fingertip, I brushed the symbol Arthur had put on my ring finger. I wanted the portrait for only my eyes, for only my memories.

At ten minutes past, I stood, feeling the shift of my knife's belt. I never took it off, not in a world dominated by men. I would be surrounded, the only woman. It was unnerving, but I'd chosen this life, this environment. And they'd be receptive to my games, I reminded myself. The men proved time and time again in the mining bars and in San Francisco they'd sit across from me.

I passed tables readied for poker and the table where I planned to deal, and then I flung open the door—of my very own establishment.

You'll work for yourself one day.

I'd run Arthur's words through my head once before, when I had been disgruntled about being under Monsieur Sullivan's thumb. His words felt repeating in this moment, too, for I'd made them a reality.

"Messieurs," I proclaimed, "I am Madame Dumont and I'd like to welcome you to Vingt-et-un. Please only bring yourselves inside. No flasks, tobacco, knives ... I do hope you get the point."

Most men were eager to comply, but the faces of some told a different story, ones questioning why they should listen to a woman.

I wanted to reply, "Because this is *my* establishment."

But I carried on, orchestrating my opening night. I directed Ernest and the first men inside toward the bar. "Champagne is a gift from me to you. Enjoy yourselves."

No man questioned me there. But they were slow to walk into the room with the feminine touches, a vase here, a pillow there, the furniture dainty. This was no saloon with spit and grime on the floors and knife marks on the tables. I even walked the room earlier spritzing from my cologne bottles to further bring to life the floral walls.

My smile spread when I saw their acceptance. These men may haul dirt and cuss like sailors at the mines, but didn't we all begin our lives pampered, suckling from a woman's breasts?

Within minutes, Vingt-et-un was bursting at the seams—the tables, the couches full. Men stood in the places in between, conversing. Poker games had begun. Champagne flutes were emptying. The violinist played "Ox Minuet." The bartender poured whiskey and champagne. And still, there was a line outside, pushing and shoving to be next inside. I returned to the door to see to the matter. Beyond the men, I saw the few wives, sisters, lovers—whomever they may be—trying not to be seen.

"You, there," I said to a man with height and girth. "Will you be a dear one and watch the door? Only let in more when others leave. And, no women or children, please."

I assured him two things: I'd pay him handsomely and I'd relieve him with another volunteer in an hour's time.

He agreed and, at the storefront window, I pulled one side of the draperies and then the other side closed.

I turned to the now-private room. I nodded to the violinists, who paused. The room grew silent. I put the hint of a smile upon my face. "Now, who'd like to join me in a game of *vingt-et-un*?"

It came as no surprise that I had takers. "Well then," I said, accepting the seat pulled out for me, "it'd be my honor to learn your names."

And so it began with four gentlemen: Joseph, Riley, Thaddeus, and George.

❤

To the men, I was a forbidden fruit with an enticing game. They learned it quickly. They soon asked for it by name. I ran game after game every night. The other tables were free for the men to use, however they liked. It mattered little to me.

All that mattered was they came. They indulged in evenings of sophisticated gambling. When at my table, I impishly smacked the hands of anyone who used profanity and referred to myself as a lady while calling the offender a *vilain garcon*. The others heckled him for being called a boy, a naughty one at that, and I wagged a finger at the jeerers, all the while asking them if they wanted to play another hand.

Every hour, I'd walk the room with a tray of cigarettes. They were complimentary, and the men seemingly enjoyed them more so for this fact, along with how they weren't readily available, how they were presented to them, and because they were hand-rolled by me.

"All I know is she's rich," I heard Joseph, one of my regulars, say as I was conversing with another group of men.

"Uninvolved?" another asked.

"Like you'd have a chance."

"Dang it all, none of us do. But I sure like trying."

Joseph toasted to the room, "To the charming, witty, vivacious, Madame Dumont!"

Madame Dumont. How glorious my name sounded. How satisfying to have created that name for myself. If only I could've suspended time or written that particular name into the history books. Of course, at that time, I didn't know a man would later alter who I was. In that moment, I modestly acknowledged Joseph's words with a dip of my head, then impishly spoke from under my lashes. "Joseph, you forgot mysterious, did you not?"

They laughed, but it was true. They made guesses about my past and where I was from, France being the most common answer. I'd heard it all before.

Additional tables were added. Another bartender, too. As luck had it, also by the name of John. Four men rotated as bruisers at the door: Henry, Thomas, Reginald, and Theo, minding the from-aways, the locals, and my regulars, Ernest included, his face continually a welcomed sight.

As always, I learned their names. None of them asked my first name, satisfied with referring to me as Madame Dumont. Only Arthur had ever asked my forename, all those years ago in the Bella Union.

If we'd met here, instead of there, where I owned the establishment, where I made the rules, would we have had the opportunity to become? Could we have created a life, where it was only he and I, no one else the wiser? And if anyone dared to squint an eye, there was Henry, Thomas, Reginald, and Theo to see to it? Or, as the only black man in town, would

Arthur always have had the limelight on him? In California, black men could own businesses, but the attitude of most was that they didn't want the competition of any black man, whether he be free or a slave. Those thoughts got me nowhere but deeper into a bottle of champagne.

Before I knew it, I woke up and a year had passed. Every night, after I locked the front door and climbed the stairs to my apartment, I fell into bed. My mind was a confusion of cards and numbers and names, but the chaos of my mind was cocooned in something novel. Happiness. Sleep found me more quickly than ever; I'd never worked so hard. All the tasks of keeping the books, cleaning the glasses, tidying the room fell on me and me alone. I relished in it, even if I largely spent my time alone.

There was no Patricia or Sophie, to play afternoon games of *vingt-et-un* in the parlor room, and no Lydia, to link arms with while strolling through town. There were only women who accused me of wanting their husbands. Like now, as I walked to the New York Hotel for a meal, a woman approached me, her dress plain, her hands chapped and with a discoloration I assumed to be permanent from laundering clothes.

I felt well rested so I'd entertain her. I didn't mean to speak ill of my own kind, but my kind did have a mind for histrionics, if I were to be honest. I spoke first. "*Bonjour*, Madame Brown."

She startled. Why yes, I'd learned which woman went with which man. It wasn't difficult when the men spoke so often of their wives, not always in the most flattering of ways. Then I'd see them about town together.

I smiled sweetly.

She did not. "You think you're a big bug, don't you? When all you've done is bring scandal to our town with your *services*."

The implication was insulting. I stepped closer, and said, "I see it otherwise. I've helped bring business to the town, in fact. Do you not own a laundry? The men who pass through, spend a night with me, then decide to spend two more. Do they not get their clothes laundered at my suggestion?"

"At your suggestion?"

"Why of course. As you've come to see, I don't allow just anyone inside Vingt-et-un."

Madame Brown shook her head. "You and your fancy words."

"French," I said. "That's all it is." I could've stopped our conversation there. This woman believing me the reincarnation of Aphrodite didn't hurt my business; any comments to her husband likely quickened his departure from her house to mine. But I felt the need to defend my honor. "And all we do is play cards."

Truly, these women were baffling. You'd think they'd be more outraged if I hired a room full of women to entertain their husbands. Somehow, me being the only woman angered them more?

As it was, she put up her nose, mumbling how she doubted we only played cards, and she went on her way. If she only knew the truth, that it'd been nearly five years since a man touched me in the way she implied. Since David.

His appetite for me had been insatiable, so much so it made me blush. He often fingered my engagement ring. During this moment in particular, he also nipped at my ear, his trim beard tickling my skin. We sat on the red velvet sofa in Papa's workshop while Papa saw to an errand. It was just David and me. It would be for some time. David knew it. He nipped away. I let out a moan.

"Simone," he'd whispered. "You shouldn't do such a thing."

I moaned again, encouraging him.

He growled, deep in his throat, and I laughed. The movement caused my chest to rise, the crests of my breasts, where they appeared from my dress, pressed into his arm draped across me.

"Simone, how long until you're mine?"

"I'm yours already," I said.

"Until we're married."

"A few weeks more. But, David," I said, my voice low in volume and tone. "Have you ever taken me for a conventional woman?"

He sat up.

I'd always been impulsive and impish. I dressed and acted like a lady not for society's sake, but for my own. I enjoyed blouses and skirts. I enjoyed to make up my face. Quite frankly, I liked the response femininity brought me. And I saw no reason for David's current response to stop, now that we were practically standing at the altar.

I tugged on his necktie.

He responded to that, kissing me, tugging at my clothing, which was surely a complex puzzle for a man.

I helped him, suggesting we lift instead of remove. David ran his hand up my leg, higher, higher, where no man had ever gone.

Maman once told me that some women saw intercourse as merely an obligation of the marriage bed. But those women were going about it all wrong with their husbands. "Trust me, my jewel. Children are a wonderful outcome, but not the only outcome." She had winked, and I had blushed at her candor.

That first time with David, my cheeks heated from his touch. *The touch of my future husband*, I had thought. Our intimacy had been off to a good start, and it only bettered, after the passing of the initial discomfort and pain. I wondered what it would've been like with Arthur.

Returning from my memories, the unhappy face of Madame Brown still stood in front of me. Clearly, she wouldn't take me for my word, that I only dealt cards to her husband. "If you'll excuse me," I said at last. "I have an evening to prepare for."

That evening turned out to be lively, especially so. Nuggets had been found in the hills outside our town. It was a time for celebration. We'd begun the evening with a toast, something the men greatly enjoyed. And now we played.

I asked Theo to let more men in than usual. Generally, I saw the same faces—Joseph and Thaddeus, for example. My regulars received preferential treatment at the door. But if additional men wished for their merrymaking to happen within my establishment, I wouldn't stand in their way. I'd sit here asking, "Will you play, monsieur?"

Like always, they would. They would indeed. The other tables had games of self-run poker and keno, while I prepared a new game of *vingt-et-un*. I shuffled, scanning the faces at my table and the men who crowded around to watch. Their clear *gaieté* caused my own smile. Nuggets were profitable for everyone. Other miners would hear of it, they'd come here. They'd sit in my chairs, purchase my whiskey.

I dealt. The cards didn't play in my favor, but that was fine. There'd be another hand and one after. I soon experienced a string of luck, while poor Howard two seats to my left, did not. He came in with light pockets, the cautious type who didn't bring a lot, but a newcomer who didn't know when to stop. His empty pockets would be his signal, it appeared. There went his last dime.

He began to stand, a bit green in the gills. But before he left me to lick his wounds, I stood, too. The violinist—and pianist when he played—often altered their rhythm to a slower one when I walked the room, to allow for conversation. The men heard the change, looked for me, eager for their next cigarette or their moment to regale me with their tales from the mines. The room quieted, and I called to John at the bar. I kept fresh milk—none of that condensed milk nonsense—to mix with the whiskey, for the aptly named milk punch. "Please, will you prepare a glass of milk for my *mon ami* Howard?" I offered dear Howard my hand and leaned closer, fully knowing others would still hear. "Any man silly enough to lose his last cent to a woman deserves a milk diet."

The men laughed, my intended effect. Laugher was contagious, and soon Howard's sour face shifted and he was laughing, too. He was accepting of his glass of milk. He held it high, offering cheers to the room. They joined him.

I'd once heard the men say, "If I'm to lose my money, it's an honor to lose it to the madame."

I hoped Howard felt honored. Then and there, I decided every pocket I emptied to completion would receive such a commotion. It was a rare thing, most people only stayed at the table that long due to inexperience or because everything else had already been lost.

With Howard lapping his milk—he indeed drank it—I walked the room. A group of men were discussing "bloody Kansas." I'd read about it in the *Nevada Journal*. Over thirty years ago, the Missouri Compromise went into effect that prohibited slavery above a latitude point. The exact point I couldn't recall. But last May, the Kansas-Nebraska Act repealed it. The pro-slavery South and anti-slavery North butted heads, violently, hence the moniker of "bloody Kansas." I was ashamed of my South, but truly thought of myself as being of the North now. Of a free state. California was greatly removed from all the country endured, playing more of a secondary role in the nation's drama. It was a state of fortune seekers. But I could help: in my apartment, I had a spare room. It'd be there, if any black man or woman should need it. I'd never seen it firsthand but I'd heard of people hiding slaves in their homes and businesses in the east. And I had money. Well, I would soon, with my funds recouping daily. I'd begin donating what I could to the abolitionists as soon as I was able. A grand would do, as my principal donation. Symbolic, I decided, to the sum I would've paid to obtain justice for Arthur.

I finished handing out my cigarettes, then returned to my table.

"Let me see who I have here," I said, taking my seat. My table sometimes changed while I walked the room. "Ernest." I smiled. I named the others—Riley and George—moving left to right. Then, I froze at the last man. My tongue felt oversized. The back of my neck prickled with heat. It was a blessing I was already seated.

"Hello, Madame," he said, his voice steady, unreadable.

Still, I couldn't find the words. My head could've been filled with cotton instead of a brain. But of course, I recognized him. His hairline had moved slightly. His facial hair was gone. Otherwise, he looked the same as when I last saw him. It triggered oxymoronic emotions that I couldn't quite place beyond how they warred within my head.

I licked my lips, feeling each beat of silence. I should've replied by now. But how? Here, before me, was a man I thought I'd left in my past. I had moved on. I was at a loss for how to address him, how he perceived me, or what to say. "Allô," I began tentatively. "How wonderful to see you again, David."

I longed for any expression from my estranged fiancé, any hint of what he was feeling. All he gave me was a flat, "Indeed."

Chapter 21

DAVID SIGNALED FOR A CARD. "Ah," he said. "It's been a while since I've done this. How I missed it."

Playing *vingt-et-un*?

Playing with me?

Banter with me?

Me—in general?

His facial expression still offered me little. His voice was void of emotion. He was playing with me, indeed. And, he succeeded at leaving me rattled. I couldn't recall, had two threes or three twos already been played this round?

Ernest picked up on my unease, but I could tell from how his eyes wandered the table he wasn't sure where it originated. I did my best to chat as I always did, with everyone.

But even as I spoke with Ernest and the other men, I felt David's eyes on me—such familiar yet unfamiliar eyes—and it took every ounce of effort not to flick my gaze toward him. He'd want that, but to what end, I couldn't tell. It was maddening. Unnerving. Sweat gathered at the small of my back.

I dealt David a new card and an imitation smile.

"Thank you, Madame," he said. "There appears to be an elegance in everything you do."

I began to reply, "*Merci*," but only spoke a syllable before he continued, "You must torment hearts everywhere you go."

The men laughed. I feigned my own giggle. "You flatter me."

"Do I?"

I licked my lips. Forced another smile. *"Je préférerais être n'importe où mais ici."*

I prayed David hadn't learned French in the time we'd been apart. But those words—*I'd rather be anywhere than here*—had never been truer, if he were able to translate.

And wanting to be someplace else, well, that left me with great irritation. This was my place. I tried to temper that annoyance because he had every right to be galled with me. But toy with me? To speak in such a manner that left his intentions and desires unclear? That was unfair. He was the one to track me down. Not in San Francisco, like I had worried he would after procuring my address. But here. And how was that even possible? He came a large distance to find and see me, or so I assumed. I knew nothing of how he had spent the past few years. But him finding me out of the blue felt familiar to how he first found me, after he'd searched every shop in *La Nou- velle-Orléans*. What lengths had he gone to find me this time? His being here wasn't accidental. I reasoned that much from his poised greeting.

His face held a puzzled look at my French, his right eyebrow slightly higher than his left. I'd seen it before, many times before, like when David had watched Papa assemble a clock-piece that he hadn't been able to figure out. David's expression—so customary of him—struck me, softened me. At his core, he was a good man. A man I once saw as my partner. A man I'd left with only false words of returning before nightfall and a left-behind engagement ring. I never said good-bye or gave him an explanation. And, it wasn't him. I didn't leave him. Not exactly. I left behind the idea of him and the life I no longer felt was mine.

And here he was, interjecting himself into a new life never meant for him. I wasn't the Simone Jules he once knew. She began to perish in *La Nouvelle-Orléans* and fully expired with a rock chipper in her hand. Eleanor was my second chance at happiness. My fresh start. Was this meant to be a second chance for us? Is that why he was here? That notion opened a sea of additional questions. My head swam. So I did what I always did, I dealt my cards.

Chapter 22

THE NIGHT CONTINUED. David and I danced around each other in words, expressions, and stolen glances. To say his presence shook me and left me off kilter would be an understatement. I didn't want to let on that I knew him beyond an old acquaintance, and he seemed to understand me and give me that courtesy.

He didn't refer to me as Simone, nor as Eleanor. Only *Madame*. His eyes flickered to my ringless finger now and again, perhaps wondering when and why I exchanged the title of *mademoiselle*, as I was so often called back home. Had I married? Or did I simply prefer the more respected title? I saw the questions in his head.

I both longed for the night to end and dreaded it. The only unwavering element of the evening was that I knew where he was at all times, whether it had been at the bar, my table, or a seat on a sofa. Our replica sofa. He lingered before sitting there. Did he remember—as I had—the one from Papa's workshop? Did he replay—as I had—our intimacy there? While he stood, I saw only his back. When he stepped forward to sit, I averted my gaze.

Later, with my tray of cigarettes, I approached him, offering the tray to David and the two men beside him. I let my eyes fall on him, but not any longer than any of the others. I didn't overlook, however, how his fingertips swirled, ever so lightly, overtop the slim velvet arm of the couch. I felt it as if it were my own skin.

I thought of it, of him, of what could've been between us if the opera house hadn't burned that day, orphaning me, along with my identity. Those thoughts only spawned to new thoughts, of Arthur, and how I never would've met him if I had carried on with my old life. Tears sprung to my eyes, at the thought of never having felt Arthur's lips on mine. But all those considerations were nothing more than a vicious circle, one leading to the next, but ones where all the people I've loved could never have existed at once. Not in my existence, at least.

At the close of the night, men stumbled toward the door. David lingered, on our couch, making as if tying a shoe. Then, it was only us. I sat beside him, leaving enough space for another person between us.

He asked, "This can't be the same couch, can it?"

So he had remembered. Of course he had. "No," I said. "But I wanted one similar. For memories." Then, it dawned on me. He wouldn't question this couch if he still had the one in Papa's shop. "Did you sell it?"

He nodded. "And moved to New York."

"Pardon?"

"I was hurt. After you left, I left, too."

My mind raced to process his words. I held up a hand. "You sold Papa's shop?"

"What did you—"

"But you wanted it." I inhaled, deeply. "Papa saw you as a son. That's why he left it to you."

"To us." He took my hand, but then as if he thought better of it, he released me. He ran the hand through his light hair. "I tried to write to tell you, but I had no idea where you'd gone."

I stilled at that—at that lie.

David misinterpreted my reaction, and further defended his decision to sell. "I wanted the shop with you, Simone, as part of our life together. But you threw that life away.

You left without a good-bye."

Why had he lied before? My mind lingered on his deceit, but my outrage at his selling of Papa's shop was stronger. "So you sold it?" I snapped my fingers.

"Simone, you left. Just like that."

This was where I apologized, or I should've done so. But I was hurt, too. The shop was an heirloom. It was my father's father's, after arriving from France. "I go by Eleanor now. Eleanor Dumont."

He sucked one cheek, then the other. "Dumont?"

"It's no one's surname but my own."

"You never married?"

I shook my head. I wasn't given the time or the liberty, with any man I'd ever cared for. I now said, "I only left because my future was so entangled with Patricia's. With her gone, I didn't know how I could go on. Or how I could marry without my sister. That was why I couldn't marry you. I should've explained."

"Yes, it took you only a handful of words."

"Now it did," I said. "Years later. But I didn't know how to deliver those words, back then."

We were silent. I was tired, feeling the exhaustion all the way to my bones, all thanks to my nightlong contradictory emotions. Even currently, I wanted David to leave my emporium, but I wasn't ready to let him go now that he sat beside me. Perhaps I let him go too hastily the first time? That moment seemed so distant. So much had happened since. I said softly, a question in my voice. "You went to New York?"

"Port trade, at first." It was what he had done back home. "Then, real estate. But I guess your family had worked their way deep into my marrow because I took to gambling. Sought it out, even. It's big there. Reminded me of you. It's how I heard of you, actually."

I cocked my head, my insides growing warm.

"Well, not you specifically, but I heard of this beautiful, mysterious, French-speaking woman out in Gold Country with a new game. They called it twenty-one. And I knew. I knew it was you."

"And you came?"

He took my hands now. "I left straight-away, and had plenty of time to doubt myself on that ship. In San Francisco, I told them the name Simone Jules, but no one seemed to know it."

"I rarely used it," I said. It was only here where I established myself and gave the gamblers an actual name to use.

"Would've made it easier if you had. But they said there used to be a woman there who played the game, until she vanished. But of late, they heard of the game being played here. I made the trip. When I saw the sign out front—Vingt-et-un—my knees quaked. I'd only ever heard the word spoken in your family's parlor. I stood outside quite a while. It was good there was a line. I needed that time to decide to come inside."

"And here you are. I'm sorry," I said it now, vaguely, encompassing all my wrongdoings. Then, "What now?"

"I'd like to get to know Eleanor Dumont. She reminds me of this beautiful woman I once knew."

In that moment, David looked like the nervous, fidgety young man who first walked into my Papa's shop. "You look familiar, too."

♠

In truth, so much of David was familiar. The way he moved, the shape of his mouth, the cadence of his voice. But did I want him here? That, I didn't know.

His first night, David stayed at Fepp's Hotel, without a hint of a suggestion of coming upstairs to my apartment. We didn't embrace when he left. With his hands in his pockets, he rocked back on his heels. "I'll come back tomorrow, then?"

I nodded, all the while my insides screamed, *No, leave me be.*

It felt selfish of me. He'd traveled all this way. But I'd traveled a great distance, too, to find my place here. And in all honesty, I never envisioned my life as Eleanor Dumont including David Tobin. He was guarded, as he should be. I was, too.

At my desk the next day, I opened my ledger and concentrated on my expenditures and income. I glanced at my wristwatch. I made a note to look into an abolitionist fund. Ernest may know of one, with his connections at the paper. I'd discreetly inquire there.

I sat back in my chair, lifting my gaze to Arthur's portrait of me when I heard a knock at my door. David, I'd been expecting him. I had a nice dress on, my face done up.

He greeted me the same way he'd said good-bye last night, with his hands in his pockets. "Does Eleanor like theater?" he asked. Then, as if realizing his mistake—that my family had died at the opera so close in nature to the theater—he said, "I'm sorry, I wasn't thinking."

"It's fine, really." I had gone to the theater a few times since living in town, and the theater's hasty construction reminded me very little of the elaborate details of the opera house in *La Nouvelle-Orléans.*

"Shall we, then?" David extended his hand.

I didn't hesitate before accepting, an olive branch of sorts, as I tried on the idea of him being here.

The theater bill consisted of two features. I'd leave after the first to be back in time to open my emporium. But for that first feature, sitting side by side with David, laughing at the dramatics on stage under the gas and limelight, I could almost pretend we were back in *La Nouvelle-Orléans* and not a second had passed. But it had.

David joined me at the emporium. Yet I was relieved to

find I felt at ease with him being there, because he held unfamiliar attributes as well. He snapped his teeth while he pondered a card. He had laugh lines around his mouth, which someone else had put there. There was more of him, in both height and width, as if he had filled out from a nineteen-year-old adolescent to a man in his mid-twenties.

The evening was filled with spirits and laughter. The nights that followed brought the same. The following week, I decided I'd make good on my intentions of donating to the abolitionists and stopped by Ernest's. I entered after a quick *knock knock*.

"I'm curious," I said. "I read in your paper how there are groups in San Francisco pushing against the Chivs for black equality. They weren't content with 'half-a-loaf' is what I believe was said."

He nodded slowly. "That's right."

"Well, I'd like to help their efforts. Financially, that is."

"Here?" he questioned. "I don't know of a black man in our town. Unless there's been one hired as a cook. Mrs. Monroe spoke of needing the help."

"Wherever's needed," I said.

"From what I've read, the black populace in San Francisco is small, but growing. Three black men registered as business owners during the last census there. Those that do come out this way are generally from New York, Boston, or Philadelphia."

Philadelphia, like Arthur. I chided myself; I couldn't recall the name of the paper that wrote an article on him. I asked, "Do you know of any abolitionist newspapers from those cities?"

"There's *The Liberator* out of Boston." I noticed a degree hung on his wall. The Harvard Law School. He went on, "The paper's run by a William Lloyd Garrison. He writes of women's rights as well."

"How perfect."

Ernest wrote down his name and an address. I'd see to it from there. On the street, I'd taken two steps from Ernest's office when David called for me. I rose a brow. "There you are again."

"Here I am," he said.

Silence stretched between us. On my side, I felt a bit lopsided that I ran into David as I was going about the ordinariness of my day, and I spent the quiet wondering what his intentions were in being here. Not outside Ernest's office, but in the greater sense. David had said he wanted to get to know me as Eleanor, but to what end?

David's question came first, "What were you doing?" He leaned to see the placard on the building's wall.

"This is the *Nevada Journal's* offices. Ernest, the paper's editor, was helping me with some business."

"Is that so?"

"Yes," I said. "Now, I must stop by the carpenter's. I'm in the need of another table."

I was relieved when David didn't offer to join.

The table arrived a week later. I was rearranging my existing ones when I heard my door creak open. "We'll open in a few hours," I called.

"Simone—Eleanor," David corrected himself. "It's only me."

"You," I said, slightly out of breath from my efforts.

"Here, let me help you." David moved to the other side of the table. "Where would you like it?"

"David," I said. "What are you doing here?"

"Helping."

I made no effort to lift my side of the table. "I meant, running into me"—I emphasized, circling my hand—"coming by most nights, calling on me."

"I told you I wanted to get to know you."

"Yes, but do you intend to stay? For any type of length, I mean."

He smiled. "For now."

"Then, for now," I said, picking up the table again, "you need a reason for being."

His smile broadened. We placed the table. He leaned over it, closer, thwacking his palms down. "You."

"No." Once again, I was happy for a table between a man and me. "Not me. I need to appear unattached." David opened his grinning mouth to speak. "No," I said quickly. "This is my business, one where I am unavailable, to anyone. And if you're going to remain, you need an occupation to fill your days, a reason for being. Other than me."

"So you've said."

I crossed my arms.

"A job, you say."

"Yes."

David crossed the room and sat down on our replica sofa. I narrowed my eyes, wondering if his choice of seats was more purposeful than a place to simply sit. Slowly, I followed, but didn't sit.

"What if..." he began. "What if we were partners?"

"Of what? You mean of Vingt-et-un?"

He nodded.

I, on the other hand, stood motionless. Finally, I rubbed an eye. "But this is my establishment. I picked the décor, the location. I make the rules."

He reached for me and pulled me into a sitting position, my hand in his, mainly because he never let it go. "I have no desire to change your rules, any more than I had the desire to change how your Papa ran things at his shop. Like then, it'd be ours. We were going to be partners once."

"But I left that life behind. I couldn't envision that life after...."

David circled a thumb atop the back of my hand. "I'm a different man now. And you, a different woman."

That was true. But was I willing to share what I'd built? Something inspired by another man? "I'll need to think it through."

Chapter 23

I KNEW THE DECISION had to be made quickly. David's routine of interpolating himself into my day would be noticed, prattle would ensue, those women would climb upon horses for the sole purpose of looking down at me and chiding me for taking one of their men. Not that David was theirs, but I doubted they clung to details.

In the end, I decided, yes, all right, having David as part of my business made sense. Papa always taught me practicality and David was a mercantile by trade, with knowledge of gambling. He could be responsible for the inventory of alcohol, the upkeep of the room, other odds and ends. Really, all the tasks I didn't have an overwhelming desire to do. I'd keep the books and run my game as Madame Dumont. Those were my interests.

"Very well," I told him, pushing back thoughts of Arthur. It was he who once stood beside me at my table and he who I had envisioned for the years to come. "Partners," I agreed to David. "But I will remain the owner."

We sat at a corner table in a restaurant. David scooped soup. He sucked it from his spoon. Then he raised his glass. "Partners."

I clinked his, smiling. He'd always been a charming man. A man—I soon found as he finished his soup and moved onto his duck—with suggestions.

"As it is, your patrons play poker and keno on their own. But it's you who is the draw, Eleanor." My name sounded intentional, a different tone from the rest of his speech. "We should add more games with you. How about roulette?"

"No," I said quickly. I spooned soup, giving myself a moment of composure. "No, not roulette, but yes, I'd be open to other games."

"Chuck-a-luck, then?"

"How's it played?"

"With dice. I can show you."

While roulette left me rattled, the idea of a dice game left my skin prickling. Hadn't Arthur painted me with dice, all from his imagination? I had laughed, telling him I'd never used dice before. He had responded, "Maybe one day."

It was as if he foreshadowed what was to come for me. In the portrait, he saw me as alive and unburdened. I smiled.

"Eleanor," I heard, but as if underwater. Then again. Finally, "Simone?"

I refocused on David. "I'm sorry. Chuck-a-luck sounds like the perfect addition."

"Wonderful. And how about other entertainment?"

I blotted my mouth with my napkin. "Well, I already have the violinist and pianist."

"Why not saloon girls?"

I thought of Lydia. "Too much of a flight risk. They'll run off with the men, and we'll have to take the time to rehire."

The tip of his tongue poked from his mouth while he thought. "Very smart, Madame Dumont. Plus, the men don't seem to miss it."

After our meal, we returned to Vingt-et-un. David wanted an official tour. I pulled open the drapery, letting light into the room. The chandeliers were unlit. David ran a hand over the couch. "This I already know."

He took in the remainder of the room. I'd opened with three tables. I now had six. The room held less open space, but people rather sit than stand, anyway.

Behind the bar, David crouched, eyeing the whiskey, the champagne, soda water, my cigarette fixings, today's fresh milk. "No ale?" he asked. "New York has plenty of brewery saloons."

"Brewery and saloon are two words I'd rather avoid."

Still on his haunches, David leaned to allow himself another view of the room. "I suppose it doesn't go with the ambience."

I smiled.

He suggested, "Maybe some ginger bottles? To mix with the whiskey?"

"Order it up."

David pointed to the first of two doors. "That where our office is?"

The second door was the office. That door led to a staircase and to my private living quarters. I had the carpenter add a door. I told him as much.

David asked, "Can I see?"

I supposed so. We climbed the stairs to a landing. From there, there was a water closet, my bedroom, and a spare bedroom. David popped his head into the water closet. "I see you've spared no expense?"

While preparing the downstairs, I also prepared the upstairs. A bathtub was installed, with a gas furnace attached to the side to warm the water. A water tank was hauled to the roof, and somehow—facilitated by a mind more inventive than my own—water came and went through pipes. The toilet worked in a similar fashion. Where it went, I wasn't sure, but the town had a system of sanitation in place.

My bedroom was next. I blanched at my unmentionables strewn about. David didn't say a word, simply walked in and out. But in the spare room he said, "No one is using this room?"

I shook my head.

"Could I? It'd be more comfortable than the hotel. And

imagine the time I'd save to and from work."

"I do believe Fepp's is only four doors down."

He winked. "Four additional minutes to spend with you."

"You've always been charming." Then, "I'll take the rent from your pay."

He laughed, stepping closer. Closer still. My back-step hit the wall. He leaned toward me, one hand extending to touch the wall beside my head. A hint of stubble covered his cheeks. He ever so slightly cocked his head to the side. "And you've always been savvy."

I was surprised to find parts of me heating that hadn't been heated in years. "Let me show you the office." I ducked free and hurried him down the stairwell and to the smaller room. "Should be enough room to add a workspace for you."

But he didn't respond. In my haste, I hadn't considered what David would find there, above my desk. The portrait of me. He asked, "Who did this? You've barely any clothing on."

"A man I once knew." I tried to erase all longing from my voice. But did David catch it? Was that why his jaw was held tight? Or, was it simply from the manner in which I was painted? From the hint of red in my hair and on my cheeks? Or from the aforementioned lack of my clothing? Or, my goodness, was his jaw tight because of the ring on my finger?

It was the ring.

That was where David's eyes were trained.

His voice deadpan, he said, "I thought you said you never married?"

I swallowed. "The ring is invented. The artist put it there."

"This man must've known you well, then, considering that and your attire."

"Also invented."

"So he imagined you this way and brought it to life so vividly. The swells of your breasts are so lifelike." He turned toward me. "I should know."

I tried to laugh away the moment. I'd grown so skilled at chuckling with men.

That evening, I continued to put the skill to use. The chip on David's shoulder was all but visible. His chest perpetually held air as he shook hands, introducing himself to our patrons. "Dave Tobin," he'd say. "Madame Dumont's right-hand-man."

At one point, as I conversed with Ernest and another man, having just offered them cigarettes, I lightly touched Ernest's arm. A breath later, David came up behind me. I yelped in shock, his arms having gone around my waist, his chin over my shoulder. His breath hit my neck as he said, "Who have we here?"

I fumed with anger, with embarrassment. I twisted free. "Ernest, Franklin, I'd like to introduce David Tobin." I added pointedly, "My business partner." The trick now was a mix of firmness but playful insouciance. "A bit overzealous, yes, but soon his decorum will resemble that of you fine gentleman."

David held up both palms, like a boy whose hands had been caught in the cookie jar, and I gently cupped his cheek before turning on my heel. I went straight for my table to begin a new game, my tension easing as I shuffled the cards.

Of course, David apologized. The portrait of me was an elephant in the room as he did so the next day. We stood in our office, his gaze twitched to and from the portrait, and he insisted the excitement got to him, but he understood I had a reputation to maintain. It was part of the allure, he admitted, that I was unobtainable. They could flirt with me, they could lose their money to me, I may even run a hand up their arm, but that was all they could have of me.

I accepted his apology. When I had walked in town earlier in the day, no one spoke of his so-called excitement. So, *laisser passer l'eau sous les ponts.*

I'd let his antics go as water under the bridge, and hope they weren't repeated for other eyes to see. But in private, would he want more? Did I? He'd come for me, after all, which I felt as a form of flattery. And I could understand his green-eyed response to Arthur's portrait. The last time David and I were in each other's lives we were bound for the aisle. I, myself, struggled with separating who we were then, and who we should be now. Truthfully, it was exhausting to reconcile. It was easier and more fruitful to focus on work. "David," I said. "Will you teach me how to play chuck-a-luck? We've a new game to add to our emporium."

♠

The next evening, I chucked the dice, with as much grace as possible. I found chuck-a-luck to be an amusing if not accurate name. The three dice poured from a cup and onto my table. A five. A one. A three.

Those who had put their money atop those numbers responded with ecstasy. Adversely, heads lowered from those who bet on the two, four, or six. They released groans. But then their heads snapped up, they rubbed their hands together, they said, "Let's go again."

"My pleasure, messieurs."

After David had taught me the game, I decided to put my own flair on it. Anyone could shake dice in a cup. But I wanted their blood to stir with anticipation. As I rattled the cup, I spoke rapidly, a wildness to my accented voice. I did so from under my lashes. I never said the same thing twice, that'd grow old, but I let some variation flow off my tongue. "Will it be you?" I said. "You, *mon homme de la montagne*. There are two-hundred-and sixteen ways I can have your money. How much of mine will be yours? Take it, I dare you. Make your bets, go on, one through six, as much as you can bear. A single, a double, big or small, how will you try to best me?"

They were quick to place their wagers, based on the

possible combinations that could appear on the three dice once I let them go.

The men couldn't wait for the release.

Before introducing the game, David had asked, "Why give them the total of outcomes? It sounds discouraging."

I shook my head, mischievousness on my face. "These men are not normal men. They are fortune seekers; you should know that by now. And, by now, every one of them knows their odds of striking it rich through gold or at my table are not in their favor. Yet, here they are. I won't downplay it. I'll use it as they puff out their chests and think they'll be the one to beat the odds."

He'd begun smirking halfway through my explanation. "Well, please, Madame Dumont. Don't let me stand in your way."

In that moment, I felt as if no one could. I rolled the dice.

It was clear my mountain men enjoyed chuck-a-luck, but it was my *vingt-et-un* that they loved, that they asked for. Not by its given name, as they endlessly butchered the pronunciation, but by the Americanized twenty-one. It was within this game, though, where they felt in control. They couldn't affect which card they received more than they could influence the weather, but they could ask for another card or they could stop me from giving them another.

No matter if I rolled or dealt, I so often felt David's eyes on me. Never beside me, but from across the room. Like now. He wasn't gambling. He sipped on his whiskey—looking as devilishly handsome as I remembered. He watched me entice the men. He, himself, looked enticed. Lord help me, the effect was emboldening. I didn't let it outwardly show. Yet, I felt its affects in my belly.

At the close of the evening, we counted our money. As he put it into the safe, I noted the amount in our ledger. Side by side, we climbed the stairs. At the landing, we parted ways,

David into his bedroom and me into mine.

This routine continued for weeks.

Next, I'd change from my blouse and skirt and tie a robe overtop my chemise, then pad to the washroom. David's personal affects were there now, too. Soap for shaving, a toothbrush, dental powder, silk dental floss. It was new for me. I'd never shared civilized space with a man.

I touched the handle of David's toothbrush.

On some nights, I passed David coming out of the washroom.

One night, I found myself lingering, waiting for the creak of his door, so I could ensure I'd cross paths with him.

"Good-night, Simone," he said with sleep in his voice, not noticing his mistake at the name. He wore only his drawers.

"*Dormez bien*, David," I managed.

His bedroom door was open when I woke the next day. "David?" I called. I walked the second then first floor, poking my head into our office. We didn't have the routine that Lydia and I had, of a meal upon waking each day. But we did dine together when it was convenient. It was likely he was meeting with a vendor, tending to our business in some way.

I began my day, walking out onto the street, quivering from the cool air, and spotting a youngster. Any would do; my favorite for favors. "Young man," I said. His tiny mouth hung open, as I wore only a robe atop my chemise. I'd brought a two-dollar note with me. "Would you be so kind as to fetch me a meal?"

A woman passing by huffed at my appearance. I smiled demurely. When I thought of my governess from my childhood days, and how greatly I'd changed, that smile broke to a laugh. The boy readily accepted my offer. I headed back inside, tidying here and there. I noticed a stain on a couch where someone had spilled. While scrubbing, there was an uneven rap at the door. I turned, expecting the young boy. But it was David.

Whatever he held, struggled with actually, knocked against the door.

I pulled the door open, David practically falling through. With him, came an enormous tree. His cheeks were pink from exertion.

"A Christmas tree?" I exclaimed. I rubbed my forehead, but from unexpected joy rather than unease. How grand. I knew the holiday was approaching, from the cooling temperatures more than anything, but the emporium had been so busy I rarely took note of the date.

"I remember your father getting one each year. I haven't had one since ... it all. But this year, I thought this year we could begin the tradition again."

I bobbed my head. "Yes, yes, that'd be wonderful."

The tree went up on a table, David and I laughing as we maneuvered it. Rather, the tree maneuvered us. It was so large the tip bent against the ceiling. But there it sat.

I said, "I'll order *Bûche de Noël* from the bakery, too."

It'd been too long since I had the sponge cake, frosted with chocolate buttercream to look like the tree bark of a Yule log.

We'd left the door open and the boy came in. I was sure he'd heard of my place, maybe even pressed his face to the windows when the drapes were open, but his wide eyes told me it was his first good look.

David slapped him on the shoulder. "We'll have a seat waiting for you in a few years."

Few years. I smiled, the grin remaining while I ate in front of the tree. I was still smiling, hummed even, while I went about the arduous task of cleaning the prior night's glasses. But David's comment and the holiday spirit had gotten to me, claimed me. So much so that even hours later, I still wore my sleeping clothes and robe.

That night, the men equally enjoyed the tree. At my emporium, at least, Christmas celebrations began a few days early.

On Christmas Day, David and I dined in town. Afterward, we sat on our couch, each taking a turn forking our Yule log cake, before opening our doors to patrons. With many miners leaving their families back wherever they'd once called home, we had many enthusiastic gamblers and drinkers, looking for companionship. Like in San Francisco, many reminisced about Christmases past.

I did my best to refrain from the same, but David at seventeen, then eighteen slipped into my mind, the memory culminating to when he'd gotten down on one knee after our carriage ride, mere hours after my coming-out party.

Across the room, David laughed with some men. As if feeling my gaze, his eyes met mine. I looked away. I so often felt like I was caught between the past and the present with him. But finally now, I could see him without seeing Patricia's Charles.

The men grew rowdy, rowdier than the ambiance of my emporium dictated—stray cats amongst doves. But there was no use trying to calm them with New Year's festivities right around the corner. Nor did I want to, truly. This was my second holiday season at Vingt-et-un, but this year was nothing like the last. I had celebrated, marveling at what I'd created. But I had done so alone. Not this year. I chuckled to myself that it felt like the men never left, their revelries continuing for days.

David was always nearby, as well, especially as the clock ticked closer to the end of the year. His presence wriggled another memory free, of each modest kiss we shared in front of my parents at the stroke of midnight. At the thought, butterflies also wiggled free in my belly.

In preparation for our midnight toast, I flitted around the room to the piano's melody. "Hold, please," I said to each man, offering a flute. Then I poured. "Wait until the bells," I instructed. Again and again, I offered, poured, recited, and popped new bottles. Ernest began following me with glasses to hand out. "How kind of you," I told him.

Then, sure enough, as bells began to chime, as glasses raised, as men cheered, David stepped in front of me.

"Simone," he whispered clandestinely. "It's poor luck not to kiss at midnight. It means loneliness for the year to come."

I overlooked the misused name; it was likely David was also feeling sentimental. "I wouldn't want that."

"No?" His hand nestled along my hairline, gently running back, then down over my ear.

"No," I said, "I don't wish for loneliness at all."

His mouth closed on mine. I kept my hand on his chest. When it surprised me how I wanted to deepen it and explore it, I fought to keep our kiss reserved.

Around us, the men responded. Hooting. Hollering.

"Hogmanay," someone called. "Madame Dumont!"

I pulled back and breathed deeply through my nose, the skin on my upper chest running hot. David shook his head. "Oh, no, no no. There will be no similar Hogmanay from Madame Dumont."

"What?" I said. "Is Hogmanay like *Hoguinané*? A gift given at New Year's?"

"If that gift is a kiss, to everyone in the room, then yes."

I laughed. "When in Rome. The New Year's kiss dates back to Ancient Rome, does it not?"

I made my rounds, pecking each man on the lips. Nobody took my face square between their hands like David had. One man seemed abashed, speaking to the ceiling about a woman back home, but did nothing to stop me. Mine were modest kisses through and through. Still, it was for the best that Madame Brown's husband wasn't here. I kissed the final two mountain men.

"There!" I called to the room. "Now none of us will suffer from loneliness!"

We raised our glasses to a new year. I drank, the bubbles

of my champagne seemingly lifting me from the ground. I rolled onto my toes, enjoying the sensation, the idea of this lightheartedness causing weightlessness. With my head back, I held my flute to my lips, allowing the golden liquid to tickle my nose before I took another sip.

David approached me. He held a beguiled expression. His words were nearly lost in the celebration. "You've never been a conventional woman, have you?"

"What would be the fun in that?"

His next breath was deep, as if considering the fun we could have, if not in a room full of people. I considered it, too. As we had in nights previous, we danced around each other with our gazes. Some hours later, David climbed upon the bar, waving a dishtowel.

"You've done it," he called over the music. It stopped. "You men have drunk every last drop we have here. Drunks, all of you." With a smile, David waved his arm, the dishtowel he held circling. The men moaned but also hailed their accomplishment with applause.

I snatched the dishtowel, then began chasing the men toward the door, snapping the towel, laughing, treating them as if they were bluebirds who wandered inside.

At last, the door was closed. The room was quiet. It was only David and me.

He nodded to the rag I now gathered in my hands. "Are you going to use that on me?"

My body still tingled from the champagne, a string of bubbles from my toes to the tip of my nose. I merely shook my head.

"My God, Simone," David said, rushing toward me. His hands, as they found my backside, lifting me up, felt larger and stronger than they had at nineteen years old. I wore no petticoat, no bustle, and no bodice as I once had, my movements less restricted. The pleats of my skirt allowed my legs around his waist.

He shuffled until his shins hit the couch. Our replica couch. I smirked. He returned it, as if reading my mind.

David nipped my ear. He kissed the swells of my breasts, lifted from the corset beneath my low-cut blouse. Did he realize their greater size, than when I was teen-aged? I hadn't grown much vertically, if at all, but my belly had softened in a womanly way and my hips had done as nature intended, widening for childbirth.

I pulled at his necktie. He dropped to his knees, gathering my chemise, my skirt. He ran his hands higher. The fabric bunched as he went. His eyebrows lifted when he found my blade.

"What's this?" he asked.

I'd forgotten the knife was even there. I shrugged. "I've been the only woman among men for a very long time now."

"May I?" he asked.

I nodded.

My knife came off. It was set aside. Then, his palms ran along to the top of my stockings. There, his fingertips pressed into my soft skin to grip the band. He pulled. A swift yank, his eagerness showing in the movement and the concentration on his face. I let out a playful yelp as I sunk deeper into the couch, more lying than sitting.

Then, taking his time, he withdrew my stockings, pulling both sides in unison, and then one leg before the other. My shoes came off, clunking to the floor, with the final yank of my stockings. He left my legs bare.

He stood to remove his own clothing. His boots came off first. I watched. David no longer kept a beard, as he had in his youth, perhaps to appear more dignified during his younger years. His hair had grown shaggy, as if accepting the lawlessness of the West. There was even a curl to his light, tousled locks. He slid one arm, then the other from his waistcoat. His braces came next. With little holding up his trousers, the pants easily fell to his ankles. He was left in a shirt, extending to his knees.

"David," I said, a purr to my voice. "You know it's only ever been you, in this way."

I left unspoken how my heart had been with another man. But David didn't know that, not with certainty at least, and every part of him swelled, obvious in how his shirt tented.

He lowered himself onto me, and I gave in absolutely to David being in my life again.

Chapter 24

IN DAVID'S ROOM, I lay in his arms. He'd carried me, taking his time, kissing me as we climbed the stairs. The evening had felt grown-up, which was an odd realization with us being in our twenties, but—before—we'd only experienced hurried, stolen intimacy when unsupervised.

David stirred. He said groggily, "Why are you awake, Simone?"

I didn't correct the name, though I wanted to. I'd let it go, as I had before. It felt hypocritical to slap his hand when my own mind kept slipping to our past and how if I'd remained only twenty-three days longer, David would've been my husband right now.

However, it wasn't Nevada where we would've shared our life together. The chances of us ever leaving *La Nouvelle-Orléans* would have been nonexistent.

"Tell me of New York," I said.

He spoke with his eyes closed. "The buildings are taller and there's more of them."

I slapped his chest. "Surely there's more to this so-called *City of Dreams*?"

He opened an eye, sighed. "Let's see, there're well over half a million people. What's that, five times the size of New Orleans? Lots of immigrants. Lots of Irish, on account of the famine overseas. You've got the poor." David lifted a hand. "And you have the wealthy. I saw both worlds. The poor were the real dreamers. But it was those with money who ruled the island. Similar to you, here, Madame Dumont." He added play-ful exaggeration to my name.

"We're doing well," I agreed.

"Do you ever think of expanding? Adding more tables? Dining, perhaps?"

I laughed. "Where would that all go? On the roof?"

"Next door."

"The restaurant? It's occupied."

His head rolled toward me. "Doesn't have to be. I have some real estate experience."

"Yes, you mentioned how you did that in New York."

"Not at first. Five Points is where all the dreamers are—and also all the gangs, thieves, destitute, prostitutes, gamblers." He motioned in a "you get my point" manner. "During a poker game, I overheard that a cousin of a friend of a friend had a real estate opportunity. I saw about it and it worked out. I'd found my way closer to the Fifth Avenuers. But at night, I seemed to find myself back at the poker tables. Good thing, too, or else I wouldn't have heard a lick about the little French woman lighting up the West." He tickled me, and between laughs, I heard him say, "I don't think the ladies of Fifth Avenue would've mentioned you with such fancy."

I wiggled free. "And what's that supposed to mean?"

"You must see how women look at you. I don't blame them. Or," he was quick to add, "you."

"Well, I'll have you know, I once had a female friend in San Francisco. Lydia."

"And what happened to this Lydia?"

"She ran off with a man. More or less."

He grinned. "Shame on her."

I pulled myself on top of him. My bare breasts pressed against his chest. "My thoughts exactly. Why should men have all the say?"

He let his arms fall wide on the bed. "You won't get an

argument from me. Though, will you think about the expansion idea?"

"I'll think about it."

I kissed him, which turned into more, which had me saying, "Now, whatever this is needs to remain upstairs. Downstairs, we're business partners."

Of course, that made my growing lust for David all the more intriguing. On any particular evening, he was forbidden, as was I, until the last drunken man had stumbled out our door. We'd shed our clothing—a shoe by the door, another by the stairs, his vest strewn on the stair's railing—until we tumbled into his bed.

We spent the winter in a perpetual state of gambling then lovemaking. We rarely left the emporium, the weather reminding me of San Francisco with all the rainfall. "Just think," David said, "if we had a cook and dining services, we'd never have to leave."

Eventually, the monsoon season passed and spring was upon us. I took it as a sign I should spend an entire afternoon outdoors. I came upon the stables, and deciding on a ride, I asked for a mule.

"A mule," the groom parroted. "Not a horse?"

"A mule will do me just fine."

Soon, with one limb on either side, I cantered down the access road. I hadn't left the town since I arrived—what was it—nearly two years ago. The weather was changing, the trees in the distance showing the initial signs of spring. The terrain where I first set out was barren, the men having stripped the hills for their mining purposes. With carefully placed feet, my mule took me down the banks of a dry riverbed, the water having been diverted elsewhere, leaving behind a sawmill with a water wheel, but no water. I crossed the dry bank and climbed the hill on the other side. The air was warm and the draft felt good, lifting stray hairs from my neck. I missed being outdoors, without knowing I even had.

I patted my mule. He wasn't cow-patterned, like the one I'd ridden in my muleteer days, but he'd do. The trail appeared well followed, with hoof tracks and fresh excrement. I veered off, moving slowly through the dense trees, using my gloved hands to push branches aside. Aimlessly, I rode, but took care in noting where I'd gone so I could retrace my mule's steps.

An hour passed, maybe two. Ahead a rolling prairie lay beyond the budding trees. I noticed movement. I stopped. At the tree line, I watched, cautious. There I saw a dozen women, Indian women. Their breasts were naked. Their lower privates covered with grass bound around their waists. The skirts extended to their knees. Their shins were dirtied from resting on the ground. Upon their backs, hung brown woven baskets that were nearly as big as they were tall. Almost in unison, the twelve women scattered seeds.

Their lithe bodies were beautiful. Their dark skin appeared as if it gathered the sun. I didn't dare make a sound. The only natives I'd ever encountered were with William, but I imagined these women would be more scared of me than I was of them. And, I was in awe of them, the fluidity of their movements, the simplicity of this exercise. I may've been a woman accustomed to fineries, who sought out those fineries, but I was also a woman who once did without.

I watched them for some time before I begrudgingly turned to return toward town. I'd meandered for only a few moments when, through the trees, I saw another woman atop a horse, not even a city-block distance away. While the native women seemed at peace, this woman was a direct contrast. Her head turned every which way. Her appearance, even while dressed in fine clothes, was disheveled. That was to be expected, I reasoned, after journeying here. I guessed her to be young, but at least sixteen, because her light hair was arranged upon her head. After sixteen, loose hair in public was unrespectable.

I picked up my reins, then stopped short, as a man emerged from within a den or foxhole. I'd heard of men hiding their money in such a way and saw the opportunity to say my hellos and invite him to Vingt-et-un. But what kept me from jabbing my heel into my mule to get him going was how the girl flinched as the man approached. He ripped the reins from the young girl's hands. With an aggression that seemed unnecessary, he yanked on the horse, the girl jostling in the saddle as the horse reacted. I softly stroked my mule's neck, keeping him quiet. He had a habit of stamping his feet when I paused.

Soon, the girl and the man were specks within the trees. I slowly followed, keeping a safe distance. By town, I'd lost the pair in the activity. With the spring came more miners.

That evening, I kept an eye out for the man from the forest, but the night had been busy and I found I had a hard time placing him, as I'd only seen him from a distance.

It took a week before I saw the mysterious pairing again. I'd pulled open the draperies of Vingt-et-un to let in the morning light, and there was a man with a young girl. Of course, it could've been a different couple, but her movements seemed forced. They were outside the grocer, across the street. The girl held his arm, rigidly, yet she leaned into him. I couldn't hear, but it appeared she giggled. He kissed her, deep and hard, before he walked off, leaving her there.

Within a single heartbeat, I saw the evolution in her. Her smile released, leaving behind a grim face, her gaze locked on his back. I leaned forward, my cheek pressed into the window, watching him go. He rounded a corner. Then, as if realizing he was gone and she could act as she pleased, the girl spun on her heel. She picked through a barrel of goods with vigor.

Her clothing looked laundered. Still, I wanted a better look at her. Her attire didn't say domestic employment to me. Again, I thought of Lydia.

"Back in a few," I called to David. He wiped glasses at the bar.

"Grab me a bite of something, yeah?"

"Mhmm." I was out the door. A steer pulling a wagon crossed in front of me. Dirt kicked up. I waved it away, dipping to see through the cloud of dust. She was still there. I felt silly for my interest in her, but it was too late for that. I stepped into the shadow of the grocer's overhang. *"Bonjour,"* I said to her back as she picked through the barrel.

The girl turned, startled. A hand went to her chest. Her eyes flicked in the direction the man had gone. She was young, younger than I originally thought. Fourteen? Fifteen? She looked up and down the street. While she'd applied rogue and blush, I still noticed a faint bruise beneath her eye, and in an instant, the niggling feeling in my stomach felt justified. Bruises weren't easily disguised, especially contrasted against her eye color, the blue of her irises brighter than any ocean or sky I'd ever seen, but I knew what to look for. Monsieur Sullivan had done well to protect the girls at the Bella Union; I'd give him credit for that, but the girls had still masked bruises from time to time.

"Shopping?" I asked her, the question obvious.

She nodded.

"New in town?" Another obvious question, considering I'd witnessed her arrival.

"Just this week."

"From San Francisco?" I guessed.

"That's right." Her nervousness showed again in how she surveyed the street. For the man from the forest?

"I once lived there." I smiled. "Did you come with your father?" The girl looked disgusted, as she should considering the kiss I observed. "Husband, then?" When she delayed, I kept going with my guessing game. "That's what he promised you? To marry you?"

Her chin rose. "He will."

I'd never doubted James's intentions to wed Lydia. But I'd

also never seen Lydia's face bruised by him. What was worse, I'd seen girls like this one before, seduced, promises made, their virginity stolen. Those women were seen as "lost." After their men tired of them, many went into prostitution. They'd end up in towns and cities, or even the mining camps, setting up their brothel tents. I'd witnessed it all first hand.

"My name's Madame Dumont." I touched her arm.

The girl sucked in a breath, but recovered, her voice sharp. "I know who you are," she said. "I asked him where he'd been."

I admired her spunk. Yet, "I see that went well for you."

She fingered the bruised skin beneath her eye. "He only acts that way when he drinks. Otherwise, he's quite charming."

That infuriated me. "May I ask your name?" She didn't answer. "Fine, may I ask the name of Prince Charming? That's an innocent enough of a question, no?"

She considered, said, "Gerald."

I smiled. "Well, I can assure you Gerald will no longer be welcome at my emporium."

The girl returned my smile, albeit timidly. People had begun noticing us conversing. Surely that wasn't good for this girl's reputation. Neither was bringing her inside Vingt-et-un, but that was exactly what I decided to do.

"Come with me, please?" I asked her. "I'm not someone who'll hurt you. Let's talk more inside."

Her mouth opened, closed, and then she stepped out from the shadowed overhang of the grocer's store. While I brought her toward my emporium, I reasoned that banning Gerald from mine would only send him to another gambling den in town. I asked her, "Would you change your mind, if you could?"

Her voice was small. "What do you mean?"

I made one more guess. "Would you have stayed as a saloon girl? Instead of leaving with him?"

Tears filled her eyes.

I opened the door. "Come inside."

David called from beneath the bar, "That was quick. What'd you bring me?" His head popped up, cocked to the side. "Not what I was expecting for lunch, I'll be honest."

I closed the door, chuckling. "I'd introduce you, but she won't tell me her name."

"Jane," she said.

I said, "Ah, there we are. David, this is Jane. Could I have a few minutes alone with her, please?"

He mouthed *food?*

I shook my head.

Frowning, he disappeared into the office.

"Just the two of us ladies," I said to Jane. "And while I've never been in your situation ..." I trailed off. "I'd like to help you, if I can." At that point, I wasn't sure how. All I could remember was being young, yet older than her when I arrived in San Francisco. I remembered the fear I'd felt at Lydia recruiting me as a saloon girl. It was likely I was projecting; Jane very well could've liked the employment but thought Gerald could've offered her more. And now regretted it. It felt like prying, but still I asked, "Would you like to leave him?"

"I can't. He said he'd find me."

"Trust me, it's very hard to find somebody who doesn't wish to be found."

Her eyes strayed from mine, taking in the décor, the first-floor of the emporium. "Your saloon is the nicest I've seen," she said.

"I prefer to call it an emporium."

"Sorry."

I waved her off. "Are you thirsty?" Then I considered. "Though we're likely only to have spirits."

"That's fine."

I laughed.

It won me a smile from Jane. "I mean to say, I've had it

before. I took sips when I served back in San Francisco."

My guesses had been correct, and the background gave me an idea. "Now, Jane, I've already told you I won't let Gerald inside. So, now that you're here, what if you stayed? What'd you make, around ten dollars a week? I'll give you fifteen. I could use another server. John and well, the second John, are always so busy at the bar."

I saw her face light up.

"The problem is," I said. "I don't employ women. Too much trouble, and you are doubly so with this man after you." I smiled, thinking of Anne Bonny, one of the renegade pirates from the book I'd read while on the California Trail. She'd disguised herself as a man. Young men Jane's age often possessed girlish features. Jane was the feminine name of John, I believed. I already had two Johns at the bar, what was one more?

"I'll hire you," I said. "Fifteen a week, like I proposed. But two conditions. The first: no sipping from my glasses. If you'd like a drink, simply make yourself one. But I won't have you becoming a lush."

Jane nodded. "And the second?"

"She's a pretty boy," David said.

Jane sat at a table. Her golden hair, once freed from its pins, had cascaded down her back. Now her hair was short, with a middle part, slicked back, and combed into a wave at the center of her forehead.

"Yeah," I agreed. "It's her eyes. Though we've yet to remove her cosmetics." I stood back and studied her. I nodded, satisfied. "I styled her to look like you, *mon cher*. She could pass for your younger brother, no?"

"So I have nice eyes?"

"She'll need clothes. Good thing you are a smaller-sized man."

And like that, David's ego punctured. I repressed a smile. Jane did not. She'd been less than eager to have her hair cut, and had squeezed shut her lids the entire time, but she was warming to us. The whiskey David gave her surely helped. Snip and sip had been her motto. David drank, too.

In private, I'd told him everything, about seeing Jane out in the woods with a man, how that man was likely hiding his loot, how that man likely abused Jane.

"I don't like it. Any of this," David had said.

"What would you have me do?"

David hadn't had an answer for that, so, that night, we'd test the waters with her new look, with Jane as John, David's younger brother come to stay with us. Until then, I'd said to her, "Let's get you settled upstairs."

"Upstairs," David repeated. It was our secret domain. Now upstairs would possess another secret, where Jane could be Jane.

I'd whispered to him, "You'll have to move into my room." We spent every night together as it was, in his room. Never mine. My room was my reserve, the last of the emporium that was wholly mine. But if it meant this child would no longer be struck at the whims of a man, then it was hers to have. I still couldn't pinpoint my immediate attachment to her, but as Maman once told me, matters of the heart need no explanation.

And my heart was in my throat as the evening was set to begin.

"This is John," I said to the Johns. "He'll be helping you however needed at the bar."

She shook their hands but didn't meet their eyes. Jane—as I'd continue to call her in my head and in private, for she deserved that dignity—appeared nervous. While the Johns gave her the lay of the land, she ran her palm up and down her new trousers. Her gaze drifted to the door, even before anyone entered. To this Gerald, Jane was likely seen as a possession, and I didn't believe him to be the sharing type. Unpredictable, cowardly, bitter? Yes. And those were the most dangerous characteristics of any human being. Hadn't I once encountered a man who thought I should be his, simply because he felt he was owed that? I often wondered what would've happened if Reuben had made it upstairs that night, if Arthur hadn't stood in his way.

I peeked through the drapes. A line stretched down Broad Street. Opening the door, I called Theo inside.

I said, "A patron complained of a man named Gerald, so he's not to be let in." I gave a description; the one Jane had provided me.

Theo said, "You've just described half the men in line, madame."

"I did, didn't I? Well, then, if you don't already know a man's name, ask it. If you greet everyone by name, it won't be odd to ask those you do not know. If you come across a Gerald, please have me fetched."

As the men entered, I saw many familiar faces. Jane stayed behind the bar. I thought it best if her visibility in the room was gradual. "Don't walk about," I told her. "Not yet."

"And my voice?" she asked.

"It's best if you talk naturally, when you do speak. But for a while, let's only nod."

She nodded. A quick learn. Though she did pat the back of her neck and head, where hair once had been. Even with a hairstyle that raised the hair off the neck, as mine did, the weight of it could still be felt. I imagined it was an adjustment, along with a waistcoat opposed to a corset. Fortunately, she had barely-there breasts.

That night, there was no Gerald. And, no one seemed to particularly notice Jane beyond serving them from the bar. If they had realized her actual gender, the whole place would've chattered. But it was only the normal noise, the exclamations of winning, the curses at losing, followed by my gentle reprimands and their quick, "So sorry, madame."

The night after, however, was a different story.

While I chucked dice, a man said, "Theo has asked for you."

Theo stood with his back to the door, the door closed.

I asked him, "He's here?"

"Right outside. I told him I had to check before letting anyone else in."

I thought on it, and the validity of Jane's disguise. The new style of her hair seemed to alter the shape of her face. There was nothing to do about her startling blue eyes, though her borrowed gray clothing didn't highlight them as fully as the colorful satin had. Without cosmetics, her face held plainness to it, her fading bruise visible. I'd wager he rarely saw it that way. Jane was truly changed, but I wouldn't let him in, not after promising her the emporium would be somewhere she'd be safe. I would, however, open the door wide. I'd allow him a look of the room. I was a woman who enjoyed reasoning, and by now, I reasoned he'd been looking for Jane. He'd found her in a saloon, so why not scour those first. They'd be empty of her, of course. The only place left in town was here. Perhaps, even, someone saw me escort Jane inside. Nevertheless, I'd let him look.

I swung open the door.

I followed Gerald's gaze around the lively emporium.

As it was, Jane's back was to the door. Had she seen him? By how she held a rag and glass, but didn't move her arms ... yes, she had.

I stuck to Theo's original statement and said, "Ah yes, I don't believe we have any more room." The men behind Gerald in line groaned. "Shush now, none of that," I said to the next man in line. "For you men, there'll be room. Just not for this man. I've made it clear I don't like violence."

Gerald narrowed his eyes at me. "She's here."

"She?" I asked.

An impatient someone from line yelled, "Step aside."

Gerald didn't take kindly to that. He yelled a threat over his shoulder, then to me he said, "She's mine."

"Forgive me, I know I'm only but a lady, but you're being unclear—and I have a business to run."

I nodded to Theo as I turned.

"Jane!" Gerald yelled.

"No," I snapped. "You will not conduct yourself in such a manner. As you plainly see"—I waved my hand toward the emporium's interior—"I am the only woman here. Now, excuse me."

Back inside, the yelling continued outside my door.

My heart pounding, I allowed myself a brief glance at Jane, but I didn't go to her. I returned to my table of well-behaved men and picked up my cup and dice. "Where were we?"

Chapter 25

AS IT TURNED OUT, Jane had talents beyond mimicking a boy. She liked to sew, and Jane asked if she could take in her hand-me-down clothing.

"Too large," David said. "Understandable."

Jane's future wasn't one we had discussed, as in: how long before she could safely leave the emporium. For now, as it was only the third day of her being under my wing, I offered to purchase supplies, including a Singer sewing machine, and ordered material for additional outfits.

The men were mostly at the mines, having brought along lunch or having eaten in town and now having returned to their work. The day was warm. I allowed a few precious seconds of the sun on my face before opening my parasol. Then I went about purchasing the items on the list Jane had given to me. School-age children mulled about. There was a woman here and there. A man lay face down on the edge of the dirt road. One of the children poked him with a stick, promptly causing a chase down the street. It was a relatively quiet start to the afternoon—until I heard my name. It was spat at me.

Frankly, I had expected him to turn up again.

The hair on Gerald's face was stuck between clean-shaven and a beard. He reeked of alcohol, the smell even greater than the nearby livestock. His clothing was the same as the evening before. I'd put him in his forties, but he wasn't aging well.

"*Bonjour.*" I did not break stride. However, I twisted my parasol to my other side to keep an eye on him.

He knocked the bag from my hands. From there our conversation resembled the night before, him accusing, me deflecting in an amicable voice, until he said, "I'd hate to see anything happen to your saloon and all those inside of it. Fires start all the time."

I kept my face smooth, as not to show the slap of his words, or how the implication of those words rattled me to my core. I'd seen the devastation a fire was capable of causing twice now. In a snap, those flames could change everything. In general, life could change in a snap, not caring what was built before or the dreams that were supposed to follow. Life was cruel that way. I had a feeling Gerald was equally unkind.

We were practically alone on the street. I brought my left foot to my right and I felt the length of my knife against my thigh. The few others slowed their pace to overhear. One man stopped, called, "Madame Dumont, is everything all right?"

I raised my hand nonchalantly to let him know I was fine, then picked up my bag. I pushed the idea of fire from my head and steeled myself. "If your threat is indeed veritable, then I'm sure the sheriff would like to know. He played at my table only last week."

I didn't wait for my own threat to land. I wanted out of this man's presence. Sweat trickled down my back. However, I didn't go to the sheriff. I went home, fighting the urge to look over my shoulder until I rounded the corner onto Broad Street. But before going inside, I lingered outside the restaurant next door.

It was occupied, as I had told David when he'd suggested enlarging my emporium. Through the windows, they prepared for the evening diners. One wall separated Vingt-et-un from it. It'd be simple to join the two, just as David had also suggested. And in the face of something—rather, *someone*—threatening to destroy what I'd built, I thought there was nothing more perfect than doing the opposite it. I'd expand Vingt-et-un.

I opened the restaurant's door, went inside. "*Allô,*" I called. My heels clicked against the flooring. The servers looked up from where they arranged the tables. "Is the owner in? Ah, Monsieur Garrison, there you are." He had stepped out from the kitchen. He smiled; pleased to see me. I took that as a positive first step.

❤

"You offered to buy his restaurant?" David pulled free a seat, sat backward on it. Jane had gone upstairs, eager to sew. I was impressed with her resolve and adaptability. Perhaps she simply felt safe, for the first time in a while. While my second stipulation to her employment was disguising her true gender, she didn't have to pretend with me. She didn't have to fake giggles, bite her tongue, or stroke egos.

"Yes," I said to David, focusing again on the business and him. "I said we'd like to come to a deal with him." I settled into my own chair. "I said you'd talk over the particulars with him. You've mentioned your experience in real estate."

"Yes. But I'm confused. It's been months since I suggested this. Then you go and do it, without talking to me? We're partners."

Was it more satisfying for him to hear *I'm wrong* or *you're right*? I went with both, foil-proof. The sentiment landed. I added, "It was impulsive of me."

"Why am I not surprised?" He came as close to an eye roll as I'd ever seen from him. "Well, was Mr. Garrison receptive?"

"He's willing to talk, so there's that." I stood and began to walk toward the office. "We'd have to enforce manners. I've seen men use a knife to both scoop and shovel food, no matter a liquid or solid, into their mouths."

"Impressive."

"Something like that. But before we do anything further,

I want a look at my books. See how much I have to spend."

"You mean, see how much *we* can spend."

I stopped, turned.

"Simone," he said. "You own this side, and that's fine. But I'd like to purchase the other side with you."

"It's Eleanor." I said. "And that feels complicated."

He followed me to the office. "How so? We split the revenue. When the time comes to sell the properties, you take all of this sale and we split the other."

"You make it sound so simple."

"Good."

"Fine," I said. "Partners."

"We're already partners."

I smiled. "Of course."

At my desk, I opened the book, flipping the pages until I reached the final entry where the current total revenue was recorded.

"Wait," David said. "What's this record? It repeats."

I bit my lip. I'd noted my payments to *The Liberator* only as *TL*.

He snatched the ledger. "It's in here weekly. Going back months. I think I have a right to know—"

"How I'm spending my half of the earnings? As you said, we split the revenue."

He dropped the book. "Will you ever let me in, Simone?"

Again with that name. Why did he not listen to me? I'd given in to David being here. But each time he called me Simone, it was like a pulley, bringing me somewhere uncertain. No, it brought me somewhere filled with pain. It transformed him from my twenty-four-year-old business partner to my nineteen-year-old fiancé. It took me back to *La Nouvelle-Orléans*, and the last time I had been there with David. Back then, Papa's grandfather clock had pounded in my ears. Then, I hadn't been able to look at David without seeing Patricia's Charles.

Then, one of the last things I had said to him was, "I need air."

It wasn't fair to him that I couldn't separate the two in moments like this. It wasn't fair to myself either. It wasn't this way with Arthur. When he called me by my birth name, I wasn't transported to my old parlor room. I had remained in the present, a sliver of my heart falling back into place at the sound of his French-speaking voice.

I took back the ledger. "I know I was once Simone to you. But here, I am Eleanor. That's who your business partner is, yes?"

His blue eyes, beautiful, but also so hard to decipher watched me. Finally, "Yeah."

I took a breath, silencing the noises in my head, then said, "The notation represents *The Liberator*. It's a newspaper in—"

"Boston," he finished. "I've heard of it."

"I'm donating to the abolitionists. I don't think any human being should be owned."

"I agree. I won't stand in your way."

"Good." I smiled. "Because I don't intend to stop."

"You've got a big heart, Eleanor. Stubborn, but large. I think our Jane John would agree. I must say… it's nice to see you take an interest in children, beyond paying them to do your biddings."

Even there, his mention of children, made me wonder if his thoughts dipped into the past, into old promises. A conversation we once had.

"Imagine," he had said. "One day our children will help us with the shop. Our boy can stock the shelves. You can teach our girl the books, like your Papa taught you. Promise me, Simone, we'll have this."

Back then, I could've whirled around the room with happiness.

Now, the memory made me want to flee. Why, after all this time, did I allow the past to haunt me? It was guilt; I knew it. I'd answered my own question. Patricia was gone, yet I remained on this earth. I'd tried to push that guiltiness away. But still, all these years later, it continued to rear up.

Like how a few days later, guilt surfaced when I signed the papers for the property next door. And again, when David popped a champagne bottle to celebrate. Once more, as the week went on, and I grew closer to Jane, those maternal feelings budding inside of me. They were all emotions and experiences my sister would never have.

But it was during all of those emotions and experiences that I decided I shouldn't stifle my guiltiness, as that felt like an insult to my sister's dreams. Instead, I tried to embrace the emotions like I would a dove and release them into the air.

I threw myself into the renovation. With a hammer, I brought down the wall. Jane wielded a hammer beside me. David, too. We were breathless by the end. But somehow we had enough breath to step back and laugh at how ferocious we'd been in our demolition efforts. The next step would be to fashion beautifully carved pocket doors. Two sets of them. When the doors were open, the two rooms would become one. During the day, the original Vingt-et-un was to be kept private, otherwise we'd be trapped upstairs or forced to social-ize all day.

Throughout it all, I never told Jane or David about my encounter with Gerald. The days went on. Everything we did, we tried to do quickly. Vingt-et-un was to be closed dur-ing the renovation. While David worked to implement the doors and connect the two spaces, I wandered town, placing orders for light fixtures, additional tables, and other pieces of decorum.

Jane's disappointment showed every time I stepped out-doors but told her she couldn't do the same. Finally, I relented and agreed she shouldn't be confined inside. There was no freedom in that.

"Keep your wits about you," I said to her. "As far as I know, Gerald's still mining here."

From the now dusty window, I watched her go.

"Gerald's been quiet." David came up behind me, his arms finding my waist.

"Biding his time," I said under my breath.

"What's that?"

I decided, yes, David should know. "Gerald threatened me on the street."

In a beat of my heart, David turned me to face him. "When?"

I exhaled. "Not long ago. He threatened to burn down Vingt-et-un. Little good that'd do him now with how we have it in shambles." I tried for a smile, to ease the lines now marring David's forehead.

"This is serious," he said. "This man could become a problem."

"He could," I agreed, which left David unsettled.

He said, "I'm going out, to keep an eye on Jane John."

David didn't join me in bed until late in the night. The next day, we woke, much earlier than I would've liked, to great noise out on the streets. On my way downstairs, flinging my robe around myself, I peeked into Jane's room. Safe and sound.

The street was alive with chatter. I waded deeper, David on my heels.

"He's down at the jailhouse," I heard.

"Stole four-hundred dollars."

"Arrested him right there at the monte table."

"To be hanged," a woman said with a gasp, but then a curt nod.

I wasn't entirely sure what to make of the gossip. The sheriff often locked up petty criminals and the drunks. Sometimes cattle were rustled. Stealing wasn't unusual. Neither was hanging those who were caught thieving.

Then came the name, the focus of all this excitement.

♦

"Gerald Hampton," the judge said. He'd been called to our town, serving multiple boomtowns, traveling wherever he needed to hold a court. A few days had passed since the uproar on the streets. During that time, Jane came and went as she pleased, as John.

David and I sat in the back of the saloon, a makeshift courtroom. Tables had been pushed aside and additional chairs brought in. Every seat was filled and every person held a drink in his hand. The saloon would make out handsomely in all of this. Only a third of the lights had been lit, keeping the room dark. That was fine. I was content sitting discreetly in the final row, fanning myself.

Gerald sat chained to a chair at the front. The judge sat at a table to his left, a glass of whiskey in front of him, too, to aid in his decision-making, surely.

The proceedings had been straightforward, with few talking. Mainly Monsieur Jenkins, who was the man who'd been robbed. He'd claimed he noticed his gold dust missing when he went to pay his boarding.

"Where did you keep your dust?" the judge asked him.

"Between my mattresses. I have two of them that I stack."

The judge gave him a look of dismissal, almost as if he expected the fool to be robbed. "How much?"

"Four hundred dollars' worth."

"And why did the defendant, Mr. Gerald Hampton, come under your suspicions?"

"He bunked across the room."

"So he saw where you kept your earnings?"

The dope shrugged. "He could've."

The judge gave him another look, one that echoed my

description of the man. Then, "So how did you come to the conclusion that Mr. Hampton did indeed take your gold?"

"I was at the saloon and someone told me that Gerald was playing large sums of money at the monte table."

"Who told you this?" the judge wanted to know.

"Can't remember. But I fetched the sheriff." He dipped his hat in the sheriff's direction.

The judge exhaled. "Fine. Was it odd for Mr. Hampton to bet large sums?"

Monsieur Jenkins shrugged again. "But it wasn't his dust. He lied and told the sheriff it was, that he took it from his stash the other day and that he had plenty more out in the woods. He says he first hid it there on his way into town. But we went searching for it—"

"When?" the judge asked.

"Right away. We lit lights and Gerald took us exactly where he said his gold would be. There was nothing there."

I glanced at Gerald. He looked as ireful as a man could look. David, adversely, had the face of a man smugly satisfied.

There was an outburst, the judge's voice rising above all else. "Mr. Hampton will speak now. Are you certain the spot you checked for your gold was correct?"

Gerald spoke through his teeth. "Yes."

"Is there anyone who can confirm this location?"

Gerald peered into the spectators. With how the room was lit, I doubted he could make out my person. But still, my skin prickled. I saw his chest rise, fall. "My girl. She was there when I hid it. But she ran off, apparently."

My breath hitched. David's face ticked to the side, half his mouth turning into a smile. I counted to ten and discreetly turned my head, finding an opened window behind us, along with a head of sandy hair eavesdropping.

My heart raced as my mind aligned the pieces—and the facilitators—of this scandal.

The proceeding had gone on. The judge was saying, "As the girl is gone and no one knows of her whereabouts, there is no one to speak in your defense, Mr. Hampton. Hanging is usually customary in this situation."

Gerald's anger turned to fear, and he bucked in his chair. Two men pressed his shoulders down. He called out how he'd been framed, how he'd been robbed. He stole nothing, he proclaimed. And I believed him. I waited for it, for him to point an accusatory finger at me, that I'd been behind the shenanigans and that Jane was now with me. I stilled my fan. I, myself, felt a bit green. But it wasn't me who had put all this in motion. And no one spoke out against me, or at least there was no opportunity, as the judged yelled, "Enough! Everything about this ..." He wagged his hand. "... this ... this mess is flimsy. I won't hang this man. He's to receive thirty-nine lashes at nine o'clock tomorrow, then he's to leave town, never to return. If he does, any man can and should shoot him, with no penalty for that person."

Gerald was taken away and the room transformed back into a saloon. I left, David lingering behind. Outside, I saw a small boy—who I knew to be a girl—running down the street toward Vingt-et-un.

She'd remain safe. So would my emporium and what I'd built there. But it wasn't lost on me how quickly one's fate could be altered.

Chapter 26

THE NEW VINGT-ET-UN would be a clubhouse for gentleman. With dining, spirits, gambling, music. Still, no women would prance around, sit on laps, or earn bite marks on their skin. No fighting, no cussing. Like previously, men were to act as if they were in the presence of ladies, even if no lady other than myself was present. And Jane, in secret.

"Why can't I be myself?" she said.

I walked the dining room, my mind hemming and hawing over the details. I straightened a floral portrait on the wall. I had additional paintings commissioned. This side would offer meals and a restaurant setting and the other side offered a *salon* setting. Though, I suspected gambling would spill to both sides each evening once the kitchen was closed. For our reopening, we decided to open at eight and only serve light food. Moving forward, the food would serve at noon, then again at six. We kept the same wait staff and cooks, and even offered the previous owner the position of manager. Neither of us wanted to work day and night.

"Eleanor," Jane said. "Did you hear me?"

I stopped fussing with an arrangement of flowers. "What's that, *ma chère*?"

"Why do I have to keep pretending to be male?"

"We've discussed this."

"What does it matter if I'm the only girl?"

She had used this argument before. I cupped her chin. "You cannot handle a room full of men on your own."

"You do."

"I don't allow them to touch me. I entertain them with cards and my words, nothing more. If I hire you as a saloon girl, I'll need to hire more. A flock of you. I do not want that. That is not what Vingt-et-un is."

"Vingt-et-un," David said, coming in from wherever he'd been. "I've been meaning to speak to you about that."

I checked my watch. We'd be holding our grand reopening in five hours. "Speak to me about what?"

"Changing the name."

"What's wrong with it?"

"Eleanor," Jane said.

"The answer is no, *John*," I said. "I do hope you'll stay. But if this position isn't what you want, there are other saloons in town. You can be yourself, there. Enough time has passed since Gerald's banishment."

She'd been enjoying her freedom, though I warned her to remain as John, when out in public. Give it time, I suggested, for people to forget there ever was a Jane and a Gerald.

Jane pouted, looking every bit her fifteen. "But I want to stay here."

"Good," I said. "I don't want you to go, either."

Over the past few weeks, we had often taken breaks together during the renovation. I taught her how to play my games. It was almost like being back in my parlor in *La Nouvelle-Orléans*. Funny, how that memory never caused me guilt. It only filled me with happiness, as if regaining something I'd lost but never thought I'd have again.

Jane said, "I'll remain as John."

I touched her chin again. "Wonderful. It'd be a pity to let all those outfits you've sown go to waste." I winked at her, and I received a smile. We'd be fine. "Have a *sieste*," I told her. "Tonight will be a lively one." She went off, and I turned my attention to David, "Now, what's this about changing the name?"

"Well, we're so much more than *vingt-et-un*. There's the dining, chuck-a-luck. And let's be honest, the men have trouble saying the name."

"Still, they ask for it."

"By twenty-one." He held up his palm. "You've made the game what it is. People know it now. Like you said, they ask for it. I bet we could go to San Francisco or to New York, even, and there'd be a man dealing your game. But you, Madame Dumont, are still relatively unknown. Which is why I think it's time you got your due. The draw shouldn't be only the game, it should be *you*."

I tilted my head. "And what is it you're proposing?"

"Dumont's Place."

I was touched. While I relished in the men calling me by the name of Madame Dumont, my desire had always been to popularize my game. But to attach my name with it in such a way, now that was a thought. There was a word for that. A legacy. Is that what I'd be creating?

Madame Dumont, the mother of *vingt-et-un*. Or if they preferred to call it twenty-one, that'd be fine. In either case, it was my game. Madame Dumont's.

The whole notion of it was intoxicating.

"Thank you," I said to David. "I wouldn't have thought of that on my own. The sign will still be wet when it goes up."

"That'll only make the outside glisten. And you'll make the inside shine."

"A woman cannot take all this flattery." I found his arms. And Lord help me, when I closed my eyes, I pictured Arthur grinning, pleased that I had found my place.

"See now," David said, "I'm only buttering you up."

I opened my eyes and shifted my thoughts and position to see David's mischievous face. "Oh?"

"Not really. But I have been thinking I'd like to deal games, too."

A reasonable suggestion. I said as much.

David mused, "Maybe monte?"

I scrunched my nose. "I don't want that game inside Dumont's Place."

"What's wrong with it?"

"Monte is nothing more than a game for cons. I won't have cons." While the odds were admittedly in my favor in the games I ran, I was honest in how I played it. "How about faro?" I compromised. "Run that game. Fairly," I added, as cheating often ran rampart there as well. "It takes two people, correct? Perhaps Jane would like to learn. You two work well together, as I recall."

He smirked, no doubt catching my drift, though we never spoke about his and Jane's involvement in Gerald's exile. Everyone was entitled to secrets. David kissed my forehead. "Grand idea."

David left on the hunt for faro equipment in town. He'd likely have to purchase it from another saloon. As he left, he told me how we were the only place in town that didn't play it. I supposed it was good we'd add it to our repertoire. The men would have no reason to leave, save for the allure of women. But I wouldn't compromise there.

Upstairs, I stood in front of a mirror, and held my dress to me. Jane had made me an ensemble of silk and lace, in emerald green, the color of my birth. I was so enamored that I purchased a jeweled ring to match in color. But what was that? I noticed a streak of gray in my hair. Another there. It wasn't enough where others would notice. But I had. And wasn't I too young, at a newly twenty-four years old, for gray to sprout on my head?

Maman often concocted a mixture to darken her hair. I consulted my wristwatch from Papa, then at a clip I went about town in search of the ingredients. I returned with gallic acid, tincture of sesqui-chloride of iron, and acetic acid. I combed the compound through my hair, just as Maman had done at her toilet-table, taking care to add oil when complete.

I worked with my window open, pausing now and again to breathe the fresh air. Outside, I heard the accumulation of men and also the sounds of bullfrog serenades. The males called with their deep *jug-o-rum* melodies. The females responded, with a sound much like that of a loose banjo string.

I'd only finished styling my hair off my neck when I heard David calling me from downstairs. I descended, David offering me a look of approval. I truly felt like a madame, the lady of the house.

And so it began.

The men were thrilled to be back, and I thrilled to have them. The night was a flourish of excitement. However, one man became too excitable. Upon losing a rather large hand, he lifted his chair above his head and brought it down upon another's. Thankfully, not mine. But the victim was an innocent, who played no part in the loser's lighter purse. Remarkably, he remained on his chair after receiving the blow. I offered him my handkercher, then nodded to my bruiser at the door.

While Theo removed the hapless, chair-wielding man, my violinist adjusted his tune to parody the exit. I hid my smile. It was likely his victim was concussed. As if reading my mind, Jane had already crossed the room with a fresh drink for him, on the house, of course.

"Let that be a lesson learned," I said to the room. The violinist resumed his original playing, and those not brandishing their seats as weapons continued on.

Night after night, Dumont's Place was a success. My name was on everybody's lips. We were open day and night, upwards twelve games going at once between mine, David's, and the games the men played on their own. After the kitchen closed and before the gambling tables filled, I fell into a routine of preparing leftovers for some of the miners to take with them at night's end. It'd do them good to wake with food in their belly to counteract the alcohol.

"A parting gift," I told one of my regulars, Thaddeus, with a grin.

"My ma would be mighty appreciative of you, Madame Dumont."

"See you tomorrow," I said, shooing him outside. I turned to find men asleep on the couches. I shook my head, though admittedly amused, while I walked past them and upstairs. However, I wasn't foolish. I'd had David install a lock on the inside of the door to our apartment.

Then, in a blink, Dumont's Place had been opened a year— a very profitable year—and the bullfrogs were bellowing again, in search of their mates.

In that regard, Jane caused me worry. In the year, she'd butterflied. It must've been gradual, but it felt sudden, all at once, as if she instantaneously emerged from the emporium with cheekbones, hips, and breasts. And, she'd taken a liking to Ernest, which I couldn't fault her for. He was handsome, educated, kind. Now, he was also confused. Jane spoke with him as John, usually while playing faro. She didn't necessarily flirt, but still, I saw how his head ticked to her voice and, then, her blue eyes. He'd immediately drop his gaze, made an excuse to be elsewhere. Sometimes he left straight away. After the last time he scurried out, he hadn't been back.

I watched her now, as we dismounted our mules. We'd spent a glorious two hours on the trails, with a breeze. The summer had grown suffocating. Jane walked with a sway of her hips that wasn't there before.

"I'm not sure we'll be able to keep your secret much longer," I said.

She forced more sway to her hips, clearly pleased.

"Stop that," I said. But I smiled. It faded as I noticed the land around us. It'd all been mined, leaving behind barren ground, piles of dirt, a dry riverbed. While Jane had bloomed, the opposite seemed to have happened to the landscape. The mining had taken its toll, using it all up. With my eyes, I followed the dry river, down and down, to where the water had been diverted. A handful of men worked there, using a novel technique. Hydraulicking, it was called, where great gusts of water tore apart California's beautiful landscape and dislodged rock and unearthed sediment for their sluices. It was nearby, in fact, that this new form of hydraulic mining had begun. The men had told me all about it, saying how it allowed them to continue mining.

But, as I trotted past the barren land, I wondered for how much longer. Would the mining expand elsewhere? One thing I could count on was the men talking. That night, I leaned in. There weren't as many new faces, but there weren't any fewer faces. Business was still booming.

I came upon my table with a demure smile, set to begin a game of *vingt-et-un*, when something humbling dawned on me. There sat Joseph, Riley, Thaddeus, and George.

"Would you look at that," I said. "I do believe my very first table comprised you four gentlemen. What are the odds, three years later, the same combination would sit across from me?"

"I'll drink to that," George said, "But, sadly, this may be it for me. In this town, at least."

"Why is that, *mon amie*?"

"She's drying up." He shook his head. I knocked the deck against the table. "Not much left to mine."

"When I first got here," Thaddeus said, "gold dust, honest to god, stuck to my shoes. That was back in fifty-one? We've taken a lot of gold from her in four years."

"Think we got it all?" Riley asked.

Thaddeus blew out a breath. He signaled for me to give him another card. He busted, sat back in his chair. "The hydraulicking will find more, but not enough for us all to stay on. I've got my fingers crossed we get word of gold elsewhere. They seem to keep finding it in the foothills."

"God Almighty let it stay that way. When I left Georgia, my daddy called me a god-damn fool, excuse my language, Madame Dumont." He filled his lungs. "I'm not ready to go back. Haven't made my riches yet, despite all the gold on my boots."

Riley laughed, whiskey on his breath. "None of us have. We're all doomed to be prodigal sons."

"Not me," George said. "But only cause I'm no son. I left my wife and daughter back home."

The table made a groaning noise, all except Joseph. The whole time, he hadn't said a word. He drank his whiskey with such consistency that I should've offered him a drinking straw.

I raised my champagne flute, forcing a stiff upper lip. "Should this be the last time the four of you sit across from me, it's been my pleasure."

"The pleasure's been all ours," Thaddeus said.

A few days later, Thaddeus was the first to go. He stayed until closing, but I never saw his face again.

Riley and George left town next. I lost both the same night.

Then, Joseph, a week later. By that point, he was nothing more than a bump on a log, with a hand for whiskey.

If my studies haven't failed me, it was Chaucer who, in the 1300s, penned the notion that everything comes to an end.

Didn't I know it? Time and time again.

♠

I walked the town, to get a feel for how it was changing. It wasn't a mass exodus, not yet, but it was coming soon. I felt it in the air. Those going west could get to where they were going, but those going east, against the grain, were likely to get blanketed in snow on the Oregon Trail if they didn't leave within days. That, of course, posed a problem for how the draft animals would eat.

Many stores had already closed, seeing the writing on the wall. Outside the theater, I noticed the lack of writing. A schedule hadn't been posted on the board. No theater companies would be using our stage to put on their shows.

Me, I wasn't sure what to do. Rifts and cracks emerged in what I had built for myself. And more so, the name I hoped to continue to build for myself. Without gold, there was no boomtown, there were no miners, there wasn't anyone to fill my chairs, there was no Madame Dumont. What a simple, yet catastrophic equation, and it felt as if it happened so quickly. As if one day the men opened their eyes, threw up their hands and said, "Well, that's it for us here."

Downcast, I returned to the emporium. Aimlessly, I wandered the room, ran my hand across the tabletops, sat on a sofa, going from one to the next, sitting in them all.

It was in the quiet that I noticed the abnormal soundlessness. Normally, voices, clatter, and footfall from the dining room could be heard. I went to have myself a peek.

The dining room was indeed empty, with the exception of David. He sat at a clothed table, candles lit, wine poured.

I asked, a chuckle in my voice from my confusion, "Are we not serving supper this evening?"

"We are, but only for the two of us."

"I can see that. May I ask the occasion?"

I hadn't entered the room beyond the initial steps I'd taken.

"Come sit. We're celebrating."

"Celebrating..." I left the word hanging. "I hardly see what there's to celebrate." I motioned outside. "Not with our patrons showing us their backsides."

"For one, we've had a very profitable year. We've recouped

all we've put in. But also, new opportunities." David stood to pull out my chair.

I sat, craning my neck to watch his face as I did. "You're clammy."

"It's warm," he said, "I'll open another window."

They were all open, but still David walked to the room's front, then back. He sat. He raised a glass. "Let's toast to what's to come."

I tentatively raised my glass.

"To our future. To us," he said. "We've made marvelous partners."

"We have."

I sipped, intrigued. Did David have a suggestion to take our business elsewhere? Somewhere more profitable? He was the orchestrator of this moment, so I'd let him orchestrate. I took a bite of my meal, waiting. Still, he hadn't spoken about why we were here. "My compliments to the chef," I said.

"Indeed."

David chewed, more than necessary, as if allowing the time for gears to shift in his mind. He swallowed, sipped his drink. "Simone." He corrected, "Eleanor, I wanted to say that I'm glad I came here. I almost didn't, but I had to see if that beautiful, mysterious, French-speaking woman was you."

"*Voilà.*" I smiled.

He returned it, and then grew more serious. "But now that things are ending here, I'd like to leave. Soon. If we don't leave within days, autumn will be upon us, then winter, and we'll need to wait until spring. We may be the last two standing, in that case."

"You exaggerate."

"Yes, but I don't know by how much. I'm not willing to find out. But that's beside the point. My point is *we*. I'd like you to go with me."

"Where?"

"Back to Manhattan."

"East," I said.

"Yes, the west is fickle. You saw how suddenly everyone jumped ship here. Manhattan is not only booming, it will continue to boom."

"There'll be gold elsewhere."

"But for how long?"

I didn't know.

He pressed, "Come east with me."

East. But I felt of the West. "What about San Francisco? It may've begun as a boomtown, but it's not going anywhere. It's the largest city of California. Or Sacramento. That city preceded the discovery of gold. Lumber is the currency there."

"But I don't wish to work with lumber. It'll run out, like the gold."

"I can't say I wish to go east again." David looked so hopeful. And, I'd be remiss to overlook how he'd originally gone west for me. "What would we do in this *City of Dreamers*? Open a new Dumont's Place?"

He took my hand. "I wouldn't want that for you."

"Want what?"

"To deal cards. I won't deny that you've thrived here. It's been exciting—for a spell. I enjoyed the break, the thrills. The danger, even. But don't you want to act like a lady and live amongst ladies again? The civilized? Maybe we can purchase property, begin again the life we were set to have in New Orleans?"

I took back my hand and scratched my hairline, feeling dumbfounded. Ambushed. My first thought was of Jane. What of her? Then, I thought of myself. I didn't think of my life here or of my work as unbecoming or shameful. I'd boarded that ship because I was lost and didn't know who I was. But I knew now. I was Madame Dumont. I was a croupier.

"David—"

"Wait." He dabbed at his forehead with his napkin. Yes, the room was too warm. "I know we're not the people we once were."

"Correct."

"We're different now."

I said more slowly, "Yes."

"I think we can create something special in New York City, but I'd like to put our best foot forward. I think it'd be pert if we arrived married."

"Married?"

"I know, that sounded … businesslike, but that's how your brain works. I know you. It's always been you. Love at first sight, remember?" He swallowed and squeezed my hand. I looked left and right, as if additional people were in the room. People I could call out to, as a way to deflect from this moment, to stop it from happening, as if I was on a runaway train and needed rescuing. But no, David held fast to my hand as his chair scraped against the floor, giving him room to dip onto one knee. His free hand slipped into his coat jacket. For the ring. I pictured him presenting me with the same gold band he had before.

I pulled my hand free. I stood. I said, "I need air."

Chapter 27

MY WORLD TILTED. David's footsteps trailed me. I quickened mine, leaning into each step. We were on the street. The sun, lowering by the minute, blinded me.

He said, "Why won't you let me make an honest woman of you?"

People stared.

My cheeks felt warm. My chest, my neck—everything except my heart. I didn't give him the dignity of a response.

"Wouldn't you rather be respected again?"

That, I responded to. I stopped, faced him. "I am respected."

I was Madame Dumont, I told myself again. I earned that name. People traveled to this town to sit at my table. My game was played across the west. That was something to be proud of, to be respected for.

David raised his arms, let them fall, as he continued to walk toward me. "You can still have your game."

"You mean in the parlor, in the afternoons?"

"What is so wrong with that?"

We stood face to face, man to woman. "Nothing, if it were all I wanted."

"What is it that you want, Madame Dumont?"

The answer was simple. "To deal, David."

He threw his hands up again and began backpedaling. "You've always been obstinate."

At least there was something we agreed upon. I watched

him walk back into Dumont's Place. The door slammed closed.

I found my way onto a back of a mule. Riding the animal had become a place of comfort for me. The slight rock of my seat, the way my limbs and feet dangled yet were supported, the thin strips of leather in my palms, offering me control. I vowed to ride more, wherever I went next.

For now, the forest was darkening. I had Dumont's Place to open. I had to face my business partner. Only, when I returned, he wasn't downstairs. Nor was David upstairs. On our bed, I found a note. It was short and simple—the exact opposite of our history together.

He told me that he gets to leave this time.

Just those six words.

Though, it was six words more than I'd once given him.

I dressed, in a summer fog, feeling the coldness of his words mix with the warmth of the room. I'd cared deeply for David, twice. Then and now. But neither timing was right, never able to be who he wanted me to be in the end. My eyes may've been blurry with tears as I moved about our room to change for the evening ahead, but I knew his leaving was for the best. He deserved to live the life he wanted, without my dictations. Just as I deserved to live mine without his.

Every chair and sofa was filled. Jane was behind the bar with the Johns. Theo was at the door. If a man came to town right then and there, then happened upon Dumont's Place, he wouldn't have known the gold was almost gone. I'd made a business of men needing a release, an escape, a diversion.

But soon there'd be fewer and fewer men with those needs. They'd move on, they've been moving on—David wasn't wrong—and I didn't wish to see my business crumble.

I let the dice slide from my cup. A two. A three. A three.

A man sprung from his chair, having made that very bet. "How lucky for you," I said to his unknown, euphoric face.

I paid him his money. A man groaned for my loss, but I gave nothing more than a careless shrug and a smile. I was indifferent to losing a bet here and there. At the end of my night, my ledger always showed a profit. I'd be fine. It was my patrons who held my worry. I also worried for Jane. Would she find work elsewhere? A saloon girl elsewhere in town, before that gambling house, too, closed? Then what, a lady of the night? I hated to even think it. I wouldn't allow it. That left her future intertwined with mine.

A future I knew wouldn't continue for me, either, in this declining town. As I rattled my cup to chuck the dice and test the luck of these men again, a decision shook loose in my head. It'd be my last evening as the madame of the best gambling emporium in northern California. Rather, the best emporium anywhere. Tonight was to be my unspoken send-off, my stage bow from Nevada, California. Then, I'd take Jane with me, wherever I went next as a croupier, dealing my game as Madame Dumont.

I completed another round of chuck-a-luck, then switched to *vingt-et-un*. I wanted my time in this town, where I truly made a name for myself, to end with my game.

Oddly, no one spoke of David's absence. Which, to me, made his absence louder, as if I was the only one who mourned him leaving. Jane would, too, I realized. She'd already caught my eye once with a question on her face as to David's whereabouts.

I didn't know, and he'd taken little with him. It made me consider... what about his half of the earnings, what about the half of the restaurant he owned?

I didn't wonder long. I opened my ledger at the evening's close, and there was David's handwriting. An address. Four numbers and a street name in Manhattan. He meant for me to send what he was owed there. I supposed he also meant for me to see to the end of things here, without him. How convenient for him, and how fortunate for him I was fair.

In the morning, I threw back my covers. My feelings couldn't quite be placed. I didn't wish to leave Nevada and what I'd built here. But I was also intrigued to take my game to another town. To ask another table of men, "Will you play?"

But first, I had to get everything in order. I knew exactly where to go.

"Madame Dumont," Ernest said in greeting, when I entered his office at the *Nevada Journal*. "Please, sit down."

I sat, crossed my limbs at my ankles. "It's fitting, me being here. You were the one to greet me at the stagecoach. This office is one of the very first places I went after my arrival. And here I am again, for the last time."

He asked, "So you're to leave, too?"

I sighed. "It's time. Will you stay?"

His response was delayed, but he finally said, "Yes. Before the gold lust, there was lumber. We diverted the water from the sawmill, but I mean to bring it back. Those who remain will be just fine. The smaller numbers will be a blessing, in fact."

"I'm pleased to hear it, and also that you planned to stay. Can I purchase one last advertisement in your journal? For the sale of my properties."

"Of course." He slid a clean leaflet in front of him. "But if they don't sell?"

I smiled slyly. "My tables and glasses never went unfilled. Any amount will be accepted."

Even without the sale, I had enough money to begin again. The only question was where.

Ernest asked, "Where will you go?"

"Well, since you're in my head, perhaps you could tell me?"

He laughed. But then it came to me. "San Francisco, I think."

It's where I began. I could stand upon my hill, honoring Arthur and my namesake of Dumont. I wondered if Clay Street was still developing. It'd been years. Six years. Only time would tell.

Ernest tapped his writing utensil against the paper. "And what of John?"

He pronounced the name oddly.

"John," I repeated. I recalled the awkwardness at Ernest's interactions with Jane. Before we left, I felt it fair to tell him the truth. "You may be surprised, and also relieved, to know that John is actually—"

"A woman." He smiled.

I huffed out a laugh. "How long have you known?"

"A while. Jane hunted me down, after I stopped coming in. And then I continued to stay away to keep her secret."

"That girl." I shook my head. But I wasn't irked. Hadn't I recognized her spunk on more than one occasion?

"Madame," he said. "I'd like for her to stay. With me, that is, as Jane." While he pronounced John oddly, he said Jane as if speaking of a goddess. He said, "She'll be safe here."

"Yes," I considered. Gerald hadn't crossed my mind in ages. Nor could he cross paths with Jane in this town.

"And we're in love," Ernest said, "She'll have a life here."

"Safely loved," I said. "Is there anything better?"

That was what I had wanted for her, from the moment I saw her atop the horse outside town. I'd miss her companionship, but I had to admit, I felt relief that Jane's future wouldn't be dependent on mine, as I chased after the miners who chased after the gold. At the idea of parting from Jane, emotion began to creep in and I stood. "I plan to leave straight away."

"Jane will be here, any minute now, actually. We were going to picnic in my office."

"Well there's no need to hide in here. Enjoy the last days of summer before the rain comes." And really, the fact Jane would be here with Ernest was ideal. I wasn't one for good-byes. "Will you do me one last favor?"

"Of course."

"Tell her farewell for me."

He cocked his head. "The way she speaks of you, you saved her."

My chest tightened. "Jane likes to sew. She's quite good at it."

He laughed, touching his pant leg. "I know from experience she does well with pants." He paused, then said, "I'll tell her."

I was quick to leave, but I lingered under the awning of a nearby building. I watched Jane, as John, approach. Her face held the hint of a smile, as if from anticipation of her clandestine meeting with Ernest. I once knew something about clandestine meetings. But I was pleased she'd be able to step out into the open with Ernest. Now she could shed her skin and be herself. As it was, Mother Nature wouldn't have allowed the secret much longer. The timing, and how the pieces fell into place, couldn't have been more perfect. I smiled as she disappeared inside.

Soon, I stood in front of Arthur's portrait of me. A few youngsters currently loaded my belongings atop a stagecoach, while a few bystanders watched, no doubt curious to the happenings at my emporium. Atop the coach, my trunk formed a base and now they struggled to balance two sofas and one of my custom-made tables, throwing twine overtop to hold it all in place.

The red, velvet sofa would be left behind. It was a couch that had served me well and held positive memories. But if I felt the need to have another, I'd find one that resembled this one and the one before.

I smiled and lifted Arthur's portrait from the wall. My heels clicked against the floor, until I reached the rugs, then again while crossing between the oriental floor coverings. Eyes forward, I didn't look upon the painted flowers hung on the walls or the gold squares on the ceiling. Those images were engrained in my memory. Under the glow of my chandeliers, I stopped at the last table. I ran my hand over the tabletop, then shook my head at my melancholy. In my best finery, I exited my emporium.

The door to Dumont's Place remained unlocked. The enduring gold seekers could scavenge the remaining tables, chairs, and paintings. It'd be my gift to them. Besides, the men thought me mysterious, unknown, and rich, and my departure would only add to the allure of Madame Dumont. They'd remember my name. They'd continue my game, wherever they went. And so would I.

PART 3

Madame Moustache

◆

1855
Columbia, California

Chapter 28

I HAD ARRIVED, but not where I had first begun or where I had expected. While I had meant to continue on to San Francisco, I veered farther south to Columbia, gold lust getting the better of me. Though, it wasn't my own gold lust: I had followed the men's. At a camp, they'd spoken with such hurrah about the Gem of the Southern Mines.

Gold had been discovered there five years prior. At first, this great length of time worried me. I'd only just experienced the failing of a mine in nearly that number of years. But this town—they insisted it'd produce gold for years to come. You can stake your future on it, they'd said.

All it took for me to say was, "Have you heard of *vingt-et-un*?" And a response of, "Can't say I have, ma'am," before I'd asked my stagecoach driver, "Will you follow them south instead?" San Francisco, and my memories there, weren't going anywhere.

I stepped off the stagecoach much as I had before, in my fineries and with coquettish words. The familiar smells of a blacksmith hit me first. The town was large, with four banks, seventeen general stores, and over forty saloons. There would be no shortage of customers. As it was, I was told the first white women had arrived in this Mexican town only four years ago. Now they had one more to add to their small total, which helped their numbers considerably in a town ten thousand strong.

In a hotel room, I hung my portrait on the wall, taking an

extra moment to stand before myself as Arthur had seen me, then my belongings and sofas were crammed into the small, yet tasteful room. Downstairs, I asked to and was much obliged to set up one of my custom-made tables in the lobby, in exchange for fifteen percent of my profits. I'd bartered well.

Both my game and me were a novelty, and it was my absolute pleasure to introduce this new group of mountain men to both, deciding to deal within the more pleasant hotel than act as croupier within a gambling den. There were transitory thoughts of purchasing a storefront and assembling a new emporium, especially after I learned of the sale of Dumont's Place, but I liked the transient nature of my current clients. I'd catch them coming or going, enticing them to play, then sending them on their way with my name on their lips and my game on their brains.

"Sit, sit, *asseoir*," I'd say as I played with my deck of cards, performing the English or the overhand shuffle, the most elementary of movements. Or I could more impressively weave, spiral, or complete the Mongean shuffle. My intent was to fix my eyes on the men, while keeping my hands and the cards in motion. "Play a round with me," I'd say, "and rest your bones a moment with Madame Dumont."

Some initially thought me a fortuneteller or a gypsy—one man even proclaimed me a magician before I had a chance to tell him my name. His jaw dropped, and he asked, "Are you the queen's Celebrated Enchantress, all the way from across the waters?"

He meant Queen Victoria; though "The Celebrated Enchantress" wasn't a name I'd heard in some time. Her Majesty, on the other hand, was a household name, who influenced much more than clothing. I recalled with fondness when Patricia and I had been ten and Queen Victoria was crowned. America had gone silly over her and *Victoria Fever* had swept the country. It certainly had swept our residence. Patricia and

I had begged and begged for *Victoria Soap*. Not to bathe with, but to simply possess. Look at. Hold in our hands. Maman, equally enamored, agreed. Poor Papa, bewildered with our request, had been the one who had to find the souvenir, no easy task.

To this day, I often scanned the headlines for the queen's name, and some time ago, I'd read of "The Celebrated Enchantress," who'd used her second-sight skills to connect Her Majesty with her deceased love, Prince Albert. The details had remained in my head. In gratitude, Queen Victoria had gifted Georgiana Eagle, which was the enchantress's given name, a gold watch.

I touched my own gold watch and responded to the awestruck man, "No, *mon nouvel ami*, I'm not skilled in similar ways, but it'd be my pleasure to enchant you with the game of *vingt-et-un*. Will you play?"

He did, along with many other risk-seeking gold seekers. In a blink, my time in the hotel's lobby had accumulated, not only to weeks then months but then to years. I was content. I even kept better hours. So, of course, that was when the universe decided to intervene and for the poet Chaucer's words to strike again.

Every good thing came to an end.

I was asleep when the shouting began. I ran to my window, only for history to repeat itself an unfathomable third time. Fire.

It felt too familiar not to feel personal. Like before, from my room I salvaged only currency, Papa's watch, and Arthur's portrait. On my way out of town, the men spoke of where to go next. It appeared we all led the lives of *les nomades*, going wherever nature dictated. This time, nature pointed the miners toward the Comstock Lode.

"Silver," one of the men said.

Another whistled. "Now that's different."

"Now that's big. The town sprang up overnight."

Just as Columbia was brought to ashes in as much time.

"Will you join us in Virginia City, Madame Dumont?" one asked.

I would. I left California for the Utah Territory. The first thing I did was hang my portrait on the wall. My second task: set up a table.

I fell into a rhythm once more. I was approaching a year's time at this new boomtown when the men began speaking of how America's north and south were butting heads along the eastern ports and rivers. We were far removed, well across the country, but with many having relations back that way, they spoke of it with vibrancy.

"War's brewing," one miner said. And as thoughts should've been turning to the holidays, they were instead affixed on an impending war, all beginning with South Carolina seceding from the Union. More southern states joined in the new year.

During our games, the men read from their letters, announcing each new state to secede. Seven in all, calling themselves the Confederate States of America. I thought little of it, as I had little to do with the east. Except, in a way, with David, if memories could be counted. Would he go to war, I wondered?

When spring came, I decided to move on to a new town, figuring it was best not to get too comfortable and risk Chaucer again. As my driver pulled into Pioche, the whole of the settlement was talking about how the north and south were officially at war. Fort Sumter had been attacked. The men spoke endlessly, receiving news daily, though our news was delayed by weeks while the Pony Express traversed the country with their mail. There were battles, more states seceding, horrific death tolls. Throughout it all, I dealt. I spread my game, the only thing I knew how to do. A solace, of sorts, while the country raged on.

When new growth began to show on the ground, I moved on once more, keen on sharing my game with more unacquainted mountain men. After spending years along the foothills, I traveled north by coach. Along the Montana Trail, war stories were inevitable at each camp, but even with all the capturing of forts, sinking of ships, and explosions, the learning that struck me most was how President Lincoln's eleven-year-old boy was lost to typhoid fever, while his youngest son barely survived. To think, the president fought battles both far and near to home, suffering losses wherever he turned. While different, I felt a kinship, knowing a thing or two about loss.

The bright spot of my journey came after joining a camp for the evening. The men and I were sitting around a fire. A man read from his letter about seventeen Union ships that had traveled the Mississippi, claiming *La Nouvelle-Orléans* for the north. *Well done*, I thought. While my family never owned slaves, plenty around us did. It was wonderful to think of those men and women now free.

In the morning, as my stagecoach driver and I began the final leg of our one-month journey the news still felt satisfying. Although, a sliver of melancholy slipped into my thoughts. While the men read from letters and spoke of home, I had no one to speak of.

"I've no one," I whispered into my empty coach, the sentiment feeling as if it needed to be spoken aloud. The only other object in the carriage with me was my portrait, propped on the bench across from me. "I have only my name and my game."

The stagecoach lurched and I shouldered into the door's frame. "Everything all right?" I called, bearing down within my side-laced boots in an attempt to ground myself.

There wasn't an answer, not to me at least. The driver encouraged our horses to go faster. Faster, still. My portrait slipped from the seat, rattling to the floor. I pulled it between my knees and tried to peer out the window, but we were jostling too greatly. My head rolled every which way. The sound of hooves was suddenly all around us, barely heard above the clattering we made over the bumpy ground. I didn't dare try to poke my head out again. I held my breath; my feet spending more time suspended than on the ground, and hoped this wouldn't be the end of me.

"Whoa," I finally heard, and we began to slow.

"What was that?" I called, a hand to my chest. It was a wonder my heart hadn't been shaken free of my body. Finally, I looked outside. We passed stables. Then, a meat market. Next, a blacksmith. At last, a hotel.

We stopped and my door opened. My driver surveyed me, and I patted my hair. "I'm all in one piece," I said.

"Sorry I didn't stop sooner," he said. "I wanted to make sure I got you here."

"Dare I ask what we ran from?"

"Bandits. There's only one way in and out of Bannack. If we had a wagon instead of a coach, we would've been gone gooses. Good thing, too, you travel light."

"Good thing," I said flatly. "Well, here we are. Though it wasn't the welcome I would've chosen for us."

It seemed rougher in these parts, remote, with nothing but an ambling creek on one side of the town, then barren ground all around, until the mountains took over. The buildings were built from logs, the reason for all the nearby desolation, with the common false fronts so readily seen in these hastily built towns. It wasn't much, but with a grocery store, a restaurant, four saloons, and a hotel—all visible from where I stood—it had what I needed.

I began with the Hotel Meade, checking into a room on the second floor. There, I hung my portrait. "Here we are," I whispered, conjuring Arthur in my mind. I swear I heard him respond, encouraging me, "Well go on, ask them to play."

The hotel's first floor didn't allow for any room for a table, so I didn't bother inquiring there. At my first steps into the first saloon, I faltered. I avoided bars and taverns when I could, the language and faces always so hostile, but this is where the miners were, and thus where I needed to be. This one, in particular, was darker than most. I claimed the first vacant seat I saw.

"*Bonjour*, gentlemen."

The faces all startled, as if I was a sudden apparition. One man's fingers inched toward his gun, right there on the table. That was a novelty for me, not a man carrying a gun or a knife or some other inventive weapon, but a man leaving it out like that. It was unnerving, but as the gun wasn't pointed at me, I went on. "My name's Madame Dumont, have you heard of me?"

My lovely tablemates offered me a few headshakes, grunts, and a loud no.

"Wonderful," I said, "then it'd be my pleasure to introduce you to my game."

As always, the responses ranged from resistance to complaisance. I learned their names. And, I went about explaining how to play. Soon, our game was lively.

I waited for the owner to tap my shoulder and demand I pay a fee, but it never happened that night or the week that followed. I never had a gun pulled on me either. It was a promising start, and I deemed that Bannack and I would get along well, despite the rocky reception from the bandits.

My reputation grew, men greeting me by name. My routine was simple, consisting of playing, eating, and sleeping. There was no Lydia here, despite there being a slew of saloon girls and bordello women. But I kept to myself, kept playing, and fortunately, we were granted a break in the war news, where for nearly two weeks the men received few letters. Too soon, the tide of letters began again, narrating a series of battles where, over a week's time, the north tried to capture the south's capital. Both armies sustained heavy losses before the north had withdrawn.

The response in the saloon was immediate, with both sides present, those from the north and those from the south. Even if they mined instead of fighting for their state, they had brothers and uncles and fathers who put their lives on the line. In one of the letters, a man learned that his nephew had fallen. It was a blessing that man didn't sit at my table. His voice—his tirade—came from the bar. He only paused to down his whiskey and reach for a girl. I felt for her, but there was little I could do.

"Frank, Henry, Joseph, Paul," I said in my easiest of voices. "Let us indulge in a distraction of cards. And, a round on me."

I, too, had myself some whiskey, not my typical drink of choice. But the room's atmosphere called for it. It continued to call for it, as the days went on, and more letters arrived. There was more news of loved ones' deaths and pleas for the miners to return to fight for their side. I thought the worst was behind us, until we learned of a battle in Maryland that claimed over twenty thousand men. Winter was upon us by then, and even those who wished to leave could not. Or should not. The whiskey both moderated and escalated tempers. In my case, the haze it brought on helped me turn a blind eye and ear to the crude language and gestures of the men at my tables.

Finally, the spring was upon us, and I hoped tensions would ease with the weather. They did, marginally, but never fully, with news of more war deaths seemingly unending, the war seemingly unending. I hadn't donated in years, but I began again, sending money each week to *The Liberator*.

One evening, those from the north and, adversely, the south clashed once more. President Lincoln had freed all slaves in Confederate states. The actual event had occurred the beginning of January, taking until the springtime to reach us. I wondered if reactions, such as ours, had happened every day since, depending on when the news arrived. Some cheered the development. Others were adamantly opposed. I suggested we play another game.

I had George, William, Marcus, and Joseph at my table. Joseph left. A man I hadn't seen before took his chair, nearly missing the seat as he sat.

"*Bienvenue*," I said to the newcomer. "And who might you be?"

He looked at me, his eyes all but wobbling in their sockets. "The name's Philip."

"Philip, how pleased I am to meet you. I'm Madame—"

"I know who you are."

"How wond—"

"Now you listen good."

His voice didn't particularly hold venom, but it was exacting. Forceful. From my right, George whispered, "Madame Dumont," with a question of concern in his words. I reached over, patted his hand, then said to Philip, "I'm listening."

Philip began, "I've got more than two hundred here. Let's get going, and I don't want to quit until you've got all my money or until I've got a considerable amount of yours." He smiled, impolitely at that, as he held arrogance in his grin. I missed the well-mannered men from my emporium. They weren't completely vacant within this town, there were sorts like George, but it'd been nearly a decade since I sat in a room of sophisticated men, who didn't smell overwhelmingly sweaty, and spit tobacco on the floor, and exhale great plumes of smoke.

"Very well." I ran a hand down my stomach, grown softer. "We're playing *vingt-et-un* here. Will that do?"

He shrugged. Inexperienced in card playing, I assumed. I took the time to explain to him the rules, though he hurried every word from my mouth. Still, I spoke softly, as softly as I could in the noisy room, and always from beneath my lashes. The past decade in this *nomade* lifestyle had aged me. I wasn't blind to it. But eyes don't age. The area surrounding them may, but rarely the actual eye. I used them to my advantage whenever I could.

"Now," I said, "Shall we play?"

He didn't answer, only motioned for me to go on. Arrogance and inexperience wouldn't work to his favor. Not at all. An hour later, I was correct, every bill and gold piece that were once his were now mine.

George whistled. "You cleaned him out."

I had. Philip was less than impressed. Not that I blamed him. He'd lost two hundred dollars. But, hadn't that been his goal? Philip had said: *I don't want to quit until you've got all my money.*

He stood, every muscle in his body tense. He returned his empty leather purse to his pocket, grimaced at me, then made to leave.

"No, no." I waved my hands animatedly. "You must not go, *mon amie*, before you've had a drink on the house. My treat." I motioned to the barkeeper, who quickly poured a glass and placed it on the table.

"Milk?" Philip said, bewilderment in his voice.

"Why yes," I said. I remembered the first time I offered milk to a man I'd bested. It'd been Howard. With a glass in hand, Howard's confusion had turned to amusement as I'd said, "Any man silly enough to lose his last cent to a woman deserves a milk diet."

I used the same line on Philip. The other men laughed. Philip was supposed to laugh, too, as Howard had done. Philip was supposed to accept the glass, hold it high, and offer cheers to the room, accepting gracefully his defeat to Madame Dumont. Just as Howard had done. Just as a handful of others had done since. "If I'm to lose my money, it's an honor to lose it to the Madame." That was what the men had always said.

But no, Philip did not respond like Howard or the others. I immediately regretted not allowing him to walk away when he tried. Philip knocked the glass over. The glass shattered, spraying milk onto my black silk dress and me. My mouth fell open. The men all jumped up, their chairs falling over. Their reactions weren't to the spilled milk or broken glass. It was to Philip's anger. They knew a man who wanted to brawl when they saw one, and it was best to be on your feet near that type of man.

I remained sitting.

"How dare you?" he spat. Color had risen to his cheeks.

The music stopped. Philip and I were on full display. I hadn't meant to embarrass him. I lowered my voice, speaking only to him. "I'll loan you a few dollars, if you'd like a chance to redeem yourself."

Philip huffed. He spoke to the room. "With you?"

I nodded.

"With the infamous Madame Dumont?" he mocked. "But look at you. Nothing more than a washed-up hag who should've quit long ago." He focused on me now. "Madame Dumont?" He laughed. "More like *Madame Moustache*."

He may not have slapped me physically, but his words struck me. Wounded me. Instinctively, I touched the skin above my lip. It had a velvet feel. Nevertheless, I gathered myself, defiantly tilted my head back, which I realized too late would have the unwanted effect of bringing more attention to my upper lip, and said, "You've been beaten. Your money is all gone. There's nothing left for you here."

He took his leave, but the damage had been done. With every eye on me, every part of me wanted to flee the room, too. But I remained sitting. I finished out the evening, though every hair on my upper lip seemingly burned. I felt every age line on my forehead, every gray hair on my head, as I hadn't dyed it in years. The area beneath my eyes, which I knew sagged, felt like great pits. My skin had lost some of its glow, from this abhorrent smoke, from the elements during travel, from this lifestyle, in general. How different I must've looked from Patricia.

She stopped aging at shy of twenty, but I'd gone on for almost another fifteen years. Even as I recalled my age, I didn't know if that was young or old. With the fire taking Maman in her thirties, I wasn't given the chance to see her age beyond my own age. What had she looked like then? Better, I guessed, but she had every convenience available to her.

At the night's end, George stopped me. "I think you're a handsome woman, Madame Dumont, no matter what Philip said."

I touched George's cheek. "Thank you, but his words mean little to me."

That was a lie for the ages.

Chapter 29

MADAME MOUSTACHE.

I woke with the moniker at the forefront of my mind. I hated to even call it a moniker. Sobriquets were used readily. And the uttering last night came from Philip's sole mouth, acting in a spiteful manner, hurling a phrase—that single time— in an effort to wound me.

He had succeeded, my appearance of great importance to me. However, I'd accept my role in this. *Aide-toi, le ciel t'aidera.* Heaven only helps those who help themselves, and, it was true I'd grown *laissez faire* with my looks.

I stretched the skin at my eyes. Once the pressure was removed, the lines returned. But what could I expect? Those lines represented nearly thirty-five years of living, the ten most recent years hard won. Ten years where I'd perpetuated my legacy. My name. A moment in time wouldn't undo all that work. Nor would a strip of hair, especially when it could be easily removed.

Voilà. With a few swipes of a razor, the fuzz was gone, and I set to finessing the remainder of my appearance. The gray streaks within my hair were darkened and I put extra effort into teasing and styling. On my cheeks, I perfected a rosy color.

Then, I was on my way to my usual saloon for this evening's revelries. I'd gone halfway there when I happened upon a debate.

"It ain't right," one said. He gestured with a newspaper. "They're lesser than us."

The second said, "So they shouldn't be able to speak the truth?"

"Truth?" the first repeated. The flapping sound he made with his lips indicated sarcasm or mockery. "Next the China-man and Indians will be allowed in court."

I slowed my gait, listening.

"Let them," the second man said. "I'm fine with blacks testifying. Us whites are just as capable of committing crimes. Besides, the law passed in California, not here. What do you care?"

The retort was that same flapping sound. If my inclination as to their conversation was correct, then I wanted to do nothing more than pinch his lips closed. Instead, I snatched the newspaper he waved around. *"Merci,"* I said and gave him my back.

I walked on, reading. And yes, my inclinations had been right. California State Legislature had granted negroes the right to testify against whites in a court of law. I swayed where I stood, then found a barrel to prop myself on.

My mind left me and traveled via memories to fifteen years ago. I was in the postal office. Arthur was across from me. His eye was bruised. I'd said to him, "You should press charges." He had replied, "Against a white man? I'm black, Simone. The law prohibits me testifying against a man like him."

But now, he could've. What if we'd met at a time where he had that right? Would Reuben have been jailed, in restraints, unable to try to claim me? Would Arthur still be alive? Would we have gone on, together, dealing cards and painting all that Arthur set his eyes on?

I would've become Madame Dumont with him at my side, just as I had dreamed. Although, perhaps I would've been Madame Jules. But that nicety was insignificant. The law had been passed too late, many years too late. And Reuben had stolen Arthur from me—with no retribution for his crime. None.

Heavy hearted, I discarded my stolen newspaper and proceeded to the saloon. There, I took my regular seat at a table now known as mine. If my attention hadn't been fixated on *what could have been* with Arthur, I may've noticed the unusual number of eyes on me—or the murmurs.

Man lacked the capacity to whisper in the manner a lady could. Ladies weren't subtle, exactly, but behind the flutter of their fans, the leaning of their heads together, and their snickering interludes, there was little doubt as to what was being spoken. Ladies were also less direct.

The poor thing, a lady would say, her head shaking in wonder. *Her attempt wasn't unsound, but what a blunder, nevertheless.*

There was the omission of proper nouns. There was the use of *it* to replace the offense.

But men—they were direct. They cut deep to the marrow. From where I sat, shuffling my cards, pretending as if nothing reached my ears, I overheard *Madame Moustache*. I heard them say *the moustache is gone*. And also, *you can't unsee the hair*. I heard *Madame Moustache*—again and again.

And I realized I had made a blunder. By removing the hair, I'd made it even more the obvious. I put the moniker—truly a sobriquet now—on the lips of every one of these men. In truth, I preferred a woman's version of gossip, where I could lift my head and bull on, pretending to be never the wiser.

I'd need to be catatonic to pretend in this room. But I tried. With my cheeks aflame, my head woozy, and my palms sweaty I asked my table if we should begin.

♠

The weeks went on. So did the nickname of *Madame Moustache*. The whispers became more discreet, in that no one spoke of my transformation of Madame Dumont to Madame Moustache any longer. Now, they simply spoke the moniker behind my back, never uttering it to my face as Philip had; what gentlemen.

As only one example, a newcomer walked into the bar, set his eyes on me, and asked a regular, "Who's that woman dealing cards?"

The regular was quick to respond, "That's Madame Moustache. She'll take your last dime."

The newcomer's eyebrows rose—to the mention of *moustache* or perhaps enticed by the challenge—I never knew which. But then that fellow found himself at my table, ever so slightly maneuvering his head this way and that to see if the light would catch on a thin strip of hair on my upper lip.

It was gone. I wanted to holler those words in his face. But I didn't.

I kept up my appearances now, even after my original misfire. I made sure that the barely-there fuzz never came back.

Even with that incident, and the others that followed, I remained at my table at my saloon, afraid, I admitted, to walk into a new room and stir the pot there. But every time I heard the name or saw a man examine my face, it chiseled away at my insides. I had traveled great distances and spent great amounts of time, energy, and money to establish the name of Madame Dumont and propagate the playing of my game.

But like my life in *La Nouvelle-Orléans* and again in San Francisco and even in Columbia, it all came undone in a single night. In truth, I had enough money to live a long life, elsewhere, never having to touch a single card again. However, that wasn't me. I was a croupier. I was the mother of *vingt-et-un*. It was all one and the same. I had no way of distinguishing myself in any other way, after all this time. Nor would I. Nor could I. I thought of Lydia's questions from long ago. "Do you cook? Laundry? Clean?" The answer was still *no*. And that was that.

Tonight's topic of conversation around my table was blessedly not me.

"What are you going to do?" Man asked Other Man. I wasn't in a mood to learn their names, besides George. I'd never forget how he called me handsome and was always pleased to see him at my table.

Other Man replied with a laugh, "Guess we'll see how tonight goes."

He meant, he'd see if he'd be able to make three hundred dollars to pay his exemption. The talk of the town was conscription, enacted by congress. All males between the ages of twenty and forty-five were to enlist—unless they paid the exemption or hired a non-exempted person to go in their stead. Other Man already made a wisecrack to an older patron, whose age exempted him. It was met with an abrupt rejection.

"And what of you, George," I asked, focusing my voice and attention on him.

"Madame Dumont, I've got to tell you, gold's in my blood. My Pop chased it in Georgia, him and his own Pop in North Carolina before that. I've no heart for war, but I do for mining."

"So you'll pay the fee and follow the gold?"

George leaned closer. "My course won't be so honorable. There's been some talk of gold." He pointed up. "So, I'm going to go that way."

I hadn't a clue what he meant. It showed on my face.

George leaned closer, whispered. "North. British Columbia."

I nodded in understanding. He meant to dodge the draft. "Your secret is safe with me."

"I knew it would be. A few others and me have put our heads together about it. Going to leave straight away." He drank. "You should come."

"Oh?" I said, the first sound that slipped out.

"Start fresh."

His words were few but the implication grand. And what an idea it was to put Bannack behind me. A mere smudge on my existence.

"Yes," I said. "I think I'll go, too."

Chapter 30

TO MY FAMILIARITY AND DELIGHT, we took a mule train. It was as if my backside remembered it from all those years ago, quickly adjusting. I rode somewhere in the middle of the pack, my portrait removed from the frame and carefully rolled. I kept touching it, a reminder of who I was.

George was part of our train, along with a slew of other men, from various mining towns. I only knew a few men, and I had a feeling George gave them a talking to, as they used *Madame Dumont* in every sentence spoken to me. I was thankful for that mercy. It'd be a challenge to begin again as Madame Dumont with whispers following me. As it was, there were only mules. And, whenever we stopped to camp, I slipped away in secret, seeing to any regrowth on my upper lip.

At one point while we trotted on, the lead rider raised his hand, a sign that we'd be halting. When he began again, he veered us in a new direction, on a less traveled path. I hadn't a clue why; until my portion of the train passed the stake the lead rider had seen in the ground. Attached to it, a warning was posted.

SMALLPOX, it read. There was an area of quarantine, marked with similar stakes every handful of paces. I shivered. Everyone knew the basics of all the diseases.

Cholera and dysentery were caused by contaminated food or drink. The effects were horrendous to the bowels, and many didn't survive. Along the trails, similar signs were used to let others know when rivers, creeks, and ponds were diseased.

Measles, a cruel fever and rash, was highly contagious, an airborne disease.

Also airborne was Consumption, which took a person's life slowly, the entire body being literally consumed by the disease.

Typhoid Fever was feared and often fatal. The president had learned that first hand, where even the President's House wasn't immune to contaminated food and water.

Then there was smallpox, which began as sores on the tongue and in the mouth. Then the sores, filled with an opaque liquid, erupted over the body's entirety, right down to the hands and feet. I heard the victim felt horrendous, racked with fever and achiness, the symptoms relentless until scabs began to form, the bumps hardening and feeling like peas beneath the skin. None of it sounded appealing, but I cringed at what came next, thinking of each hard scab falling off the body. A person was contagious until the last bit of the scab fell off the skin. For those who survived, the whole ordeal took over a month, though smallpox scars could last a lifetime and some victims even lost their eyesight.

I wondered how long the disease area had been quarantined. We detoured well around it, adding a full day to our journey. I readily accepted the delay, even with the trip being upwards of five hundred miles. We reached Wild Horse River in just over a fortnight. Already, the settlement was in the process of becoming a town, with a handful of buildings erected and a number of structures in varying states of completion. Standing there, I eyed the very place I'd erect a new Dumont's Place and I presently went to post a letter to the bank in Bannack to request the sum of my savings.

As it was the onset of autumn, with winter on its heels, the men worked fanatically to prepare for the spring mining season, including claiming their stretches of land they'd soon mine, marked with stakes in the ground. Even now, I felt the chill, but, for the most part, the biting cold was the wind's punishment only, lowering the temperature from sixty to forty degrees, or so I was told from a toothless man native to the area who found my reaction to the weather comical. I smiled him off, too busy trying to fight the gales and keep my feet on the ground.

Rain was added soon. Then by November it began to snow; but, to my surprise, it was never more than a dusting at a time. So far north, I thought I'd be buried in snow, but we were nestled between mountains, much as I was in the foothills. However, the foothills never reached temperatures this low, digits dropping to ten degrees, or lower.

For a few hours each day, I dared winter to introduce the men to my game and me, the saloon one of the first establishments raised. Otherwise, I kept indoors in my cabin, which was little more than a shanty of logs and bark, and in the company of two other women, the only other women at the camp of a thousand men. However, the one woman was very much still a child.

"Catherine," she said her name was, although she'd spoken her name as if she'd done so only a handful of times.

Meekly, I offered, "I shall call you whatever you'd like, if you'd prefer to go by another name."

The girl's smile was slow, but she said, "Chunhua."

I repeated it. Anna did too, the other woman who completed our trio.

"My husband thought Catherine would be easier."

The mention of a spouse was surprising, for various reasons. For one, she was here, in the female cabin instead of with her husband. But also, "You're so young," I said.

"Nearly thirteen," she answered. "My mother was forced from China to San Francisco. The appropriate number of months later, I was born. I was raised in a bordello with my mother, but we worked the laundry. Then Edward—that was my husband's name—came in. He saw me when I brought fresh linens to the room he spent the night in. He insisted on marrying me." She shook her head, as if still confused or surprised by this development. "By that time my mother had passed. Edward and I came here straight away, but by the time we got here, he was halfway in the ground. He had Consumption. Must've contracted it before."

"My condolences," I said. I wasn't sure I meant them, but it felt like the proper response.

Anna said, "Mine, too."

"Thank you, but I barely knew him. And all he did was transport me from there to here."

There being the bordello.

Here being a place where men expected much the same of women.

As it was, Anna counted on this behavior from the men. She returned to us every night she worked, but she otherwise saw men in her tent. She took Chunhua's hand. "Your fate's not set for you here, honey."

"What would you like to do?" I asked, the question striking me as similar to the one Lydia had once asked me.

Chunhua shrugged. "Laundry. My mother and I used to hum while we worked." Her voice quieted some. "It's all I know."

And I chose to deal cards, as something I'd always known and something that'd been dear to my maman and to me.

I claimed Chunhua's remaining hand and nodded curtly. "Laundry, then."

❤

There was little to our days until the fourth of March. On that day, it marked a full forty-eight hours of the temperature rising above freezing. Thus—boom—our town of Kootenay sprang to life.

The three of us women emerged from our cabin, our Fortress of Mistresses we had coined it as winter began to take its toll on our minds. Though, to be honest, a swift kick could've dismantled our fortress. The wind had tested it a time or two. But now, on top of a nearby dwelling, a weathercock was hard-pressed to complete a revolution.

"Chunhua," Chunhua said in her soft voice, her gaze far off. She laughed at my reaction, which was laced with confusion and perhaps concern for her mental health. "Spring flowers." She pointed toward buds. "It's what my name means."

I smiled and tilted my head to more directly feel the sun. "Mine means shining one."

The three of us linked hands. I said, "Shall we begin?"

The croupier, the laundress, and the courtesan.

We were the most unlikely, but the most splendid, of trios. Each, with a knife sheathed to our inner thigh; weapons I had won during my recent card games. We'd stick together and help one another establish our new enterprises. After spending the winter with the men, Anna's venture was well underway. Now, she'd help Chunhua and me, by encouraging her clients to launder with Chunhua and by spending their remaining spare time with me, once the new Dumont's Place was built.

It was a thrill as my new emporium was raised, log by log, brick by brick, then window panes, doors, the bar, tables, and chairs. For the sake of practicality, the new Dumont's Place had less frills than the original. I wanted the structure raised as quickly as possible and, also, it was an eight-hundred-mile round trip to Walla Walla, the largest town in the Washington Territory. Little was imported. Instead, most everything was built here.

I swallowed down any downheartedness that arose when I compared this emporium to the one before it. There really was no similarity to the decorum and, I wagered, to my future clientele. I hardly could've expected model behavior when my gambling den looked no different than the others, though lacked certain so-called gratifications. Nevertheless, I held firm to the business acumen I'd followed before: I'd employ no saloon girls. While I knew I wouldn't have the same allure here, there remained the draw of a female dealer, still unique. And booze.

Within weeks, my new emporium was done. I took care while unrolling my portrait. I had no frame, so rocks held the corners down, stretched out over my new desk in my new office. "And we begin again," I whispered, in the way I've always done to Arthur.

Truly, the timing of my building's completions was *idyllique*, as it aligned with the mass arrival of men and mail. The latter gave me full access to my savings, not a moment too soon. The cost to build was extortionate, leaving me in debt, but I'd taken it all on the chin, confident I'd pay my loans and earn back my money within a few years' time. With a bonanza beneath us in the ground, there was no reason not to believe it.

Chapter 31

"MY NAME'S MADAME DUMONT," I said in greeting to my latest table of men, then, as per my recent routine, I promptly watched their reactions for any recognitions, be it of my spoken name or the association with an unspoken moniker. It never appeared to be the later and warmth built inside of me, released in the form of a smile. "Very good, will you play?"

They did, and it seemed hundreds more of potential *vingt-et-un* players arrived each afternoon as spring turned to summer. The American newcomers spoke of anti-draft riots, along with the north's great victory in Gettysburg. However, in general, the arrivals consisted of many Europeans and the Chinese and there was less war talk and a greater focus on unearthing gold. Each had their claims along the river, where they'd panned the waters and shoveled loads of dirt into rockers. Diligent miners, they were, which poorly affected my business, as my *vingt-et-un* players came in most largely on Saturday evenings. Still, men came in.

One night, a woman did, too.

She was a pretty thing, young, with a ruffled blouse and a high collar, tucked neatly into a skirt. Her hair was so unnaturally red it must've been manufactured. Manufactured, that was, to catch the attention of men. I wasn't one to talk, as my hair color was also applied. However, this girl didn't alter her appearance to save her looks, as I had, but rather to enrich her beauty. The men were certainly enriched. Every head and body turned toward her.

With each step she took toward me, I felt my own beauty diminishing. But then I chastised myself for such a thought. She was but a girl, in a sea of men. We were alike in that way. I recognized her uncertainty but also her resolve.

I signaled to my table that I'd return in a moment and suggested they freshen their drinks at the bar, then I rose to meet her.

"Madame Dumont?" the girl said.

"That's me. May I help you with something?"

"I hope so." She held eye contact. "I'd like a job."

"Here?" I began to edge our conversation toward the exit. "There are four saloons a stone's throw away. In those, as I'm sure you've noticed, they employ women."

"It's not the type of job I want."

I paused. "Oh?"

"I want to deal."

"Cards?" I asked, admittedly surprised. Remarkably, in my many years as a croupier in gold bars, towns, cities, and settlements—you name it, I'd worked them all—I'd never seen another woman brandishing a set of cards. I knew other female dealers were out there. I'd heard mention of them, but never by name. And never my game. They played poker or faro.

The girl raised her chin. "Poker."

"You know how to play?"

"My daddy works a saloon in California."

"Where's your daddy now?"

"Still there. It's only the two of us. He sent me up here to prospect, see what kind of life could be had for us here."

"I see."

And, I thought on it. This girl, surely tough as nails if she'd made it this far on her own, could very well deal poker in the other establishments here. She'd likely face resistance. The arrangement would surely be unfair, outrageously favoring the owner. It'd be a difficult start.

I knew from experience.

However—I shifted my weight from one side to the other—I could help her sidestep those hurdles. My grandfather had paved the way for Papa, who had planned to pave the way for me. Life zigzagged, but had it not, that courtesy would've been extended to me.

I didn't beat around the bush. I offered the girl the same sixty percent and salary of ten dollars a week that I had finagled from Monsieur Sullivan as I was beginning.

And thus began our partnership. Well, after I asked her name.

Florence, as it turned out, was one of the savviest business decisions I'd ever made. Men were drawn to her, to put it plainly. She dealt, with none of the fancifulness I weaved into my games, but it also wasn't necessary. She was a goddess in their eyes, the reincarnation of Aphrodite.

I recalled how I once thought of myself in that manner, after a wife—Madame Brown, if my memory hadn't failed me—confronted me in the streets outside my original Dumont's Place. But now that I thought on it, she linked my allure not specifically to my beauty, but to my French tongue and how I held myself and how her husband spent more time with me than with her.

I still held the capacity to do all those things. I wagered I always would hold such a power. And for those reasons, I tempered any resentment that the men rightfully drooled over Florence, while treating me in a more mature, maternal manner. In fact, I welcomed Florence into additional folds of my life. More specifically, into the Fortress of Mistresses.

Florence had been staying at a hotel, as did any additional women who had arrived. It was only our original trio who'd chosen to remain in our cabin, bark walls and all.

It was the afternoon. Chunhua was off laundering. But Anna, Florence, and I sat in a circle, seeing to the welts upon our bodies. The biting insects in British Columbia were the worst I'd ever experienced. While we slept in the mornings, the no-see-ums slipped through the cracks of our crude cabin and breakfasted on us. During the day, the horse flies and buffalo gnats emerged. At dusk and into the night, the role of stealing our blood was passed to the mosquitos. Relentless creatures.

I dabbed a concoction of wild geranium and lemongrass on one bump before moving to another. Chunhau had created the ointment for us. She'd turned our fortress into a sort of flower nursery. There were fresh flowers in mason jars and drying flowers hanging from crevices. All of them had uses. By the window, in a small pot, Florence had beets growing.

She pulled two and rejoined us on the floor. There she mashed the beets into a bowl of honey. "I'll need more soon. Think any of these gold hunters double as honey hunters?"

I laughed. "Let's ask at our tables tonight."

She smiled, then began to apply the mixture to her hair. I'd darkened mine the other day, with ingredients I'd brought from Bannack. Anna stood to help Florence, but Chunhau returning home swiftly stole her attention.

"Did you do it?" Anna asked. The anticipation in her voice was comical. Cruel, and also justified, but comical. You see, one of Anna's clients became too rough with her the other evening. Sweet Chunhau had a solution. This afternoon, while laundering the man's pants, she rubbed stinging nettle and dried Baby's breath all over the loins area, where his buttocks and his member were surely to touch—and thus itch and rash, like the Dickens. We all surmised the discomfort and embarrassment would keep him from Anna's tent. And naturally, there was never a shortage of the plants.

Chunhau said in a serious tone, "It's done."

Then we all burst into laughter. And, I marveled at how fortress-like our appointed fortress really had become, as we all prepared to enter again into this man's world.

♣

By the time summer turned to fall the population along the river had soared. What had begun as a thousand men was now over five thousand. The populace was mainly of European and Chinese descent, but there were Americans, too.

Already, the men claimed they'd taken millions of dollars' worth from the ground. I encouraged them to find more, then to celebrate at Florence's and my tables. It'd been a year since I'd heard the moniker of *Madame Moustache* uttered and I enjoyed each *Madame Dumont* spoken since.

Soon, the grizzlies turned in for the winter and the miners hung up their caps and spent more time indoors. Hallelujah for that. With my emporium built—and substantially warmer than our cabin—the girls and I saw fit to raise a wall, creating a room that we outfitted with cots. Even with the warmer accommodations, we once again celebrated the temperature doubling from one digit to two and then finally above freezing. And thus, another mining season was upon us.

I was content, which should've been my first cautionary clue.

One day, as the day finally cooled from the summertime sun, it was all over.

Mike, who I preferred to call Michael, was the first to break the development to me. "This'll be my farewell game, Madame Dumont."

"How sad, Michael. It'll be a shame to lose you."

He asked for another card. "Me and hundreds of others."

"Pardon?"

"Everyone's moving on."

I looked around the room. My table was full. The room seemed as crammed as usual. "Doesn't appear that way to me."

"You'll see. Come morning. A mule train is passing through and I plan to hitch a ride. Aren't you fellas leaving, too?" he said to the others at my table.

"John, William, Charles?" I asked.

They all confirmed they'd be leaving as well.

I asked, "But why? To where? Just today a small nugget was found."

"Small," Charles said with a nod. "But down in Carpenter's Bar, the prospects are huge. We all want a piece of it. Sounds too good not to see with our own eyes. And we got to move quick before the claims are snatched up. Besides, word came in that slavery is done. An amendment was passed. War can't go on much longer now. Back to our country we go."

They all confirmed, once again.

While I was quite pleased about the amendment, I shook my head in regard to their gold lust. David had been correct. Mining, and those who mined it, were fickle, fickle beasts. But still, I couldn't fathom the entirety of the town would leave, on a whim.

Turned out, it wasn't the whole of town, but more than half deserted. It was astonishing, really.

The girls and I had to determine what to do, with all the men we depended on now leaving. Florence was quick to say she'd return to California and her father, which we all thought a wise decision.

Anna looked at me and said, "Will you stay?"

I shook my head. "There aren't enough men to support a business here. I've no choice but to sell and cut my losses." Quite substantial losses, unfortunately.

"Well," Anna said, "I'm going wherever you go, Eleanor."

I took her hand, squeezed. "The men swear up and down there's gold all over the Montana Territory. So we'll follow, I guess. And what of you, Chunhua?"

"I think I'll stay," she said, but kept her gaze low.

"Chunhua," Anna said, drawing out her name.

The girl looked up.

Anna pressed, "There's a boy, isn't there?"

Chunhua's porcelain skin deepened with a red hue, and I swatted at Anna, saying, "Leave her be." There were many Chinese who remained, a clear decision to keep their numbers large, as a way to protect one another from the hostility often shown to their race. To Chunhua, I said, "I'm happy for you. I was never given the chance to be with the man I cared for."

The girls were silent; perhaps surprised I said even that much about my past. I spoke rarely of it, only in a short burst such as that. But Florence had seen my portrait one time and said simply, "How stunning you are."

"Thank you," I'd said, my mind returning to the night in Arthur's room, and how his eyes had roamed my body.

Anna had then asked me who painted it with such familiarity of me.

I'd answered, "The man I was supposed to spend my life with." I had debated stopping there, but I shared more. And what I shared still applied now. I thought it always would. I had said, "But instead, I spend my life fulfilling his depiction of me. That's my consolation."

Chapter 32

MY TIME IN BRITISH COLUMBIA had left me destitute, but fulfilled. *Bonne renommée vaut mieux que ceinture dorée.* A good name was better than great wealth.

And, my name had been restored.

I'd also extend that maxim to friendship as being greater than riches. I'd enjoyed the camaraderie I'd shared with my women, and was thrilled that Anna currently occupied the animal behind mine within our mule train.

We worked our way south, with me finding flat surfaces on which to deal cards and Anna finding flat ground to erect her tent. Our destination, we decided, wouldn't be a gold mine, after all, but the more tried and true town of Fort Benton in the Montana Territory. It had been settled as a trading port well before gold was announced in San Francisco, and we were both drawn to the certainty that the town wouldn't be forsaken in a year's time. Gambling was also rampant there.

The day was hot. Sweat dripped between my breasts, down my back, gathered at my elbows and knees. All over, I was achy. I coughed dust from my lungs, my eyes watering. My mule progressed into some blessed shade from a cliff face and I circled my lips to let out a relieved breath. It was in that moment that I began to sway on his back.

There wasn't much I remembered after that, only minute moments, along with the oddest of details. I recalled Anna's face leaning over me, her blonde hair, down instead of up, swinging with her movements. I recalled being in her tent.

The shade of it changed, from a burnt color, so bright I squinted, to a dull tan, then to the darkest brown, where my mind contrived that I was deep underground. The colors looped, interchanged.

I thrashed some. Anna said *shh* often. She dabbed my forehead. At times, she held my arms down. When I was conscious, my head rolled from side to side. But mostly, I must've slept, or there would've been more I recalled.

Finally, I more sturdily saw Anna above me, my vision blinking clear.

"Measles," she said in a whisper, the same softness to her voice she had used with all her *shh* sounds. "You're all better now."

"Anna, no," I croaked. "You'll catch it."

She shook her head. "I had it when I was young. I can't get it again."

I licked my dry lips. "Where are we?" I looked around the tent. It was the burnt color again; the brightness now discerned to be the sun's illumination, even brighter along the tent's seams.

Anna explained all that had happened. After I fell from my mule, the signs of measles were apparent. Fever. Cough. Red, watery eyes. Then, the telltale sign of tiny white spots within my mouth. Two others showed the symptoms, too. Immediately, we were asked to leave the mule train. Anna pitched her tent, hidden amongst growth along the trail, and took care of me. With how she spoke, I knew it was worse than she was letting on.

I asked, "How long?"

"A little over a week. But you'll be pleased to know," she said, "I don't believe an inch of your skin will scar. You wanted to scratch, but I wouldn't let you. You're quite strong, for your size, I must say."

I laughed, still feeling weak. "Thank you."

"You can thank Chunhua, too. I was able to find her geranium and lemongrass flowers to help soothe the rash."

I closed my eyes and, indeed, sent Chunhua a thank you. As vain as it sounded, scars on my arms, my face, my hands—all I presented to the men at my tables—would've been detrimental to the image I clung to of myself as the beautiful, mysterious, French-speaking woman dealing cards. I owed Anna a great debt.

♦

It took another day for me to regain my strength enough to walk. Fortunately, I'd fallen ill on the final leg of our trip, and after our calculations of how far we'd gone; we decided we were within reasonable distance of completing the journey by foot.

It wasn't safe to travel as two solitary women, even two solitary women with knifes sheathed to their legs. When I spoke the concern aloud to Anna I included the word *per se*. It wasn't safe, per se....

Anna raised her perfect brow and countered that it wasn't safe, at all.

But we had little other choice than to chance any aggressive humans or rattlers, mountain lions, bears, wolves.

Anna added, "Moose, too."

We stuck close together, arms linked for my support as much as for the feeling of our shared safety. As night fell, we came upon a camp, desperate for sustenance. While I'd been sick, Anna made fish broth for my fever. How she did so and how she knew how to do so, I was unsure; Anna spoke little of her background, and I'd let her have her silent memories just as I had mine. But she must've been ravenous. She'd eaten barely more than strips of dried meat, carefully at that, so animals wouldn't come sniffing around, expecting her to share.

The first night at the camp, we did little more than eat, set up Anna's tent, and sleep, fire crackling nearby. The sound and the additional bodies were a comfort, as long as they remained outside our tent. And, they did.

In the morning, we took stock of the other campers and they took stock of us. I imagined our appearances left much to be desired. But then a man came closer, as if he needed a better look at us. More specifically, at me.

"I thought so," he said, his hat shadowing his face. Anna and I exchanged uncertain glances. "You're Madame Dumont." Then he whistled. "Aren't you a courageous little thing? Both of you."

A laugh slipped out, the effort weakening me further. But that laugh was worth it. So was hearing that name. I'd been recognized. Recognized as Madame Dumont, on the side of a trail, after being tent-ridden with a weeklong illness. I felt as if I could drift straight up to the clouds and perch there, smiling like a fool.

"Can we play?" he asked.

We most certainly could.

Although, I lost: my head not all the way back. To our good fortune, the man—Frank was his name—was on his way to Fort Benton and agreed to take us along, asking no short of three times if we were certain we wanted to go there, citing how a marshal once had the entire town encircled by his cavalry so warrants could be served to five of Fort Benton's inhabitants.

Surely, Frank had been exaggerating, but I swore the sun went hiding as soon as we walked into the town. Then the first sound we heard, honest to goodness, was gunshot. Had we more strength, Anna and I would've turned on our heels. But we did not, and we let Frank and his friends escort us down Front Street. While there was a fort, with bastions flanking its sides and portholes for canyons, Frank informed us the fort's interior was used mostly for trade, with a trade store, trader's quarters, a warehouse, a blacksmith and carpenter's shop. Front Street was used more for entertainment.

One side of the road held two-story brick and wood buildings. The other side stretched alongside a levee where the calm Missouri River was the only agreeable welcome to town.

Frank bent closer to us, saying, "This road here's earned the title of 'bloodiest block in the West' so keep your head down and keep to the middle of it when you can."

He'd only just said it, but Frank did little to heed his own advice. He greeted those we passed, perhaps living the adage of killing with kindness. At any rate, Anna and I may as well have been on parade; the feeling heightened when Frank took us into a saloon known as The Jungle and introduced us to every Tom, Dick, and Harry.

Anna and I untangled our limbs from each other to say our hellos, transforming ourselves into a confident croupier and courtesan. Frank continued his hobnobbing and, before we knew it, Anna and I were both asked if we wanted jobs at the establishment.

The Jungle offered food, music, organized fistfights and Indian wrestling, sex, and gambling. What more could a patron want? I hoped, for a civilized game of cards. However, I felt no encouragement of refinement with how the men kept six-shooters on the tabletops.

Frank assured me the use of such weapons was—what was the word he used—discouraged. It wasn't as if I hadn't seen guns in plain view at the table before, because I had in Bannack, but here it was as if the most horrific man of each town across the West was selected, and all those worst men were transported to this singular town, this singular saloon.

Nevertheless, Anna and I agreed to the employment, both a bit dumbfounded that the wages fell into our laps, but hadn't we earned a bit of luck after our Kootenay failure and the measles? And, didn't we desperately need income?

Our apartment, once bartered for, required our week's rent to be paid within four days.

It was on the third night that I faced a great set back. The evening began well enough. News that General Robert E. Lee surrendered his Confederate Army to General Ulysses S. Grant arrived via steamboat. The war was blessedly over. The Jungle celebrated, too much, in fact, with the men's emotions at an all-time high. A man was shot, with one of those so-called never-used guns. Another was stabbed.

I smiled when smiled upon but otherwise kept a low profile and dealt, speaking in a greater amount of French than usual as not to incite more conversation than needed. My pile was growing, and I calculated that if my night continued as such and if Anna's night was also profitable, we'd be on target to pay for our room after only one more night of working.

A man named Pete, who corrected my tried use of Peter, was new to my game. Most were, though I was delighted to find some came already knowing how to play *vingt-et-un*, even while referring to it as twenty-one. It brought me satisfaction, picturing my game being played across the West.

This particular round was favoring me, and not Pete. In fact, I soon took his last dime, cautiously adding his money to my pile. "It's been a treat to play with you, monsieur," I said in my most earnest of voices. I infused it with no honey or sweetness, nothing he'd be able to confuse with patronization on this celebratory night of high emotions.

He began to stand. Another player, Geoffrey, chimed in, "You're not going to offer him milk, Madame Dumont?"

This stopped me. Elation had surged through me at Frank's recognition of me along the trail, but as he was such a friendly man, I thought it a special circumstance. And since then, my name had been spoken, but I figured on account of Frank's liberal introductions. But now here, again, Geoffrey—this rough-and-tough man—recognized me. But not only that; he also knew my ways. A delight filled me.

I smiled at Geoffrey, then I focused on Pete, to explain to him my cheeky consolation prize of milk. I wouldn't put him on the spot the way I had with Philip, whose spiteful reaction was so heartless, petty, and cruel.

Pete didn't let me explain. He spoke first. "I'll accept your milk."

Oh, I thought, so he also knew of my gag. I hadn't been expecting that.

Pete added, "Madame Moustache."

At first, I was sure my ears had deceived me. But my eyes couldn't miss his face. And his face also held condescension, with his right eyebrow raised, as if poised for my reaction.

I wouldn't give him the one he wanted. I raised an arm, signaling the bartender. "May I get a glass of milk, please? I've taken this man's last dime. For that, he deserves a milk diet."

Outside, I held Pete's gaze.

Inside, my mind raced. In loops, my thoughts repeated, *no, this couldn't be happening again.*

Chapter 33

WHAT WAS I TO DO?

I sat in my apartment, hands clenched in my lap. Last night, I had finished out the evening. I'd remained in my seat, asking the men to play again. They had, a new man taking Pete's seat. But I felt the words *Madame Moustache* move about the room as if words could be tangible. As if the words manifested into an invisible band wound tightly around my chest and neck. Through it all, my cheeks had colored and I'd restrained from touching my upper lip. I knew there was no hair there. I'd only just removed it that morning.

But men were petty beings, doing whatever necessary to pet their own egos. Though, to be fair, not all men held that distinction. There were men like my Papa. Men like Arthur, who saw more in me than I saw in myself. There was William who helped me become Eleanor and there was David—for a spell—who had helped me establish that name. I recalled the others—Ernest, George, Frank—who helped positively perpetuate who I wanted to be.

I was fortunate to have men lifting me up, to counter those who sought to bring me down. The same could be said for women, and I thought fondly of my friendships with Lydia, Jane, and my Fortress of Mistresses, Anna especially.

I hadn't told Anna about the moniker of *Madame Moustache*, not when we were living in our fortress and not after last night's happenings. But she'd hear it. At The Jungle, she spent her time upstairs, but on one of the occasions she was in the main room, the whispers would reach her. She'd be furious on my account.

Across our small parlor, she knitted. Though her glance kept falling upon our door.

"What is it?" I asked her. "Something is wrong."

She rubbed her lips together, then finally said. "The men in these parts are mean. We've no choice but to be meaner. But this girl, Emma, who I'd met my first night, doesn't have it in her. Last night she got knocked around. I should've asked you first, but I invited her to stay with us for a few days while she recovered."

"You should've asked me," I said, "so that I could've said, of course, Emma is welcome here."

Anna relaxed in her chair. "Thank you. I worried you'd think I was trying to turn our apartment into a bordello."

I laughed. "I could imagine much worse places."

Right now, imagining a worse place was particularly easy. I had no desire to return to The Jungle tonight and subject myself to hours of behind-my-back whispers. I thought again, *what was I to do?* In my head, I extended the question to Arthur, and waited for some great inspiration to flood my thoughts.

Instead, there was a knock at the door. Anna answered and Emma entered. With her battered face, it looked like Emma had first made a stop in Hell. I subtly shook my head, but did nothing more to display pity. No woman wanted that. Jane never had. She only needed somewhere safe to be.

And that was exactly what Anna was doing for Emma, while the worst of Emma's wounds healed. If the men saw her this way, there'd be two outcomes. The first, the men would refuse to hire her. Or, the second, Emma would accumulate bruises, the men feeling as if they could treat her as others had.

I felt as if I'd fall victim to the latter behavior if I dealt at The Jungle, or any other establishment in town again. The name Madame Moustache would swiftly replace all I'd built as Madame Dumont. I could leave. Wasn't that my pattern? I'd skip town then begin again, figuring out who and where and what I was supposed to be.

But as I looked at dear Anna, to whom I owed a great debt, who depended on me to work this evening to pay for our apartment, and Emma, who depended on this apartment for her well-being, what choice did I have but to break my pattern of running away—and allow the tarnishing of my name. William had once said not to chase my past, but to find my purpose and create my future.

I stood, running a hand down my uneasy stomach. "If you'll excuse me, I must ready myself for work."

❤

The tarnishing continued, for I kept going back, kept over-hearing the moniker. Like before, besides the initial gut-punch of it being spat at my face, it wasn't spoken to me, only around me. In a way, it made it worse, as if I was doing a disservice to my portrait and to Arthur's memory. I was not the free, unburdened woman he'd captured in his brush strokes.

However, I was a woman who helped to keep a roof over Anna's head and the poor battered souls she brought home. First there was Emma, but there were others after that. Many others, as the weeks and months went on.

Anna relished in being able to provide this aid. "I was an orphan," she said one day, "sent to an asylum by some distant relative. When I aged out, I followed the buzz westward. I took the first job presented to me."

With her looks, I wagered the work came quickly and easily.

"I don't mind the job," she said. "Though, I'd be quick to work for myself, managing the girls, seeing to our clientele.

That way I'd have control over which men went near the girls."

Yes, I thought, and the word *control* spoke to me. I let it settle into my reflections as I dealt, as I ate, as I fought for sleep each night. In the end, it was quite simple. *Control* was why I had gone into business for myself, all those years ago, thirteen years to be exact. I'd strived to govern the men's manners and conduct business exactly as I had wanted. Then, later, when Philip, then Pete, then the entire saloon uttered the sobriquet of Madame Moustache, it'd stripped away the control I felt over who I was and what belonged to me as Madame Dumont.

My game. My occupation as a professional croupier.

But perhaps it was the game and not me that was to be my legacy. In that case, did it matter what name I was called? Or, adversely, could a moniker perpetuate my game to an even greater degree? Now that was a notion.

A person doesn't often choose their nickname. These dreaded monikers were often bestowed. But that was what made the name memorable, I reminded myself. There was *Ivan the Terrible*. *The Do-Nothing* was given to one of the Louises of France. And Charles II was known as *Charles the Bald*, though in actuality he was rumored to be sufficiently hairy and the nickname of baldness was a reference to his landlessness.

Nevertheless, it was pleasing to know men weren't exempt from deplorable nicknames, even if mine was so clearly linked to my appearance and theirs to their abilities. However, *Bref, c'est la vie*. In short, that was life.

And, I decided there was simply no other resolution than to not only accept but to embrace the sobriquet of Madame Moustache. I think Arthur would've approved of that owner-ship, the decision a freeing one. I touched my lip. It was smooth. But I'd let the hair grow. I'd no longer shave the dark fuzz away.

I once heard that moustaches held no practical function.

A moustache was merely a symbol. Military men often grew them and, during battle, in combination with their prominent uniforms, a moustache was meant to strike fear into their enemies. So, what should my moustache symbolize? That I wouldn't allow a man to derail me?

Instead, I'd carry on.

In fact, the whole country would. President Lincoln had been assassinated weeks ago. A single shot to the head by a singular man. But then Andrew Johnson took office, the last of the Confederate forces surrendered, and there was a victory parade in Washington to boost the country's morale.

As it was, my own morale had been uplifted, albeit morbidly, around that same time. And, I'd felt as if I experienced my own victory. Again, albeit morbidly. The night had begun normally enough. Anna and I arrived at The Jungle together. She squeezed my hand, as was her custom, before we parted ways, Anna going upstairs and me to my table, which sat on a raised platform at the room's middle.

Tonight, she squeezed, but didn't release her grasp.

My eyes dropped to our intertwined hands, before rising to her face. Her jaw was tightened. Anna's eyes were narrowed.

"What is it?" I asked her.

"Him," she said.

I followed her gaze. The man smiled, the cockiest of grins, his upper lip lost within his moustache. A woman passed, him swatting her backside as she went. He followed the slap with a laugh, a crude remark, and a swallow of his drink. At once, the recognition struck me. The familiarity of the man soaked me with memories—the worst kind of recollections—while also twisting my insides, like a dishrag that'd been wrung out.

"He called on me last night," Anna said, the anger barely contained in her usually melodic voice. "The kind of man who thinks rules don't apply to him."

I knew that all too well. More so, I knew this man all too

well. At once, thoughts of vengeance sprung to mind. It'd been over fifteen years since I'd laid eyes on him, but once reminded, how could you forget someone who murdered the man you once believed you'd spend your remaining days with? How could you forget someone who thought you were his property, simply because he felt he was owed that?

Reuben.

All the way in Fort Benton. Serendipitous, really, as all those years ago I'd wondered if he'd come to this merchant town. Instead, I'd chosen to follow my own path. I'd reduced Reuben to a dreadful part of my past, while keeping Arthur alive in my ongoing decisions, my thoughts, my heart. But now, here was Reuben, in the present, with the same arrogance he'd once displayed.

Or, I could assume he hadn't changed by the behavior I'd just witnessed, that he hadn't altered his ways after taking another man's life, that he wasn't deserving of mercy, but instead, of his comeuppance—of justice.

Justice, I thought, that could be delivered by my own hand, in one of two ways.

The first was the arrangement of Reuben's return to San Francisco. Arduous, the process felt. Though, satisfying.

The second, also satisfying—but in a more callous, yet expedient manner—was the ending of Reuben's life. An eye for an eye. So I had to ask myself... could I take the life of another human being?

Anna whispered how she needed to slip upstairs before Reuben saw her; she didn't wish to service him again. As she went, I feared Reuben would see me, too, before I decided on my course of action. Alas, I had nowhere else to go but to my table, elevated on the platform, at the room's center. Players awaited me there. I asked them, "Shall we play?" even while my attention remained on Reuben across the room.

As if he felt my eyes on him, he looked straight at me.

Reuben's recollection of me wasn't immediate. Long ago, I doubted he'd know the reds, yellows, blues, and whites that made up my skin color, especially when I had stood amongst the muleteers as I searched the faces for his. But here—now—I was still the card-playing French woman. I doubted he'd seen another like me, even in fifteen years.

My assumption became warranted with the slow, steady, spreading of his lips into a grin. No, a smirk.

I couldn't help the shiver that spread over me.

"You all right, Madame?" asked Matthew, one of the men at my table.

I forced a smile. "Of course."

Matthew said, "He gives me the woollies, too." And I realized Matthew had witnessed my reaction to Reuben.

I asked. "Do you know him?"

He responded with his words proceeded by a harrumph, "Came in night before last like he was the second coming of Christ himself. That kind of swine will get himself killed if he sticks around."

I nodded and rubbed my lips together. This was indeed the self-proclaimed "bloodiest block in the West." I wagered there was the chance Reuben's actions—all on his own—could have him pushing up daisies within the week. And, as a betting woman, I guessed it'd take little encouragement from me to help that imminent process along. A nudge, if you will. *Justice*, I reminded myself. Or perhaps, revengeance, if such a word existed. For me, it did, and I said, "I can't say I'd be surprised if he found himself backed into a corner. Talk on him is that he's a snake. Quick to throw a fit"—like he had with Arthur and James on the minefield—"quick to take what doesn't belong to him"—like he'd wanted to do with me—"quick to squeal"—like his false accusations that I'd card-sharped—"and even quicker to sink a knife in a man's gut."

Matthew, along with the three others at my table, shook

their heads. One tapped his knife on the table and said, "Best way to see to a snake is to cut off its head before it can strike."

I met Reuben's eyes again, that smirk still on his face, and I gave a noncommittal shrug to my table. I had only told my truth.

The next morning, Anna and I heard the news. The newcomer in town hadn't backed himself into a corner, as I had suggested, but Reuben had been backed into an alley, where his body still remained.

That was that. And while it wouldn't bring Arthur back, it felt gratifying to know Reuben's malefactions were at an end. Anna agreed, and within a year's time, she opened her own parlor, to similarly put a stop to the cruelty of men like Reuben.

By that time, I'd become an afternoon fixture at The Jungle as Madame Moustache, deciding it was futile to replicate the civility of Dumont's Place in this town.

From time to time, I still heard my name of Madame Dumont, and of course it was how I introduced myself, but I didn't allow the sound of *Madame Moustache* to pummel my emotions or threaten the playing of my game.

Every day, I dealt to the men. I asked them in my harmonic voice, "Will you play?" and then, from beneath my lashes, I explained to them my rules, adding a smattering of French. It was my way.

And the men loved it. Once upon a time, I was a novelty for simply being a woman croupier—the very first one of the West. Now there were other females dealing card games. But men still sat at my table, so they could say they played a round with Madame Moustache. Who knew a strip of hair would become my new novelty? I often wondered what would have become of my game and me if I had fled this time around.

One afternoon, as the sun was beginning to sink, a new disturbance stirred outside The Jungle. As seen with the response to Reuben, fights broke out routinely. Furthermore, gunshots were an all-too-common and a look-the-other-way occurrence. But today's commotion still had a curious soul pushing to his feet to peer out the window.

"Got a boat coming in," he relayed. "Dock master don't want him to."

That piqued my curiosity as well. Last time there was a fuss on the river it was because a man fell overboard. His body was never found. Before that, a native's body was dumped in the river, retaliations occurring right there on the street. Anna and I had kept indoors for two whole days until the worst passed.

I liked to know what dangers were headed my way, so I stood and went to the window. Others did as well, shouldering each other for a better view, wondering what catastrophe was unfolding this time.

Mountain boats came up the river throughout the day, docking at our ports to conduct their trades. It wasn't a surprise to see a steamboat now. However, the alarming aspect was the yellow flag that hung from the bowsprit. It signaled the ship was under quarantine. The question was, from what?

Someone hushed the music. The men currently arm wrestling called a truce. We all strained our ears, listening to the exchange of the dock master and the boat's captain. There was little I made out, until I heard the word *smallpox*. Then I witnessed the onset of greater hubbub, with the town's men running to defend the dock and the captain desperate to leave the diseased mountain boat.

The idea of smallpox was horrifying. If it were to infect Fort Benton and if I contracted the disease, it'd surely be worse than the measles. It'd mean a month of sores and rashes, fever and achiness. If I survived, my body would undoubtably be scarred, a horrendous thought as my vanity had always been of importance. But arrogance aside, smallpox could take my eyesight. Then, that would surely be the end of me playing my beloved *vingt-et-un* and all that my game stood for.

I raised a hand to my mouth, quaking at the thought. Too many times I'd been unsettled just as I'd become settled. I needed to act first. My gaze fell on the guns on a tabletop. I snatched two, one in each hand, and then I rushed from the saloon.

I wager I appeared mad, my hair coming loose, dressed in my fineries, a frantic look in my eyes, swinging two pistols as I ran. But I didn't stop until I stood at the dock's edge, the *Walter B. Dance* steamship only feet away.

I stretched out my arms, the pistol pointed at the boatman. "You'll come no farther."

He had little clue what to make of me.

The men behind me backed me up, saying, "That's right. You best listen to the Madame. She'll shoot."

Would I? Perhaps. I technically had been the gunpowder behind Reuben's death. But before I pulled the trigger, I looked down both barrels and said, "I've no time for your sad tales. Keep on going up river. You're not welcome here until that flag rightfully comes down."

"All right," the boatman said, his eyes dancing over all five feet of me. "We'll go."

I feared Fort Benton's men would hoist me on their shoulders. On second thought, the excitement caused me such relief and exhaustion that being carried would've been nice. I settled for a seat at my table, cards in my hand, and the men making toasts to "the Madame."

Of course, around the room, in the retelling of the incident, most men referred to me by my moniker. I didn't mind, not when everything else that left their mouths was flattery. Perhaps I would be remembered for more than a dainty strip of hair upon my upper lip. Perhaps, I was even still the woman in Arthur's portrait, the canvas now wrinkled and worn from years of travel and abuse. It was like me in that way.

I overheard *Madame Moustache* said once more. And this time I smiled. There it was, my sobriquet, for better or for worse, but forever the mother of *vingt-et-un* and the West's first betting woman, should history decide to write me into her pages.

The End

A Note from the Author

MY INTEREST IN ELEANOR DUMONT'S story bloomed as I began researching the women of the California gold rush. It wasn't long before I came upon a name unknown to me, *Madame Moustache*. As it turned out, Madame Moustache was the sobriquet for Eleanor Dumont, who was born as Simone Jules, and who had popularized *vingt-et-un*, now known as blackjack.

The presence of three names for a single woman intrigued me. I wondered how one name bled into the next and how life winded to a nickname—one I didn't initially find particularly endearing—that Eleanor lived with for over a decade. I wondered if she endured the moniker for all those years or if she was accepting of the name, which was spat at her after taking a man's last dime during a game of *vingt-et-un* and offering him a glass of milk, Eleanor having been claimed to have said, "Any man silly enough to lose his last cent to a woman deserves a milk diet."

In all the anecdotes I found of Eleanor, she was warm-hearted, quick-witted, business savvy, courageous, and tenacious. The attributes led me to believe that perhaps Eleanor didn't tolerate the nickname but instead embraced it, and I knew that Eleanor owning the sobriquet was how I wanted my story of her evolving identity to conclude. As far as the novel's start, I began with her first identity of Simone Jules, though for simplicity I'll refer to her throughout this note and the Reader's Guide as simply Eleanor.

Eleanor was touted as being "mysterious" and "private" and I soon found that to be accurate. There wasn't a lot of information about her earlier life. I didn't alter any conclusive details I unearthed, though that left much to be imagined and expanded on, which is the equivalent of striking gold for a fiction writer.

What I could conclude about Eleanor was that she was originally born in New Orleans or France, with more sources pointing to New Orleans. While it was unknown why she left her birthplace for San Francisco, my depiction of a fire at Théâtre d'Orléans was quite realistic, as the building was burned down in 1819 and again in 1866. Creating a fire around the median of those two years worked well for my story.

Eleanor arrived in San Francisco around 1849, in her late teens or early twenties, using her birth name of Simone Jules. She rented a table at the Bella Union Hotel and began a game of *vingt-et-un*. Soon after, Simone officially took a job dealing cards and, in that moment, she became the first known professional croupier of the game—man or woman. How cool.

During the time she would've worked at the Bella Union, two events occurred. First, on December 14, 1849, Arthur C. M. Reynolds was stabbed and killed by Reuben Withers, a mercantile from New York. A reward of $1000 was posted for Reuben's capture, though I couldn't find any conclusive details on whether anyone ever brought Reuben to justice. Second, on December 24, 1849, a fire devastated Portsmouth Square. Both events greatly influenced Eleanor's early storyline. And, of course, the real-life Arthur inspired a great deal more of the book, taking on the role of Eleanor's love interest and muse.

The portrait referenced within the book is real, but I romanticized Arthur as the artist, as the real-life Arthur C.M. Reynolds was in fact a painter, who hailed from Philadelphia, my own hometown. It was also said the real-life Arthur went by the nickname *Bones* because he played the instrument in an all-black band.

One of the assumed reasons for Eleanor's departure from San Francisco was due to accusations of card sharping. The next conclusive town I placed her in was Nevada (now Nevada City), California in the 1852-1854 timeframe. To account for the time between Eleanor leaving San Francisco and her arrival in Nevada, I integrated Eleanor's story with the current happenings of the United States, which was the great migration west along the Oregon and California Trails, with the California trail branching off to various goldfields. William was inspired by a real-life guide of those times, a Native American in his fifties, who spoke several languages, and who had been a wanderer for many years. It is my hope I didn't minimize or misrepresent his Native American character and any inaccuracies are my fault alone. The rock in which Eleanor carved her name was inspired by Independence Rock, which was called the "Great Register of the Desert." It contained more than five thousand names of early emigrants.

In Nevada City, Eleanor checked into the Fepp's Hotel, not as Simone Jules, but as Eleanor Dumont. She never used the name Simone again, as far as I can tell. There, she opened Vingt-et-un, before opening Dumont's Place with a man named Dave Tobin, who was a gambler from New York. I added depth and a background to his character, in which I'm certain I imagined historical inaccuracies.

I also came across the name Jane in my research; however, I found nothing more telling than the mention of her name. The court scene while in Nevada City was inspired by a real case and circumstances, though Eleanor, Jane, and David's involvement was fictionalized.

Eleanor and Dave held their partnership for over a year, and some claim they were secretly romantic, also inspiring their storyline, before the gold in Nevada City dried up. At that time, Eleanor and Dave went their separate ways, Dave back to New York City, where he died in 1865, and Eleanor to Carson City, where she owned a cattle ranch for as short as three months. During that time, Eleanor (unbeknownst to her) married a con man named Jack McKnight who swindled Eleanor of everything she owned. As the duration was so short and as this occurrence felt like a departure from my storyline, I excluded it. But, I'll have you know, many claim that later in Eleanor's life she tracked down Jack McKnight and shot him in the gut.

Eleanor is next documented as dealing cards in Columbia, California (1857), where a fire leveled the town during the time Eleanor would've been there; Virginia City, Nevada (1859); Pioche, Nevada (1861); Bannack, Montana (1862), where it's said Eleanor received the nickname of Madame Moustache; Kootenay, British Columbia (1864); and Fort Benton, Montana (1867). I did my best to align the storyline with these years and her known locations.

Another rumor I left out of my novel was that of Eleanor owning a brothel. Some believe, and my beliefs follow suit, that there was confusion with the terms *madame* and *madam*. The word *madam* was originally from Old French *ma dame*, meaning "my lady." In the sixteen century the term broadened to any woman, but mainly a married or matronly woman. Cited from an etymology dictionary, it wasn't until the eighteenth century that madam, in relation to a courtesan or a prostitute, was first recorded. Then madam, in reference to an owner of a brothel, was attested by 1871. The latter date aligns with Eleanor's popularity as Madame Dumont and Madame Moustache. And, original sources have only ever spoken of Eleanor dealing cards.

As said earlier, I chose to end my novel with Eleanor's acceptance of the sobriquet of Madame Moustache, but in a memorable way, bringing to life one of her claims to fame, which is commemorated in Fort Benton on a sign that summarizes the town's Old West history, including how *Madame Moustache brandished Colts to halt the landing of a steamship carrying smallpox.*

Beyond my novel's timeline, Eleanor was said to have dealt her game in Idaho (Salmon, Silver City, and Boise City), Utah (Corinne), Montana (Helena), Nevada (Eureka), South Dakota (Deadwood), Arizona (Tombstone), and California (Bodie). Tombstone was considered the last boomtown of the gold rush. In Deadwood, Eleanor was believed to have met and befriended Calamity Jane. I very much wanted to include Calamity Jane within the novel, but as they didn't meet until a decade after my conclusion, I felt the revision of Calamity Jane's history was too great in transporting her to a different time and place.

Eleanor's life ended in September of 1879. It was said that after losing her last dime, Eleanor walked a mile outside Bodie, California and drank a vial containing claret wine and morphine. Next to her body was a note saying she was tired of life. Eleanor was approximately forty-five years old. At the time, the average lifespan was thirty-four. It's said that Eleanor's funeral was the largest ever held in Bodie, California.

Within her eulogy, it read, "Truthful and honest, whatever other faults she might have had, always smiling, never forgetting the politeness of her native [birth place], and her purse ever open at the appeal of sickness or suffering, 'Madame Moustache' leaves friends in almost every class of Western society to regret the sad closing act of her life's drama."

While I didn't include the end of Eleanor's life in my novel, nor do I wish to glamorize her actions, I have imagined her final moments, as authors do. I saw Eleanor lying back, her head resting on a stone, arranging her skirts, closing her eyes, and raising the vial to her lips. Then, Eleanor was twenty again. She was smiling demurely. A man with blue paint along his jawline looked at her like she was the eighth wonder of the world, and the first thing Eleanor said to Arthur was *will you play, monsieur?*

Reader's Guide

Questions for Discussion

1. Eleanor suffered from survivor's guilt on more than one occasion. What choices and actions do you feel were impacted by this emotion?

2. Eleanor mentioned their shared French language as a reason that she was drawn to Arthur. What else do you feel drew her to him? And him to her?

3. While Eleanor traveled with William as a muleteer, he said, "A name evolves with the person, depending on the season of life and what the season means." Discuss the catalyst for each evolution of Eleanor's identities (Simone Jules, Eleanor Dumont, Madame Dumont, and finally as Madame Moustache).

4. Were you as shocked and unsettled as Eleanor when David reentered her life? If you were Eleanor, would you have let him back in? Would you have made a similar decision not to leave with him?

5. While Eleanor lived in a man's world, various female relationships were explored within the novel. Which friendship of Eleanor's did you connect with most, and why?

6. Putting yourself in Eleanor's side-laced boots (i.e., her shoes), would you have also embraced the moniker of Madame Moustache? Why or why not?

7. Depending on your interpretation of the cover, Eleanor's gaze may depict confidence or deep longing. Which do you see? Or, does another emotion come to mind for you?

8. While Eleanor's character included a number of positive attributes, such as tenacity, compassion, and intelligence, she was also crafted to be a self-centric individual. Do you feel this characteristic was crucial or a hindrance to her survival and likewise to her accomplishments?

9. Even after Arthur was taken from Eleanor, she continued to audibly speak to him. In what other ways did Eleanor keep Arthur alive in her heart and in her mind throughout the novel? How did the memory of him influence her decisions and actions?

10. The search for her identity was a central theme for Eleanor throughout the novel. What were the most memorable moments for you from our protagonist's time as Simone, as Eleanor, and as Madame Moustache?

11. Lastly, Eleanor's focus on establishing a legacy and her place in history was another theme of the novel. If Eleanor's portrait hung in a gallery, what one-to-three-sentence caption would you use to accompany the artwork?

About the Author

JENNI L. WALSH worked for a decade enticing readers as an award-winning advertising copywriter before becoming an author. Her passion lies in transporting readers to another world, be it in historical or contemporary settings. She is a proud graduate of Villanova University, and lives in the Philadelphia suburbs with her husband, daughter, son, and various pets. Jenni also writes nonfiction and historical fiction for middle-grade readers. To learn more about Jenni and her books, please visit jennilwalsh.com.

CPSIA information can be obtained
at www.ICGtesting.com
Printed in the USA
BVHW081000220321
602863BV00016B/12